Language and Politics

Language and Politics

Edited by MICHAEL J. SHAPIRO

New York University Press
New York 1984

First published in 1984 in the U.S.A. by
New York University Press, Washington Square,
New York N.Y. 10003

Library of Congress Cataloging in Publication Data
Main entry under title:
Language and Politics.—(Readings in social and political
 theory)
 Includes bibliographical references and index.
 1. Languages—Political aspects—Addresses, essays,
  lectures.
 2. Languages—Philosophy—Addresses, essays, lectures.
 I. Shapiro, Michael J.   II. Series
 P119.3.L3   1984   401'.9   84–16498

ISBN 0-8147-7838-0
ISBN 0-8147-7839-9 (pbk.)

Typeset by Katerprint Co. Ltd, Oxford
Printed and bound in Great Britain

Contents

1
Introduction

MICHAEL J. SHAPIRO

An anthology is a hyper-realist genre of writing. Not only is the 'author' of the anthology necessarily construed in a presentational mode — 'here they are', he/she says, 'a series of essays on language and politics' — but, in addition, there are no statements crafted by the author/compiler/entrepreneur (how should we speak of him/her?) to offer clues that there is a measure of rhetorical force which belies claims to innocence of involvement in argumentation. Thus an anthology is at one remove from ordinary realism. In ordinary realist genres — for instance a treatise on railway networks — the 'author' is thought to play a *minimal* role. It is generally conceded that very little intrusion into the subject matter is maintained when one confines the discursive selection to descriptively oriented utterances. In the case of the anthology, it would appear that the 'author' plays *no* role inasmuch as the spaces he or she occupies are outside of the main text, being restricted to such places as this introduction.

But more than 'Here they are . . .' is being said in this volume. There is an argument *in* the text, not just in the 'pretext' (an apt designation for 'my' introduction). To understand the argumentation, it is necessary to overcome two prejudices. The first is related to the traditional conception of authorship. As we have learned from post-structuralist thinkers (represented in this volume by de Man and Foucault), authorship is a function rather than an initiating activity. The idea that a single author is wholly responsible for a text is belied, first of all, because any writing begins and proceeds within a heritage of speech acts and discursive practices. As Derrida has pointed out, it is difficult to regard a single author as responsible for even those statements to which he is the sole signatory. For example, speaking of John Searle's reply to his essay on Austin, Derrida refers to the difficulty he has in identifying Searle as the author of that reply, '. . . not only because of the debts acknowledged by John R. Searle *before even* beginning to reply, but because of the entire, more or less anonymous tradition of a code, a heritage, a reservoir of arguments to which both he and I are indebted'.[1] Secondly, in addition to Derrida's point that all statements are to a large degree pre-scripted is the argument elaborated by Foucault that there are conventions for designating authors, conventions which are products of the discursive practices within various historical epochs. These conventions lack consistency from one period to another, and even within a particular civilization, the rules for authorship vary from one genre to another and change over time. For example, literary texts, which now always have authors, at one time, 'were accepted, circulated, and valorized without any question of the identity of their author'.[2] What does this conventionalizing of the author mean for present purposes? It indicates that the meaning and/or force of a text is not simply the result of some initiating intention. To find a polemical practice in a piece of writing (or in this case in a series of writings) is not dependent upon locating a single author with a hand in each of the text's statements as well as an overall purpose or aim guiding the direction of the text. Argument is sedimented in language in general and speech practices in particular; it does not require a present, immediate speaker/author. The flow of statements and meanings in any discursive practice, even the more austere, descriptively oriented ones are part of historically engendered, social practices which precede any speaker/author and, in addition, guide interpretive practices deployed on texts once they are produced.

The second prejudice is one which accepts a radical separation between realist and non-realist genres. Because the essays which follow go a long way toward dispelling this prejudice, I shall simply note here that even the more descriptively oriented genres such as historical accounts can be shown, as Hayden White has done, to have plots.[3] All stories and accounts, no matter how much their style might protest innocence, contain a mythic level – that is they have a job to do, a perspective to promote, a kind of world to affirm or deny. Seemingly neutral accounts of activities deliver, by dint of their grammatical and rhetorical structures, implicit political arguments, either legitimations for entrenched authority or polemical critiques which seek to demystify or disestablish existing structures of power and domination. A demonstration of this latter point occupies much of my closing chapter. The point that emerges for purposes of this introduction is that this anthology has a plot. The plot is revealed both by virtue of the 'content' it contains – what is said in each essay and, to some extent, *how* it is said – and by virtue of its syntax, expressed primarily by the order of presentation of the various essays.

Much of the plot in this volume is taken up with the issue of politicizing language, with developing a philosophical vantage point from which the things and identities of persons sequestered in language become politically problematic and/or with presuming that vantage point and discussing the political relations involved within a particular speech practice. I shall review this aspect of the plot briefly below as I refer to each of the various essays. The issue I want to address here is only implicitly apparent as one moves from the opening to the closing chapters of this volume, but it constitutes the major plot. This is the issue of the relationship between Anglo-American and Continental traditions in the philosophy of language. Whereas some philosophers of social science, steeped in the Anglo-American tradition, have tried to construct a rift between the functional approaches to meaning of Austin and Wittgenstein which emphasize the contexts of action within which utterances have meaning and the semiological/post-structuralist approaches which emphasize the language system as a play of differences and the purely conventional relationship between the signifier and the signified, the argument of this volume acts to bring them into closer harmony.[4] This task is much simplified by the inclusion of Fredric Jameson's essay which reviews and juxtaposes the Anglo-American approach which, as he points out, has been caught up with the problem of the referent, and those approaches influenced by Saussure which he sees as, 'deflected by his terminology from the whole question of the ultimate referent of the linguistic sign'.

Jameson provides an excellent overview of the differences in the heritages of both traditions, but it should be noted that despite these differences, recent Anglo-American linguistic analysis, particularly that influenced by Austin and Wittgenstein, shares a lot with contemporary Continental emphases. For example, Wittgenstein, like Derrida, a post-structuralist very much influenced by Saussurean linguistics, affirmed the position that there is no need to invoke a conscious subject to account for the meaning of a statement or proposition. As Allison has pointed out, Wittgenstein, like Derrida, reacted against the traditional account of language which animates both empiricist and phenomenological approaches to understanding: 'Derrida approaches language by criticizing a theory of expression and Wittgenstein approaches it largely by rejecting a theory of representation.'[5] What is perhaps most important for comparing the contributions of Wittgenstein and Derrida is that both offer a view of language which not only removes the problem of meaning from the idea of the referent or object of language, which is privileged in the empiricist approach,

but also removes the aim or intention of the subject/speaker from
the privileged position it achieves in Husserlian/phenomenological
approaches. A conscious, willing or intending subject is not, for
either Wittgenstein or Derrida, the essential ingredient in the production of meaning.[6] What *is* privileged is the linguistic structure
within which subjects are caught up.

If there is a seeming divergence between the two traditions –
recent linguistic philosophy following Austin and Wittgenstein and
post-Saussurean analyses such as those of Barthes, Derrida and
Foucault – the differences can be laid to the emphasis on speech
practices in the former tradition and on writing practices in the
latter. Even though Austin and Wittgenstein were aware that linguistic practices represent institutionalized or sedimented practices
with import beyond anything controlled within an interlocutory
relationship, their emphasis on the action context of an utterance
can obscure the prior context of possibilities from which verbal
performances are developed. In the case of the written sign, we have
something which, as Derrida has pointed out, carries with it a force
that breaks with its context, that is with the collective presences
organizing the movement of its inscription.[7] The written mark or
statement is thus more clearly 'weaned' from its referent and from
its initiating subject.[8] But, as Derrida goes on to point out, every
spoken utterance can break with any given context – for example a
spoken statement can be 'cited, put between quotation marks; in so
doing it can break with every given context in a manner which is
absolutely illimitable'.[9]

The point is not that there is no context for an utterance but
rather that, like the written statement, the utterance has many
possible contexts which exceed any limitation imposed by the
speaker, listener(s) or any aspect of the interlocutory structure.
And, what is more important about the structure of locution –
Austin's almost exclusive focus – is that it is predicated on another,
prior structure. This is what Derrida refers to as the 'system of
graphemic predicates', the linguistic system which provides the
possibilities for both 'normal' and 'deviant' (in Austin's terms,
'infelicitous') utterances. Thus the risks and accidents to which all
speech acts fall prey (e.g. the performative utterance, 'I now pronounce you Man and Wife' failing to take effect when spoken by
the wrong person), essential parts of Austin's analysis, are not
simply brought about by something extrinsic to the act. Austin
referred almost exclusively to conventions surrounding enunciation. What Derrida, and those within the Saussurean linguistic
tradition add to Austin's kind of analysis is a sensitivity to the

conventions constituting the linguistic system predicated in all speech acts. As Derrida puts it, 'Austin ... appears to consider solely the conventionality constituting the *circumstance* of the utterance [*énoncé*], its conventional surroundings, and not a certain conventionality intrinsic to what constitutes the speech act [*locution*] itself, all that might be summarized rapidly under the problematic rubric of the "arbitrary nature of the sign", which extends, aggravates, and radicalizes the difficulty'.[10] The treatment of these more radical difficulties is evident in Continental emphases on writing or discourse, and I shall summarize them briefly below in connection with the essays by de Man and Foucault. At this point, we can turn to a consideration of C. Wright Mills's essay, a contribution written early enough to be innocent of both the Anglo-American and Continental traditions. Nevertheless, Mills's insights articulate well with both of these philosophical traditions and with the overall plot of the volume.

Mills, like such thinkers in the English linguistic tradition as Austin, Hart and Ryle, rejects the notion that language is to be understood primarily from the point of view of its referential function. Statements of motive are therefore not to be understood as statements about prior, causal elements in the mind which explain observable behaviour. Employing a sociological perspective on the way language is used, Mills locates the meaning of statements in the social functions they perform. He thus anticipates Austin and Wittgenstein's position that language is best understood in terms of its use, the action framework within which it is deployed: 'As over against the inferential conception of motives as subjective "springs" of action, motives may be considered as typical vocabularies having ascertainable functions in delimited social situations'.

Once we agree with Mills that statements about motives are 'imputations', the frame of the analysis shifts. Rather than understanding human action as a problem of causal explanation – e.g. considering 'harmful acts' as a function of the motive, 'desiring to cause injury' or 'wanting to do evil' – the problem of understanding focuses on historical processes, the coming into being or extinction of various vocabularies of motive. Within such a focus, one's attention is turned to the problem of authority and power. We are led to ask, for example, what it tells us about the development of legitimized control when we note that we seem to have lost the 'desire to do evil', which functions within a religious vocabulary of motives, and have acquired desires which function within pecuniary and hedonistic vocabularies of motive. Mills's suggestion is therefore that we study motives not to find out why a given person engaged in a particular act but to learn about the kinds of justifications for action that are legitimized in a society at a given time.

J. G. A. Pocock's essay *is* specifically edified by English linguistic philosophy, particularly Austin's notion of speech acts, and it shares with Mills's contribution a rejection of the idea that a speaker or actor is wholly in control of the meaning of his or her articulations: 'Each of us speaks with many voices, like a tribal shaman in whom the ancestor ghosts are all talking at once; when we speak, we are not sure who is talking or what is being said, and our acts of power in communication are not wholly our own'. Pocock is more explicit than Mills in noting that language is a repository of sedimented power and that to understand the language-power relationship attention should be focused not on the intention of the individual user but rather on the inheritance of practices and conceptions that precede what comes out of the speaker's mouth. The language in use constitutes for Pocock a series of role assignments. Anticipating part of what has more recently constituted Foucault's political problematic – how to resist those assignments – Pocock speaks of resistance in the form of 'reshaping' language in order to reshape how we can define ourselves and thus how we can act. Interestingly, however, rather than emphasizing the historical context of linguistic inheritances (something he has done in his other writings), Pocock, under the influence of speech act theory, emphasizes the immediate, interlocutory relationship and its attendant conceptions like 'communication'.

Murray Edelman's essay differs in perspective from those of Mills and Pocock. While it is perhaps even more *politically* sensitive, it is even less historically sensitive. Its focus is primarily on the strategic use of language. Edelman, like others influenced by modern philosophy of language, moves away from the idea that language is a series of terms which represent some aspect of reality and toward the notion that it functions in various ways which are constitutive of realities. From this perspective, he shows, specifically, how the language used by a particular class of persons both constitutes a kind of political reality that enables or empowers the helping professionals and disenables their clientele. Edelman's frame of analysis is thus strategic rather than historic. We do not get an appreciation of the conditions and practices responsible for the emergence of therapeutic language and of the subjects, objects and relationships it contains, but we are offered a clear and effective perspective on the political reality that therapeutic discourse produces. He shows us how the 'terms' (that part of linguistic practice that absorbs all of his attention) in the helping professions 'evokes in our minds a world in which the weak and wayward need to be controlled for their own good'.

In addition to pointing out the distribution of empowering (in the case of helping professionals) and disempowering (in the case of their clientele), Edelman contrasts the virtues of a politicized language. When those who control and limit others do so within the linguistic universe of therapeutic discourse, there are no seemingly legitimate devices to oppose their power or authority. In contrast, Edelman notes that the use of political terms – e.g. regarding the authority of a psychiatrist over mental patients in a hospital as 'tyrannical' – legitimizes opposition. It has the effect of turning a 'clientele' into a potential 'political opposition'.

Kenneth Burke's review of *Mein Kampf* provides an interesting contrast with Edelman's construal of the language-politics relationship, for his focus is on rhetorical structures rather than individual terms. Like Edelman, he sees the political language of the domain he investigates from a strategic perspective, but anticipating the emphasis we now observe in modern post-structuralism, Burke minimizes the author's position in the strategic action and privileges the mechanisms in the text. Rhetorical mechanisms are not only the *object* of Burke's analysis; they are its vehicle as well, for Burke is a writer whose style comprises much of the argumentation. The vandalism metaphor with which he begins constitutes the opening for his argument that criticism consists not in attitudinalizing but in close attention to the mechanisms with which a text does its work. In constructing models of Hitler as alternatively, a 'medicine-man' and the 'folkish architect of the Folkish State', he lends coherence to the text as a strategic document, and the rest of his analysis is directed toward a highlighting of the ways that Hitler's strategy – or the strategies that operate through Hitler – works. What Burke demonstrates, among other things, is that an appeal to mass attitudes is effective not simply by virtue of its exhortation and attitudinalizing but by connecting itself to rhetorical structures which are already a part of general discursive practices and thus of generalized understandings. Under this kind of analytic discipline, the central strategy of *Mein Kampf* becomes the appropriation of 'church thought' with its already established script for relating economic ills to problems of personality. This sets the rhetorical stage for both scape-goating the Jews and for exalting the dignity of the Aryan, and, ultimately, for legitimizing violence in order to effect the desired movement in status: 'This sinister secularized revision of Christian theology thus puts the sense of dignity upon a fighting basis, requiring the conquest of "inferior races".'

Following Burke's essay with Tracy Strong's presentation of Nietzsche's view of language is propitious because what Nietzsche offers, among other things, is an epistemology of rhetoric, a position that knowing is not tied to a relationship between a cognizing subject and a world of objects but rather to the production of things in the tropological structure of language. The 'truths' we know are, according to Nietzsche, illusions, 'about which one has forgotton that this is what they are; metaphors which are worn out and without sensuous powers, coins which have lost their picture and now only matter as metal, no longer as coins'. This perspective of Nietzsche, as Strong brings out, lines him up with Wittgenstein and others who see language not as a form of transaction between thoughts and things but as a domain of human practices. To inquire into what people say is to learn *how* they construct their worlds. As Strong points out, Nietzsche is not simply saying that *we* are caught in language; he is pointing out that the 'we', the kind of subject we become is engendered within our linguistic practices.

Nietzsche's extension of the idea of the fetish to the subject as well as the object, showing how we mistakenly view human identities as universal predicates of knowlege rather than as linguistically engendered contrivances, was clearly influential in Foucault's argument that various historical ages constitute types of persons. And Nietzsche's idea of the subject as a fetish is central to Strong's presentation of Nietzsche's systematic critique of the epistemological tradition in Western philosophy, his attack on the subject-object distinction, the concept of free will and the concept of causality. Most important from the point of view of political understanding is what Nietzsche substitutes by way of a model for inquiry after tearing down the epistemic structures embedded in traditional views of language. Because for Nietzsche the language of people's transaction is, both grammatically and rhetorically, a set of contrivances which locks people into identities and gives them objects and kinds of action with predetermined value, his attack on entrenched authority had to take the form of both recommending new linguistic practices and of writing in a distinctive, convention-rejecting style (e.g. the purposeful contradictions he perpetrated to represent the idea that truth is rhetorically produced).[11]

Foucault's 'Order of Discourse' is appropriate reading after Strong's presentation of Nietzsche on language. It takes up some of Nietzsche's more important themes and marks Foucault's intellec-

tual movement from the archaeological perspective of his earlier
writings to the Nietzschean, genealogical perspective that informs
his subsequent work. First of all, he reaffirms his focus on discursive formations, a focus best explicated in his *Archeology of Knowledge* where he claims, 'To analyse a discursive formation . . . is to
weigh the "value" of statements, a value that is not defined by
their truth, that is not gauged by the presence of a secret content;
but which characterizes their place, their capacity for circulation
and exchange, their possibility of transformation, not only in the
economy of discourse but more generally, in the administration
of scarce resources.'[12] Here is clearly both a concurrence with
Nietzsche's replacement of the idea that language is to be evaluated
on its truth as correspondence with the idea that language creates
value and a highly politicized way of looking at that value creation.

Secondly, Foucault anticipates the genealogical perspective in his
later studies in which he characterizes the development of prevailing discursive practices constituting understanding in the modern
age. These practices, which he treats in his studies of punishment
and sexuality, are the result of the historical production of ways of
thinking/speaking which contain identities designed to be docile in
the face of power.[13] Because the political contributions of
Foucault's more recent writings are developed in Connolly's essay
which follows and in mine, which concludes the volume, there is no
need to elaborate them here. The linking of Foucault's interest in
discourse and the genealogical perspective is very well stated in the
essay:

> Thus the critical and genealogical descriptions must alternate
> and complement each other, each supporting the other by
> turns. The critical portion of the analysis applies to the system
> that envelops discourse, and tries to identify and grasp these
> principles of sanctioning, exclusion, and scarcity of discourse.
> Let us say, playing on words, that it practices a studied casual-
> ness. The genealogical portion, on the other hand, applies to
> the series where discourse is effectively formed: it tries to
> grasp it in its power of affirmation, by which I mean not so
> much a power which will be opposed to that of denying, but
> rather the power to constitute domains of objects, in respect
> of which one can affirm or deny true or false propositions.

William Connolly's 'The Politics of Discourse' is a particularly
important contribution to the plot of this volume because it promotes its theme in the context of a critical confrontation between

Anglo-American and Continental positions. Connolly's major impetus is to politicize. Arguing that 'the language of politics is not a neutral medium that conveys ideas independently formed', but is, rather, 'an institutionalized structure of meanings that channels political thought and action in certain directions', he mines both traditions in order to oppose understandings which would aid and abet existing power and authority by depoliticizing our view of concepts. Connolly's encounter with Foucaultian thinking is an extraordinarily productive one because it illustrates an important shift in notions of human agency as one moves from the Anglo-American to the Continental tradition. In the earlier part of the essay, Connolly emphasizes what can appropriately be said about the power that persons exercise over each other. Even though, within this discussion, he recognizes that the notion of the human agent or subject which such a discussion assumes is part of a traditional grammar of power, and he finds himself resisting the linguistic constraints – e.g. the 'definition' – which constitute this tradition, the style of his discussion remains faithful to the tradition. As he moves to his later section in which he elaborates the Foucaultian view of the subject as an artefact of power rather than its agent, his terms and rhetorical style change. He thus employs alternatively two kinds of language to speak about power, the Foucaultian in which power is, 'not a possession of agents who exercise it to define the options of others, but a set of pressures lodged in institutional mechanisms which *produce* and *maintain* such privileged norms as the subject or the primacy of epistemology', and the Anglo-American in which the self is an agent, 'capable of forming intentions, of deliberately shaping . . . conduct to rules, of appreciating the significance of actions for others . . . of exercising self restraint'.

This critical encounter serves not only to highlight the differences between two traditions but also effectively to raise the issue of the *value* of alternative conceptions of the subject. Connolly, by virtue of the way he addresses this value question, invites us to reconsider our political discourses, to consider them, as Foucault has done, from the point of view of the resources they deploy, the capacities and incapacities they distribute.

The importance of Fredric Jameson's essay to the plot of this volume has already been elaborated above. In addition to the role that he has performed in contrasting Anglo-American and Continental linguistic traditions, he has contributed, in numerous other writings, to our understanding of how the style of a text harbours political commitment.[14] In the essay in this volume we get a hint of

Jameson's contribution to a politicized epistemological stance which combines the structuralist and Marxist notions that political consciousness is a consciousness of the totalities within which individual objects and kinds of persons have meaning. Attacking Anglo-American empiricism, Jameson refers to it as a kind of thinking, 'characterized by a turning away of the eyes, a preference for segments and isolated objects, as a means to avoid observation of those larger wholes and totalities which if they had to be seen would force the mind in the long run into uncomfortable social and political conclusions'. Jameson thus provides here an interesting counter-point to the post-structuralist rejection of empiricism, seeing empiricism as depoliticizing not because of its neutral construal of the subject but because of its failure to grasp *the* totality which Jameson construes in a Marxist sense.

With Paul De Man's essay we move unambiguously into the Continental tradition. De Man's analysis, which is typical of current post-structuralism, shows how a text does much more than its writers thinks it does. He shows, first of all, that Locke, in his *Essay Concerning Human Understanding*, delivers himself of a theory of tropes even though, 'He would be the last man in the world to acknowledge this.' What De Man does in his reading of Locke (and of Condillac and Kant) is to pay attention not only to the 'explicit statements' ('especially to the statements about statements') but also to the 'rhetorical motions' of the text. This sets the stage for his 'deconstructions' which he carries out on the Locke, Condillac and Kant positions on figurative language. All of these thinkers end up being rhetoricians in spite of themselves. Their texts make use of metaphors in the very act of trying to promote modes of understanding whose representations are thought to be literal or non-figurative. What one gets from De Man's practice as he carries out a literary reading of philosophical texts is not only a deep suspicion of all attempts to distinguish between literal and figurative statements but also a new respect for the worthiness of the literary enterprise in domains connected to problems of epistemology and inquiry. Inspired by this insight, I apply a literary practice to a typical genre in political analysis in the concluding essay of the volume. Given my celebration above of the post-structuralist notion that texts say more than their writers think, I shall let the final essay speak for itself.

NOTES

1 Jacques Derrida, 'Limited Inc a b c', *Glyph* 2 (Baltimore: Johns Hopkins University Press, 1977), pp. 162–254.

2 Michel Foucault, 'What is an Author', in D. F. Bouchard ed. *Language, Counter-Memory, Practice* (Ithaca, N.Y.: Cornell University Press, 1977), p. 125.

3 Hayden White, 'Historicism, History and the Figurative Imagination', in *Tropics of Discourse* (Baltimore: Johns Hopkins University Press, 1978).

4 Anthony Giddens mistakenly distinguishes Derrida from Wittgenstein, arguing that Wittgenstein's view of language is superior because it emphasizes the 'involvement of language with social practices'. *Both* Wittgenstein and Derrida arrive at an emphasis on this relationship because they both react against views that privilege individual consciousness. See Giddens's 'Structuralism and the Theory of the Subject', in his *Central Problems of Social Theory* (Berkeley and Los Angeles: University of California Press, 1979), p. 46.

5 David B. Allison, 'Derrida and Wittgenstein Playing the Game', *Research in Phenomenology* 8 (1978), p. 93.

6 Ibid., p. 105.

7 Jacques Derrida, 'Signature, Event, Context', *Glyph* 1 (Baltimore: Johns Hopkins University Press, 1976), p. 182.

8 Ibid.

9 Ibid., p. 180.

10 Ibid., p. 189.

11 See Jacques Derrida, 'The Question of Style', in D. B. Allison ed. *The New Nietzsche* (New York: Delta, 1977), pp. 176–89.

12 Michel Foucault, *The Archeology of Knowledge* (New York: Pantheon, 1972), p. 120.

13 See Michel Foucault, *Discipline and Punish: The Birth of the Prison* (New York: Pantheon, 1977), and *The History of Sexuality* (New York: Pantheon, 1978).

14 See Fredric Jameson, *The Political Unconscious* (Ithaca, N.Y.: Cornell University Press, 1981).

2

Situated Actions and
Vocabularies of Motive*

C. WRIGHT MILLS

The major reorientation of recent theory and observation in sociology of language emerged with the overthrow of the Wundtian notion that language has as its function the 'expression' of prior elements within the individual. The postulate underlying modern study of language is the simple one that we must approach linguistic behavior, not by referring it to private states in individuals, but by observing its social function of coordinating diverse actions. Rather than expressing something which is prior and in the person, language is taken by other persons as an indicator of future actions.[1]

Within this perspective there are suggestions concerning problems of motivation. It is the purpose of this paper to outline an analytic model for the explanation of motives which is based on a sociological theory of language and a sociological psychology.[2]

As over against the inferential conception of motives as subjective 'springs' of action, motives may be considered as typical vocabularies having ascertainable functions in delimited societal situations. Human actors do vocalize and impute motives to themselves and to others. To explain behavior by referring it to an inferred and abstract 'motive' is one thing. To analyze the observable lingual mechanisms of motive imputation and avowal as they function in conduct is quite another. Rather than fixed elements 'in' an individual, motives are the terms with which interpretation of conduct by *social actors* proceeds. This imputation and avowal of motives by actors are social phenomena to be explained. The differing reasons men give for their actions are not themselves without reasons.

First, we must demarcate the general conditions under which such motive imputation and avowal seem to occur.[3] Next, we must

*C. Wright Mills, 'Situated Actions and Vocabularies of Motive', reprinted from *American Sociological Review* 5 (December, 1940), pp. 904–13.

give a characterization of motive in denotable terms and an explanatory paradigm of why certain motives are verbalized rather than others. Then, we must indicate mechanisms of the linkage of vocabularies of motive to systems of action. What we want is an analysis of the integrating, controlling, and specifying function a certain type of speech fulfils in socially situated actions.

The generic situation in which imputation and avowal of motives arise, involves, first, the *social* conduct or the (stated) programs of languaged creatures, i.e., programs and actions oriented with reference to the actions and talk of others; second, the avowal and imputation of motives is concomitant with the speech form known as the 'question'. Situations back of questions typically involve *alternative* or *unexpected* programs or actions which phases analytically denote 'crises'.[4] The question is distinguished in that it usually elicits another *verbal* action, not a motor response. The question is an element in   *conversation*. Conversation may be concerned with the factual features of a situation as they are seen or believed to be or it may seek to integrate and promote a set of diverse social actions with reference to the situation and its normative pattern of expectations. It is in this latter assent and dissent phase of conversation that persuasive and dissuasive speech and vocabulary arise. For men live in immediate acts of experience and their attentions are directed outside themselves until acts are in some way frustrated. It is then that awareness of self and of motive occur. The 'question' is a lingual index of such conditions. The avowal and imputation of motives are features of such conversations as arise in 'question' situations.

Motives are imputed or avowed as answers to questions interrupting acts or programs. Motives are words. Generically, to what do they refer? They do not denote any elements 'in' individuals. They stand for anticipated situational consequences of questioned conduct. Intention or purpose (stated as a 'program') *is* awareness of anticipated consequence; motives are names for consequential situations, and surrogates for actions leading to them. Behind questions are possible alternative actions with their terminal consequences. 'Our introspective words for motives are rough, shorthand descriptions for certain typical patterns of discrepant and conflicting stimuli.'[5]

The model of purposive conduct associated with Dewey's name may briefly be stated. Individuals confronted with 'alternative acts' perform one or the other of them on the basis of the differential consequences which they anticipate. This nakedly utilitarian schema is inadequate because: (a) the 'alternative acts' of *social* conduct 'appear' most often in lingual form, as a question, stated by one's self or by another; (b) it is more adequate to say that individuals act in terms of anticipation of *named* consequences.

Among such names and in some technologically oriented lines of action there may appear such terms as 'useful', 'practical', 'service-able', etc., terms so 'ultimate' to the pragmatists, and also to certain sectors of the American population in these delimited situations. However, there are other areas of population with different voca-bularies of motives. The choice of lines of action is accompanied by representations, and selection among them, of their situational termini. Men discern situations with particular vocabularies, and it is in terms of some delimited vocabulary that they anticipate con-sequences of conduct.[6] Stable vocabularies of motives link antici-pated consequences and specific actions. There is no need to invoke 'psychological' terms like 'desire' or 'wish' as explanatory, since they themselves must be explained socially.[7] Anticipation is a sub-vocal or overt naming of terminal phases and/or social conse-quences of conduct. When an individual names consequences, he elicits the behaviors for which the name is a redintegrative cue. In a *societal* situation, implicit in the names for consequences is the social dimension of motives. Through such vocabularies, types of societal controls operate. Also, the terms in which the question is asked often will contain both alternatives: ,'Love or Duty?' 'Busi-ness or Pleasure?' Institutionally different situations have different *vocabularies of motive* appropriate to their respective behaviors.

This sociological conception of motives as relatively stable ling-ual phases of delimited situations is quite consistent with Mead's program to approach conduct socially and from the outside. It keeps clearly in mind that 'both motives and actions very often originate not from within but from the situation in which indi-viduals find themselves. . . .'[8] It translates the question of 'why'[9] into a 'how' that is answerable in terms of a situation and its typical vocabulary of motives, i.e., those which conventionally accompany that type situation and function as cues and justifications for normative actions in it.

It has been indicated that the question is usually an index to the avowal and imputation of motives. Max Weber defines motive as a complex of meaning, which appears to the actor himself or to the observer to be an adequate ground for his conduct.[10] The aspect of motive which this conception grasps is its intrinsically social char-acter. A satisfactory or adequate motive is one that satisfies the questioners of an act or program, whether it be the other's or the actor's. As a word, *a motive tends to be one which is to the actor*

16 C. Wright Mills

*and to the other members of a situation an unquestioned answer to
questions concerning social and lingual conduct.* A stable motive is
an ultimate in justificatory conversation. The words which in a type
situation will fulfil this function are circumscribed by the vocabulary of motives acceptable for such situations. Motives are accepted
justifications for present, future, or past programs or acts.

To term them justification is *not* to deny their efficacy. Often
anticipations of acceptable justification will control conduct. ('If I
did this, what could I say? What would they say?') Decisions may
be, wholly or in part, delimited by answers to such queries.

A man may begin an act for one motive. In the course of it, he
may adopt an ancillary motive. This does not mean that the second
apologetic motive is inefficacious. The vocalized expectation of an
act, its 'reason', is not only a mediating condition of the act but it is
a proximate and controlling condition for which the term 'cause' is
not inappropriate. It may strengthen the act of the actor. It may win
new allies for his act.

When they appeal to others involved in one's act, motives are
strategies of action. In many social actions, others must agree,
tacitly or explicitly. Thus, acts often will be abandoned if no reason
can be found that others will accept. Diplomacy in choice of motive
often controls the diplomat. Diplomatic choice of motive is part of
the attempt to motivate acts for other members in a situation. Such
pronounced motives undo snarls and integrate social actions. Such
diplomacy does not necessarily imply intentional lies. It merely
indicates that an appropriate vocabulary of motives will be utilized
– that they are conditions for certain lines of conduct.[11]

When an agent vocalizes or imputes motives, he is not trying to
describe his experienced social action. He is not merely stating
'reasons'. He is influencing others – and himself. Often he is finding
new 'reasons' which will mediate action. Thus, we need not treat an
action as discrepant from 'its' verbalization, for in many cases, the
verbalization is a new act. In such cases, there is not a discrepancy
between an act and 'its' verbalization, but a difference between two
disparate actions, motor-social and verbal.[12] This additional (or '*ex
post facto*') lingualization may involve appeal to a vocabulary of
motives associated with a norm with which both members of the
situation are in agreement. As such, it is an integrative factor in
future phases of the original social action or in other acts. By
resolving conflicts, motives are efficacious. Often, if 'reasons' were
not given, an act would not occur, nor would diverse actions be
integrated. Motives are common grounds for mediated behaviors.

Perry summarily states the Freudian view of motives 'as the view that the real motives of conduct are those which we are ashamed to admit either to ourselves or to others'.[13] One can cover the facts by merely saying that scruples (i.e., *moral* vocabularies of motive) are often efficacious and that men will alter and deter their acts in terms of such motives. One of the components of a 'generalized other', as a mechanism of societal control, is vocabularies of acceptable motives. For example, a business man joins the Rotary Club and proclaims its public-spirited vocabulary.[14] If this man cannot act out business conduct without so doing, it follows that this vocabulary of motives is an important factor in his behavior.[15] The long acting out of a role, with its appropriate motives, will often induce a man to become what at first he merely sought to appear. Shifts in the vocabularies of motive that are utilized later by an individual disclose an important aspect of various integrations of his actions with concomitantly various groups.

The motives actually used in justifying or criticizing an act definitely link it to situations, integrate one man's action with another's, and line up conduct with norms. The societally sustained motive-surrogates of situations are both constraints and inducements. It is a hypothesis worthy and capable of test that typal vocabularies of motives for different situations are significant determinants of conduct. As lingual segments of social action, motives orient actions by enabling discrimination between their objects. Adjectives such as 'good', 'pleasant', and 'bad' promote action or deter it. When they constitute components of a vocabulary of motives, i.e., are typical and relatively unquestioned accompaniments of typal situations, such words often function as directives and incentives by virtue of their being the judgements of others as anticipated by the actor. In this sense motives are 'social instruments, i.e., data by modifying which the agent will be able to influence [himself or others]'.[16] The 'control' of others is not usually direct but rather through manipulation of a field of objects. We influence a man by naming his acts or imputing motives to them – or to 'him'. The motives accompanying institutions of war, e.g., are not 'the causes' of war, but they do promote continued integrated participation, and they vary from one war to the next. Working vocabularies of motive have careers that are woven through changing institutional fabrics.

Genetically, motives are imputed by others before they are avowed by self. The mother controls the child: 'Do not do that, it is greedy.' Not only does the child learn what to do, what not to do, but he is given standardized motives which promote prescribed actions and dissuade those proscribed. Along with rules and norms

of actions for various situations, we learn vocabularies of motives
appropriate to them. These are the motives we shall use, since they
are a part of our language and components to our behavior.

The quest for 'real motives' supposititiously set over against
'mere rationalization' is often informed by a metaphysical view that
the 'real' motives are in some way biological. Accompanying such
quests for something more real and back of rationalization is the
view held by many sociologists that language is an external manifestation or concomitant of something prior, more genuine, and
'deep' in the individual. 'Real attitudes' versus 'mere verbalization'
or 'opinion' implies that at best we only infer from his language
what 'really' is the individual's attitude or motive.

Now what *could we possibly* so infer? Of precisely *what* is
verbalization symptomatic? We cannot *infer* physiological processes from lingual phenomena. All we can infer and empirically
check[17] is another verbalization of the agent's which we believe was
orienting and controlling behavior at the time the act was performed. The only social items that can 'lie deeper' are other lingual
forms.[18] The 'Real Attitude or Motive' is not something different in
kind from the verbalization or the 'opinion'. They turn out to be
only relatively and temporally different.

The phrase 'unconscious motive' is also unfortunate. All it can
mean is that a motive is not explicitly vocalized, but there is no need
to infer unconscious motives from such situations and then posit
them in individuals as elements. The phrase is informed by persist-
ence of the unnecessary and unsubstantiated notion that 'all action
has a motive', and it is promoted by the observation of gaps in the
relatively frequent verbalization in everyday situations. The facts to
which this phrase is supposedly addressed are covered by the statements that men do not always explicitly articulate motives, and that
all actions do not pivot around language. I have already indicated the
conditions under which motives are typically avowed and imputed.

Within the perspective under consideration, the verbalized
motive is not used as an index of something in the individual but *as
a basis of inference for a typal vocabulary of motives of a situated
action*. When we ask for the 'real attitude' rather than the 'opinion',
for the 'real motive' rather than the 'rationalization', all we can
meaningfully be asking for is the controlling speech form which
was incipiently or overtly presented in the performed act or series of
acts. There is no way to plumb behind verbalization into an individual and directly check our motive-mongering, but there is an
empirical way in which we can guide and limit, in given historical
situations, investigations of motives. That is by the construction of

typal vocabularies of motives that are extant in types of situations and actions. Imputation of motives may be controlled by reference to the typical constellation of motives which are observed to be societally linked with classes of situated actions. Some of the 'real' motives that have been imputed to actors were not even known to them. As I see it, motives are circumscribed by the vocabulary of the actor. The only source for a terminology of motives is the vocabularies of motives actually and usually verbalized by actors in specific situations.

Individualistic, sexual, hedonistic, and pecuniary vocabularies of motives are apparently now dominant in many sectors of twentieth-century urban America. Under such an ethos, verbalization of alternative conduct in these terms is least likely to be challenged among dominant groups. In this milieu, individuals are skeptical of Rockefeller's avowed religious motives for his business conduct because such motives are not *now* terms of the vocabulary conventionally and prominently accompanying situations of business enterprise. A medieval monk writes that he gave food to a poor but pretty woman because it was 'for the glory of God and the eternal salvation of his soul'. Why do we tend to question him and impute sexual motives? Because sex is an influential and widespread motive in our society and time. Religious vocabularies of explanation and of motives are now on the wane. In a society in which religious motives have been debunked on rather a wide scale, certain thinkers are skeptical of those who ubiquitously proclaim them. Religious motives have lapsed from selected portions of modern populations and other motives have become 'ultimate' and operative. But from the monasteries of medieval Europe we have no evidence that religious vocabularies were not operative in many situations.

A labor leader says he performs a certain act because he wants to get higher standards of living for the workers. A business man says that this is rationalization, or a lie; that it is really because he wants more money for himself from the workers. A radical says a college professor will not engage in radical movements because he is afraid for his job, and besides, is a 'reactionary'. The college professor says it is because he just likes to find out how things work. What is reason for one man is rationalization for another. The variable is the accepted vocabulary of motives, the ultimates of discourse, of each man's dominant group about whose opinion he cares. *Determination of such groups, their location and character, would enable delimitation and methodological control of assignment of motives for specific acts.*

Stress on this idea will lead us to investigations of the compart-
mentalization of operative motives in personalities according to
situation and the general types and conditions of vocabularies of
motives in various types of societies. The motivational structures of
individuals and the patterns of their purposes are relative to societal
frames. We might, e.g., study motives along stratified or occupa-
tional lines, Max Weber has observed:[19]

> . . . that in a free society the motives which induce people
> to work vary with . . . different social classes. . . . There is
> normally a graduated scale of motives by which men from
> different social classes are driven to work. When a man
> changes ranks, he switches from one set of motives to another.

The lingual ties which hold them together react on persons to
constitute frameworks of disposition and motive. Recently, Talcott
Parsons has indicated, by reference to differences in actions in the
professions and in business, that one cannot leap from 'economic
analysis to ultimate motivations; the institutional patterns *always*
constitute one crucial element of the problem.'[20] It is my suggestion
that we may analyze, index, and gauge this element by focusing
upon those specific verbal appendages of variant institutionalized
actions which have been referred to as vocabularies of motive.

In folk societies, the constellations of motives connected with
various sectors of behavior would tend to be typically stable and
remain associated only with their sector. In typically primary,
sacred, and rural societies, the motives of persons would be regularly compartmentalized. Vocabularies of motives ordered to different
situations stabilize and guide behavior and expectation of the reactions of others. In their appropriate situations, verbalized motives
are not typically questioned.[21] In secondary, secular, and urban
structures, varying and competing vocabularies of motives operate
coterminously and the situations to which they are appropriate are
not clearly demarcated. Motives once unquestioned for defined
situations are now questioned. Various motives can release similar
acts in a given situation. Hence, variously situated persons are
confused and guess which motive 'activated' the person. Such
questioning has resulted intellectually in such movements as
psychoanalysis with its dogma of rationalization and its systematic
motive-mongering. Such intellectual phenomena are underlaid by
split and conflicting sections of an individuated society which is
characterized by the existence of competing vocabularies of motive.
Intricate constellations of motives, for example, are components of

business enterprise in America. Such patterns have encroached on the old style vocabulary of the virtuous relation of men and women: duty, love, kindness. Among certain classes, the romantic, virtuous, and pecuniary motives are confused. The asking of the question: 'Marriage for love or money?' is significant, for the pecuniary is now a constant and almost ubiquitous motive, a common denominator of many others.[22]

Back of 'mixed motives' and 'motivational conflicts' are competing or discrepant situational patterns and their respective vocabularies of motive. With shifting and interstitial situations, each of several alternatives may belong to disparate systems of action which have differing vocabularies of motives appropriate to them. Such conflicts manifest vocabulary patterns that have overlapped in a marginal individual and are not easily compartmentalized in clear-cut situations.

Besides giving promise of explaining an area of lingual and societal fact, a further advantage of this view of motives is that with it we should be able to give sociological accounts of other theories (terminologies) of motivation. This is a task for sociology of knowledge. Here I can refer only to a few theories. I have already referred to the Freudian terminology of motives. It is apparent that these motives are those of an upper bourgeois patriarchal group with strong sexual and individualist orientation. When introspecting on the couches of Freud, patients used the only vocabulary of motives they knew; Freud got his hunch and guided further talk. Mittenzwey has dealt with similar points at length.[23] Widely diffused in a postwar epoch, psychoanalysis was never popular in France where control of sexual behavior is not puritanical.[24] To converted individuals who have become accustomed to the psychoanalytic terminology of motives, all others seem self-deceptive.[25]

In like manner, to many believers in Marxism's terminology of power, struggle, and economic motives, all others, including Freud's are due to hypocricy or ignorance. An individual who has assimilated thoroughly only business congeries of motives will attempt to apply these motives to all situations, home and wife included. It should be noted that the business terminology of motives has its intellectual articulation, even as psychoanalysis and Marxism have.

It is significant that since the Socratic period many 'theories of motivation' have been linked with ethical and religious terminologies. Motive is that in man which leads him to do good or evil. Under the aegis of religious institutions, men use vocabularies of moral motives: they call acts and programs 'good' and 'bad', and impute these qualities to the soul. Such lingual behavior is part of the process of social control. Institutional practices and their vocabularies of motives exercise control over delimited ranges of possible situations. One could make a typal catalog of religious motives from widely read religious texts, and test its explanatory power in various denominations and sects.[26]

In many situations of contemporary America, conduct is controlled and integrated by *hedonistic* language. For large population sectors in certain situations, pleasure and pain are now unquestioned motives. For given periods and societies, the situations should be empirically determined. Pleasure and pain should not be reified and imputed to human nature as underlying principles of all action. Note that hedonism as a psychological and an ethical doctrine gained impetus in the modern world at about the time when older moral-religious motives were being debunked and simply discarded by 'middle-class' thinkers. Back of the hedonistic terminology lay an emergent social pattern and a new vocabulary of motives. The shift of unchallenged motives which gripped the communities of Europe was climaxed when, in reconciliation, the older religious and the hedonistic terminologies were identified: the 'good' is the 'pleasant'. The conditioning situation was similar in the Hellenistic world with the hedonism of the Cyrenaics and Epicureans.

What is needed is to take all these *terminologies* of motive and locate them as *vocabularies* of motive in historic epochs and specified situations. Motives are of no value apart from the delimited societal situations for which they are the appropriate vocabularies. They must be situated. At best, socially unlocated *terminologies* of motives represent unfinished attempts to block out social areas of motive imputation and avowal. Motives vary in content and character with historical epochs and societal structures.

Rather than interpreting actions and language as external manifestations of subjective and deeper lying elements in individuals, the research task is the locating of particular types of action within typal frames of normative actions and socially situated clusters of motive. There is no explanatory value in subsuming various vocabularies of motives under some terminology or list. Such procedure merely confuses the task of explaining specific cases. The languages of situations as given must be considered a valuable portion of the data to be interpreted and related to their conditions. To simplify these vocabularies of motive into a socially abstracted terminology is to destroy the legitimate use of motive in the explanation of social actions.

NOTES

1 See C. Wright Mills, 'Bibliographical Appendices', Section I, 4, 'Sociology of Language' in H. E. Barnes, ed. *Contemporary Social Theory* (New York: Becker & Becker, 1940).

2 See G. H. Mead, 'Social Psychology as Counterpart of Physiological Psychology', *Psychol. Bul.* VI (1909) pp. 401–8; Karl Mannheim, *Man and Society in an Age of Reconstruction* (New York, 1940); L. V. Wiese-Howard Becker, *Systematic Sociology*, part I (New York, 1932); J. Dewey, 'All psychology is either biological or social psychology'. *Psychol. Rev.* 24, p. 276.

3 The importance of this initial task for research is clear. Most researches on the verbal level merely ask abstract questions of individuals, but if we can tentatively delimit the situations in which certain motives *may* be verbalized, we can use that delimitation in the construction of *situational* questions, and we shall be *testing* deductions from our theory.

4 On the 'question' and 'conversation', see G. A. DeLaguna, *Speech: Its Function and Development* (New Haven, 1927), p. 37 (and index). For motives in crises, see J. M. Williams, *The Foundations of Social Science* (New York, 1920), pp. 435 ff.

5 K. Burke, *Permanence and Change* (New York, 1936), p. 45. I am indebted to this book for several leads which are systematized into the present statement.

6 See such experiments as C. N. Rexroad's 'Verbalization in Multiple Choice Reactions'. *Psychol. Rev.* 33 (1926), p. 458.

7 Cf. J. Dewey, 'Theory of Valuation', *Int. Ency. of Unified Science* (New York, 1939).

8 K. Mannheim, *Man and Society* (London, 1940), p. 249.

9 Conventionally answerable by reference to 'subjective factors' within individuals. R. M. MacIver, 'The Modes of the Question Why', *J. of Soc. Phil.* (April, 1940). Cf. also his 'The Imputation of Motives', *Amer. J. Sociol.* (July, 1940).

10 Max Weber, *Wirtschaft und Gesellschaft* (Tübingen, 1922), p. 5. '"Motiv" heisst ein Sinnzusammenhang, Welcher dem Handelnden selbst oder dem Beobachtenden als sinnhafter "Grund" eines Verhaltens in dem Grade heissen, als die Beziehung seiner Bestandteile vons uns den durchschnittlichen Denk- und Gefühlsgewohnheiten als typischer (wir pflegen in sagen: "richtiger") Sinnzusammenhang bejaht Wird.'

11 Of course, since motives are communicated, they may be lies; but this must be proved. Verbalizations are not lies merely because they are socially efficacious, I am here concerned more with the social function of pronounced motives, than with the sincerity of those pronouncing them.

12 See F. Znaniecki, *Social Actions* (New York, 1936), p. 30.

13 S. E. Perry, *General Theory of Value* (New York, 1936), pp. 292–3.

24 C. Wright Mills

14 Ibid., p. 392.
15 The 'profits motive' of classical economics may be treated as an ideal-typical vocabulary of motives for delimited economic situations and behaviors. For late phases of monopolistic and regulated capitalism, this type requires modification; the profit and commercial vocabularies have acquired others ingredients. See N. R. Danielian's *AT&T* (New York, 1940) for a suggestive account of the *non-economic* behavior and motives of business bureaucrats.
16 Znaniecki, *Social Actions*, p. 73.
17 Of course, we could infer or interpret constructs posited in the individual, but these are not easily checked and they are not explanatory.
18 Which is not to say that, physiologically, there may not be cramps in the stomach wall or adrenalin in the blood, etc., but the character of the 'relation' of such items to social action is quite moot.
19 Paraphrased by Mannheim, *Man and Society*, pp. 316–17.
20 Talcott Parsons, 'The Motivation of Economic Activities', in C. W. M. Hart, *Essays in Sociology* (Toronto, 1940), p. 67.
21 Among the ethnologists, Ruth Benedict has come up to the edge of a genuinely sociological view of motivation. Her view remains vague because she has not seen clearly the identity of differing 'motivations' in differing cultures with the varied extant and approved vocabularies of motive. 'The intelligent understanding of the relation of the individual to his society . . . involves always the understanding of the types of human motivations and capacities capitalized in his society . . .' 'Configurations of Culture in North America'. *Amer. Anthrop.* 25 (January–March, 1932); see also: *Patterns of Culture* (Boston, 1935), pp. 242–3. She turns this observation into a quest for the unique 'genius' of each culture and stops her research by words like 'Apollonian'. If she would attempt constructively to observe the vocabularies of motives which precipitate acts to perform, implement programs, and furnish approved motives for them in circumscribed situations, she would be better able to state precise problems and to answer them by further observation.
22 Also motives acceptably imputed and avowed for one system of action may be diffused into other domains and gradually come to be accepted by some as a comprehensive portrait of *the* motive of men. This happened in the case of the economic man and his motives.
23 Kuno Mittenzwey, 'Zur Soziologie der psychoanalystischer Erkenntnis', in Max Scheler, ed. *Versuche zu einer Sociologie des Wissens* (Munich, 1924) pp. 365–75.
24 This fact is interpreted by some as supporting Freudian theories. Nevertheless, it can be just as adequately grasped in the scheme here outlined.
25 See Burke's acute discussion of Freud, *Permanence and Change*, part I.
26 Moral vocabularies deserve a special statement. Within the viewpoint herein outlined many snarls concerning 'value-judgements', etc., can be cleared up.

3

Verbalizing a Political Act:
Toward a Politics of Speech*

J. G. A. POCOCK†

In this paper I propose to talk about the verbalization *of* a political
act and verbalization itself *as* a political act. I shall not withhold a
measure of sympathy from those who feel there are simply too
many words floating around already, and that the nöosphere is in
danger of becoming as badly polluted as the atmosphere, biosphere,
and geosphere. A man in Los Angeles said to me: 'You're under no
obligation to verbalize your life-style'; and on the way down life's
staircase since, it has occurred to me that the proper answer would
have been: 'A very strong inner compulsion at least; and I suspect
that Thomas Hobbes could even have found an obligation.' There
have been schools of political philosophy whose doctrine was
founded on the rejection of the word; I think I know of two such in
ancient China. The Confucians held that shared patterns of ritualized behavior communicated and internalized values more harmo-
niously and with fewer contradictions than did verbal imperatives;
while the Taoists withdrew in disgust from the monstrous edifice of
fictions, confusions, and lies which words entailed, to pursue an
anti-politics of transcendence.[1] But it seems that both schools were
reacting, from different sides, against the discovery that it was next
to impossible to construct any verbal statement in terms such that it
could not be refuted or distorted. Refutability was to the Confucians a stumbling-block and to the Taoists foolishness; but there
has been enough of Karl Popper in my upbringing to commit me to
the view that refutability *macht frei*. I shall in due course argue that
it is the imperfect character of verbal statements which renders

*J. G. A. Pocock, 'Verbalizing a Political Act: Toward a Politics of Speech', reprinted
from *Political Theory* 1 (February, 1973), pp. 27–43, by permission © Sage Publica-
tions, Inc.
†AUTHOR'S NOTE: An earlier version of this paper was delivered to the Confer-
ence for the Study of Political thought at City University of New York Graduate
Center, April 1971.

them answerable and human communication possible, and there may be said to exist a Hobbesian kind of obligation to verbalize my acts toward my neighbor so that he may have the opportunity of answering them; and I shall say this in the context of a consideration of politics itself as a language-system and language itself as a political system. I ought also to say at this stage that I do not claim competence in theoretical linguistics and that those who have such competence may well be able to correct me. And although my politics will initially develop as a classical structure of shared power, I shall – in order to make it quite clear that it is power that is being shared – start with a consideration of words as actions and as acts of power toward persons.

Shakespeare's Brutus declares – and it is significant that he does so in a soliloquy:

> Between the acting of a dreadful thing
> And the first motion, all the interim is
> Like a phantasma or a hideous dream
>
> Julius Caesar, II, i: 63–65.

R. G. Collingwood argued with characteristic ingenuity that 'the acting' meant the initial conception and 'the first motion' the first step in actual performance.[2] The point need not be settled in order to realize its significance, which is that the framing of the intention is part of the total process of the act. English treason law, of which Shakespeare will have been thinking, used to insist that to 'compass or imagine' the death of the king was as treasonable as to kill him; and the point was not entirely unsound, even if J. Edgar Hoover did agree with it: but the law used further to insist on two witnesses to an overt act as proof even of the compassing or imagining. Words, however, might well be taken as proof of the act of intention, and this step takes us near the heart of the complexities of our subject. But unless some zealous Cuban has bugged the garden where Brutus utters his soliloquy, he is not at this moment acting by communicating his intention to others; he is talking to himself. Given the ambiguity of speech as both expression and communication, both a private and a public act, it is appropriate to begin a study of the politics of verbalization with a man in a moment of self-communion.

The words quoted indicate to us what Brutus is doing. He is trying to escape from a hideous dream by verbalizing his action to himself, and this means two things: verbalizing his intention to act, and verbalizing the quality of the act he intends (which is, *inter alia*, to provide it with a rationale). Under the first aspect, verbalization is immediately performative: by saying 'I intend to kill Caesar', Brutus confirms – he completes forming – that intention, and this performance is part of a series of performances which constitute the totality of the act of killing Caesar. It is at present part of the hideous dream that Brutus does not know for sure that he is really going to kill Caesar, or that he really intends or wants to kill him, until he hears himself say that he intends to do so. This is why he is talking to himself; the communication is part of the performance. But under the second aspect, verbalization is much more complex though still in part performative. Brutus may now say: 'I intend to kill Caesar because he is a tyrant', and this utterance is more than simply explanatory or justificatory. 'Caesar is a tyrant' is an assertion, an act of definition, not the simple recital of a previously accepted datum. In defining Caesar as a tyrant, Brutus is not only justifying the act he intends, but is also qualifying it; he is saying that to kill Caesar is to kill a tyrant, so that what he intends when he says 'I intend' is 'to kill a tyrant'. The statement 'Caesar is a tyrant' and the implication 'it is right to kill tyrants' are both present and may perhaps be articulated and further explored; but equally they may be left behind, embedded in the structure of the utterance in such a way that it will become increasingly hard to go back and examine them. Brutus may subconsciously intend to make it hard for himself to do this, given that throughout the utterance he is engaged in burning his boats. But the assertions and assumptions he is found to have been making are in no case separate from the formation of an intention by verbalization. In qualifying the intention, they help make it by making it what it is, and so form part of – and help form – both the immediate and the prospective performance, even though none of them by itself may constitute a performative statement.

But the intention and the performance require, to give them meaning, the sort of qualifying context which the words invoke; they require it for reasons lying deeper than even the need for justification. In using so potent a word as 'tyrant', Brutus invokes a whole world of reference structures, into which his other words, his intended act, and his verbalized state of consciousness now enter in such a way that it qualifies them all; so that 'Caesar', 'kill', 'intend', and even 'I' take on new meanings retrodictively as they enter the world that 'tyrant' invokes. Because of the magic quality of speech, the worlds you invoke are very likely to appear around you. Speech-acts of this kind are notoriously difficult to revoke – not least so, perhaps, as Brutus may very well intend, when uttered in soliloquy. For the hideous dream, they substitute what is verbalized and presented as a terrible reality.

Brutus is using language; he is communicating with a hearer, who happens to be himself. He is acting upon himself – the first person 'I' – by forming his intention as an act of verbalization; but this he does by communicating information concerning that intention to a second person – himself as hearer – who is in turn acted upon by being made the receiver of information which is bound, as it is intended, to modify his perceptions of the world. In archaic and formal English, a communication of information was sometimes introduced by the imperative verb: 'Know that' and the message would follow; the imperative left no doubt that to inform might be to act upon and to command. If we imagine Brutus communicating his intention to a second person existing independently – let us say his wife – the situation would be complicated by the immediacy of her self-willed responses, which would immediately modify Brutus's perception of his intention through perceiving her perception of it. But let us not exaggerate the scale of this complication; in the first place, Brutus's message would be designed to predetermine Portia's response to it; and, in the second place, I used to give a lecture entitled 'Playback, or you never know who's listening', with the theme that in any message you had always one auditor – yourself – whose responses might be those you could least determine or predict. Meanwhile, at a distance, a third person – Caesar – is being acted upon in two ways: he is being defined in the imparted perceptions of the first and second persons (a) as the object of an intended act, 'killing'; (b) as the sort of person, 'tyrant', who qualifies the act as the sort of act it is henceforth intended and understood to be. Verbalizations we now see, act upon people – and so constitute acts of power – in at least two ways: either by informing them and so modifying their perceptions or by defining them and so modifying the ways in which they are perceived by others. Either of these acts of power may be entirely unilateral and arbitrary: performed, that is, by the will of one person only.

In discussing verbalization *of* an act as part of the act performed, we have also begun discussing verbalization *as* an act or performance – indeed, an assertion of power – in its own right; that is to say, we have examined the relation of 'means' to 'ends' in examining the intention as part of the action. We will also be considering the relation of 'theory' to 'practice' if we imagine Brutus pausing – as he does pause – to explore and clarify the meanings and implications of the words he is using; but to set up this relation as a worthwhile problem we shall have to suppose that clarification of language may become an intended act distinguishable from the intended act which the language has been verbalizing. If we imagine the secondary statements composing theory merely as qualifying the primary verbalizations of intent which constitute practice and concerning which the former are made, then theory must be seen as re-entering the complex of verbalization, intention, communication, and action which constitutes what we call practice. But, in introducing the distinction between first-order and second-order verbalizations, we have introduced another problem, of equal if not greater importance.

Brutus's language is not his own. He would be unable to talk about it if it were composed purely and exclusively of his declarations of his intentions. He has been asserting, or defining, his intentions, his role, and the roles of second and third persons, and acting upon all three, in a language which he has not made, but which consists largely of the sedimentation and institutionalization of speech-acts performed by other persons, upon other persons, and with other intentions.[3] Very complex processes of assumption, mediation, and conventionalization have gone on to bring this language to him as a structure of givens, and, as a result, it is usually not possible to say with simple factuality what their authors intended the speech-acts originally fed into the language to effect; who meant what by them. For this very reason, Brutus's language is not his own; he did not make it and he does not know who did, and given – what for a variety of reasons we must concede – that there is much implicit in language which becomes explicit only when it is explored after being used, a consequence for Brutus is that, in willing to impose a variety of roles upon himself and others, he is discovered to have been entering into a most complex collaborative fiction with co-authors whose names, intentions, and communicative devices are removed from him along an ever-receding series of mediations. Each of us speaks with many voices, like a tribal shaman in whom the ancestor ghosts are all talking at once; when we speak, we are not sure who is talking or what is being said, and our acts of power in communication are not wholly our own. Theory may be said to consist in attempts to answer questions of this order, to decide what power is being exercised over us when we seek to exercise it.

At this point, it becomes possible – though only, I think, on Platonic, puritan, romantic, or existentialist grounds – to accuse Brutus of bad faith. To assert his intention, role, or identity in language made up of others' assertions of their intentions, roles, and identities is to allow his act of power to be taken over by the

ghosts and to disguise their power as his; he is accepting a false
identity, subjecting himself to an alien power, and allowing it to be
supposed that the alien agency is his active self. To reduce speech-
acts to acts of power is to point toward this result, because power is
desperately hard to reconcile with fiction or identification with
another. I cannot say that another's power is my power; I may
indeed own that another's power is to be treated *as if* it were my
power, but how I come to perform this is one of the darkest
mysteries in *Leviathan.*[4] Brutus, then, is saying 'this is mine' when
actually what he is saying is another's. He is performing a fiction.
But the accusation of bad faith is valid only if he does not know or
will not admit that he is performing a fiction or that the conditions
of utterance are such that the fiction he intends to perform cannot
be the fiction he is performing. The language he uses is not of his
own making; it has been made by others. But if he knows to the full
what others have intended – or, to telescope the whole series of
mediations in a single metaphor, what is intended – by the language
he uses, then he knows to the full what the action is that he intends
by means of fiction to perform; whereas if – as is far more probable
– he knows that he does not know fully what his language means,
then he knows that he does not know the full meaning of the act he
intends; and theory becomes the honest exploration of the limits of
his intention and action, the pursuit of the Socratic and Confucian
wisdom of 'knowing what one does not know'. It is, of course,
difficult to be, or to endure being, as conscious of one's medium as
this; but it is mere intellectual snobbery, posing as anti-
intellectualism, to pretend that the number of people who can be so
is insignificant.

At this level, too, what appeared to be Brutus's disguising of
others' power as his own may become his acceptance of others'
power as a qualification and limitation of his own. I want next to
put forward a picture of language operating, as a two-way communication system, to transform the unilateral assertion of power
in action into the shared exercise of power in a polity. I shall be
saying that there is polity where people succeed in communicating –
that is, in making and replying to statements in such a way that
there is some not too remotely discernible relationship and continuity of medium between statement, reply, and counter-reply –
and I shall postpone consideration of the somewhat too easily
rhetorized situations which exist when this is not the case.

I shall continue to assume that men communicate by means of
language, and that language consists of a number of already
formed and institutionalized structures. These embody and perform

speech-acts, but they perform the intentions of the user only through words formed by sedimentation and institutionalization of the utterances performed by others whose identities and intentions may no longer be precisely known. There is a double sense, then, in which the words that perform my acts are not my own: in the first place, they are words used by others and only borrowed by me, and in the second place, they have been institutionalized to the point where they cannot be finally reduced to the speech-acts of known individuals. My acts, therefore, have been preinstitutionalized; they must be performed by institutionalized means. But language-structures which have been institutionalized are available for use by more than one person, operating with more than one purpose and in more than one situation; they are never free from ambiguity in the sense that they can never be reduced to the performance of any one person's intention. To perform my speech-act I must borrow another's, and he was in exactly the same predicament; all verbalized action is mediated. But next, institutionalization makes my language available to the person to or about whom I speak for purposes of reply and refutation; he can, as we put it, answer me in my terms. Communication rests upon ambiguity. From the premiss of institutionalization, it follows both that we can never fully understand one another (or even ourselves) and that we can always answer one another (and in soliloquy, we can answer ourselves). There is a certain refraction and recalcitrance in the medium which ensures that the language I bend to perform my own acts can be bent back in the performance of other's acts against me, without ceasing to be available for my counter-replication. Language gives me power, but power which I cannot fully control or prevent others from sharing. In performing a verbalized act of power. I enter upon a polity of shared power.

Two incidents in *Alice Through the Looking Glass* would seem to be making this point.[5] Humpty Dumpty, as is well known, avers that 'when I use a word, it means what I want it to mean, neither more nor less. . . . The question is who is to be master, that's all.' This poor being is in the linguistic equivalent of a Hobbesian state of nature; it has not occurred to him that words subject to one person's totally arbitrary control may become unintelligible to those hearing them, and so of very little use for purposes even of mastery. As his conversation with Alice develops, he is increasingly unable to retain the master's posture and is forced to resort to obfuscation. 'Impenetrability! That's what I say.' Finally Alice gets tired of him and simply walks away, and as she does so he falls off his wall. At a later stage in the story, the Red Queen remarks:

'When you've said a thing, that fixes it and you must take the consequences.' Without going too deeply into her use of the word 'fixes', we can intepret her as meaning that to use language at all, you must make commitments. You have not merely performed upon yourself; you are inescapably perceived as having performed in ways defined by others' acceptances of the words you have used. You have performed upon them, but the means by which you have performed are in some degree not at your power but at theirs. An act of power verbalized is, in this perspective, an act of power mediated and mitigated.

There is, of course, one fairly evident possible flaw in this presentation, and I will come to that. First, however, I need to explore some further theoretical implications of the perspective in which language is seen as polity. It involves seeing language as a medium which cannot be wholly controlled by any single or isolable agency; we rest this assertion on the premiss that language is institutional. Institutionalization breeds ambivalence, or rather multivalence. Where Humpty Dumpty went wrong was in averring that his words meant what he wanted them to mean, 'neither more nor less'. In language, it must be declared, we have to be content with saying both less and more than we mean: less, because our language will never immediately convey our meaning or perform our acts of power; more because it will always convey messages and involve us in consequences other than those we intended. And it is our willingness to be involved in these unintended consequences, to commit ourselves to what others may make of our words, our intentions, our performances, and our *esse* as *percipi*, that makes communication and even action possible. I am clearly not presenting language as a neutrally objective medium, though I will at need argue from these premisses that there are neutral and objective operations that can be performed with it. This theory of language is essentially Clausewitzian. Clausewitz perceived that it was the relative non-conductivity of the medium in which violence was conducted that made it conceivable that war might be conducted as an intelligent, and so intelligible, communicative, political mode of behavior. Because there were frictions between my intention and its performance – because, that is, I was not Humpty Dumpty – I had a problem in relating means to ends. To that problem I might intelligently address myself; my adversary, perceiving and interpreting my actions, might infer from them what my ends and means were; and I might direct my actions toward him as messages of a special sort designed to influence his will, as he might do to me. We entered the chess-playing stage, of seeking to impose strategies on one another by means of symbolic communications which were also acts of power; and none of this would have been possible had either of us possessed the power of immediately performing our intentions. Because there were frictions in the medium, we were compelled to accept mediation of our acts; because the acts and the frictions were observed and utilized by two mutually perceptive intelligences, they became modalities of communication and neither intelligence could exclude its adversary from the medium or the mediation.

It now becomes possible to regard verbalization as a singularly effective device for introducing frictions into a medium and thus rendering it communicative. Language is an effective medium for political communication and action, on this interpretation, not because it is neutral but because it is relatively uncontrollable and so hard to monopolize. Whatever biases I impart to the medium, it is hard for me to prevent others not merely from imparting their own biases but actually from using my imparted biases to construct and impart their own. We thus have to devise strategies, and in observing one another's strategies, we begin to communicate. If we reach the point of uttering statements about the medium, its frictions and our strategies in making use of these, which are not merely moves in the power game but clarificatory utterances simultaneously usable by both players, we have reached the point of theory – of making utterances about utterances which possess a certain objectivity that permits them to perform a further mediatory and communicative function. The institutionalized speech-structures which the language polity requires us to employ carry a certain load of utterances of this secondary kind, which have themselves been institutionalized.

I am aware that the emphasis I am laying upon interposing frictions in the way of action will have a conservative ring in some ears, and since my intentions are only incidentally conservative, if at all, I feel slightly apologetic about this. I do think it desirable to slow down the action to the point where it can be conceptualized and criticized and we can relate ourselves to it; I have anti-McLuhanist preferences, and if this be conservatism, make the most of it; but my main concern is for the preservation of a structure of two-way communication, which appears to me a necessary feature of any form of human freedom, and I am stressing the introduction of frictions into the medium with that end in view – and equally, I am seeking to slow down the power act so that it ceases to be immediate and unmediated. This is why I prefer my politics verbalized. But I am also probably exposing myself to what has lately

become the accusation of pluralism in stressing that mediation has
to go through the medium of a relatively slow-changing authority-
structure, and the time has come to show that I am under no
illusions about the tendency of institutionalized authority to get out
of hand and become power – either somebody's or nobody's. So far
I have been dealing with a language polity and talking in terms of
the classical politics, which is the appropriate vocabulary to use
when we believe ourselves to have equals; the players of my language game are performing the linguistic equivalent of Aristotle's
'ruling and being ruled'. It is now desirable to examine the linguistics of unshared power.

When I said there was a flaw in the theory of the language polity,
I had in mind that Humpty Dumpty need not be an isolated
eccentric sitting on a wall. He may command the services of all the
king's horses and all the king's men; and he may use them to
convey, and to compel acceptance of, his arbitrarily varied speech
acts. The two-way character of communication will be entirely lost
when there are those who have the meaning of their words decided
entirely for them, and reply to the speech-acts of those in command
of the language only, if at all, in terms which the latter have
determined and to which they impart nothing of their own. When
we define the situation as precisely as that, we can ask whether it
ever exists in definitional purity in the real world; but there is an
impressive array of rhetoric to remind us that real-world situations
can come close to it. We therefore need to understand both the
linguistics of this situation and the linguistics of getting out of it.

If the point is reached where I exist, even in my own perceptions,
solely as defined in terms set by others, my condition may be called
that of the slave. My masters may be visible or invisible, personal or
impersonal. There may be some identifiable Humpty Dumpty with
power to fix or change the language at will; there may be some
institutionalized language independent of any will now existing,
but permitting some to perform all the speech-acts and others only
to suffer them; or I may, as in *1984* find myself subject to an
invisible but highly effective bureaucracy of manipulators who
maintain their power by varying the entire language structure in
directions and at moments that cannot be predicted. What I know
is that speech-acts are being performed on me, and that I am
performing none of them myself. Now let it be assumed that I begin
to liberate myself from this slavery, and that I do so partly by the
performance of speech-acts which begin to be my own in the sense
that they perform my intentions and I intend their performance.

The questions now arise; how do I acquire the linguistic resources to perform these acts and on whom do I perform them?

There is an important body of theory which says: I must acquire the linguistic means of liberation from my former master; and I will acquire them by using, in the world of experience into which he has thrust me, the means of verbalizing that experience which he has imposed upon me, but which can no longer be used as a means of such verbalization without setting off conceptual consequences unforeseen and undesired by him. Something has happened, unintended by the master, in the material world which my speech verbalizes; we proceed to provide a theory of change in the world, brought about in consequence of the relationship between me and my master, which will explain and predict how this unintended result happens. But if it is to be asserted that my self-liberating speech act is a simple reversal of his speech-acts toward me, simply my expropriation of his language defining me in order to perform my definition of my self, the master must be locked into the relationship between us in such a way that he cannot move from it or redefine it; his language must imprison him as rigorously as does the same language when imposed upon me. He may be allowed to find new ways of enjoining me to consider myself a slave, or tell me the outright lie that I am not a slave if this can have the sole and exclusive result of manipulating me to remain one; but if he is able to perform any speech-act the effect of which is that I become other than a slave, then I am no longer liberating myself by the simple negation of his language that enslaves me. On the other hand, if I am doing this I am not engaging in two-way communication with him. Essentially, I am talking about myself to myself, and if I say anything to him it is probably said in order that I may hear myself denouncing him. I cannot be engaging him in dialogue if I am engaged in destroying the means of his speech-acts, and thus in destroying him or transforming him into something other than he is. If, in making myself other than a slave, I am making myself other than a thing, I am liable to find that this involves treating him as a thing, or at any rate a third person or *alter*.

The proposition 'the master must be a master if he is to cease being a master' is, I suppose, a dialectical tautology; but it becomes a good deal more than a tautology if the master–slave relationship, while real, is not the whole of the reality about us. That is, if the ruler is not entirely contained and imprisoned within this or any other categorization of the ruler–ruled relationship, he can act – which includes the performance of speech-acts – outside that categorization. Moreover, unless he can wholly control the communications universe in which he acts, he will speak outside that role, and some of his words will reach the ruled in forms not wholly intended by the ruler or expected by the ruled. To these, the ruled will reply, and the context he sets up by doing so will modify the linguistic exchanges intended and expected to be otherwise. In proportion, as this happens, we enter a situation of language power very different from the simple dialectic of the master–slave relationship. The master is no longer wholly a master, or the slave wholly a slave, since the master no longer enjoys unmitigated linguistic authority to define the slave; and on the other hand, the ex-slave has lost the absolute freedom to annihilate the master by defining him as a nonmaster (or *ci-devant*). The master has lost and gained; he is no longer imprisoned within an absolute and one-dimensional power; in admitting that he is not only a master, he has acquired additional freedom of action. He may well think the deal worth making, especially if he retains 99% of the advantages of being a master. The ex-slave still has a long way to go. But from the moment the two of them accept mitigation of the master–slave relationship, the furthest reversal or transformation of their relationship begins to move from a pattern of dialectical negation toward one of Clausewitzian communication. They have strategies and counter-strategies for working on one another's wills; and when will is working on will by means of the sending of messages, they are in second-person communication.

There is theory which will deny this, on the grounds that the freedom of maneuver they have acquired is illusory; socially constricting forces are at work which will force them back into the relationship of master and slave. This may very well be; the prediction sets up a pattern of warnings which should receive serious attention. But the statement that it must be so – that I am imprisoned within a certain categorization because there is no alternative – begins to resemble the sort of holistic utterance I was taught to regard as non-refutable and non-investigatable. At best it is rhetoric, introductory to an investigatable statement; and operational and performative rhetoric can lead to methodological naivete. I recall picking up some Soviet-Marxist tract of the bad period and finding in the opening pages an assertion to the effect that bourgeois societies believed themselves to be founded on absolute and unchanging laws. Reflecting that this anyway was false, I turned to the last page of the book and found there something about the eternally viable laws of Marxism-Leninism. The first fallacy probably had something to do with generating the second.

Those with a keen ear for ideology will have noticed that I am changing roles and speaking now as the recipient or target of the liberating statement. If someone insists that I am imprisoned within the structure of my own reifications and goes on saying so even when, after self-examination and reflection, I am convinced that I am not, we may reach the point where I am convinced that there is no way to persuade him that I am not; and about this point, I may begin wondering about the performative character and intent of his statements. Are they error, myth, or strategy? He may be prevented by some intellectual blockage from seeing that I am not imprisoned; he may be cheering himself with the illusion that I am imprisoned in the master–slave relationship and so possess greater power and less freedom to manage it than I believe; or he may be seeking, by means of performative statements, to imprison me in that relationship, and in the role of master, for reasons arising from his own notions of revolutionary strategy. We have begun talking about the politics of polarization. One-dimensional rulers have the choice of remaining the rulers they are or ceasing to be at all. Sensible rulers try to avoid giving themselves that choice and may accept the alternative of becoming rulers who are also ruled, which is, or may be to say, citizens in a polity. But the revolutionary strategist tries to thrust the one-dimensional choice upon them and to deny them the alternative. In the case I am supposing, he is to be found attempting to do that by means of performative speech-acts.[6] He is either compelling recognition of the world as it really is or forcing the world into a one-dimensional shape for his own one-dimensional purposes. The chances that he is attempting the former increase in proportion as he has left room for deciding whether or not the world is as he says it is; room, that is, for recognizing the possibility that it may not be as he says it is; but performative statements – especially those which perform upon the hearer rather than the speaker – are extremely difficult to construct in a refutable form. If someone says – performatively – that I am what I am not, how am I to reply? If someone is performing speech-acts whose effect, if unmitigated, would be to terminate communication between us, by what speech-acts shall I mitigate his performance and keep him in communication against his intent?

The problem of the legitimacy of polarization raises the problem of distinguishing between true and bogus revolutions. If the ruler is really a slave-master or is deceived in thinking that he is not, it is hopeless to attempt mediation between master and slave; a false structure of two-way communication may have to be broken down. But the bogus revolution is found when the revolutionary in bad

faith is attempting to impose one-dimensionality where this is not
sufficiently imposed by factors outside his own speech-acts. The
distinction is highly recognizable in principle but very hard to draw
in practice; especially if we phrase it as a distinction between
absolute and relative, between situations where the partners really
are as master and slave and situations where master and slave
represents part but not all of the truth about them. I may have
unfairly suggested that this is as the distinction between ideal and
actual, and that therefore purely revolutionary situations never
exist, and revolutionary strategy is never justified, in real life; but
this is not the contention I am arguing for. The message I am trying
to convey is that the distinction is hard to draw, and that while it
remains hard to draw there will be bogus revolutions as well as real
ones, and situations in which it will be hard to decide whether we
are playing bogus or for real. Enough of us have faced nasty little
Antigones trying to make us behave like Creon for their own
nefarious purposes to know what the bogus situation is like; and it
is only one more step to the situation in which Antigone, with the
utmost integrity, of course, is so certain that we *are* Creon that we
are beginning to have doubts ourselves and may react so energeti-
cally that we prove her right. If she is wrong and we are not Creon,
we urgently need means of converting tragedy into comedy. There
may be an unnecessary tragedy if we lack them, since tragedy is
necessary only if she is right.

We inhabit an overcrowded, overcommunicative, intersubjective
world in which people easily become convinced of each other's bad
faith, and these suspicions are often justified and often self-
fulfilling. There has come to be a politics of bad faith, consisting in
the performance of speech-acts in which I define you as acting in
bad faith in such a way that your only means of being in good faith
is to give me what I want (possibly your abdication or self-
annihilation). If you are in bad faith, you deserve this treatment and
cannot escape it; if not, you need means of replying to my statement, which it must be remembered is performative rather than
descriptive. Because I disbelieve your good faith, I have placed you
in the position of being in bad faith; I have performed an act of
power designed to reduce your freedom of action. Your reply –
which I am busy reducing your freedom to make – will have to be
similarly performative, upon yourself and on me. But speech of this
kind is both self-actualizing and escalatory. The trouble with
escalation is both that it is counter-productive and that is makes an
end of two-way communication. In a conversation where each of us
is constantly moving into denying the legitimacy of the other's

contributions, we have to test whether such denials must continue, whether the contest between us is dialectical or Clausewitzian, whether the escalatory tendency in our speech has to run its course. Come, let us delegitimize together. The crucial question will be whether it is possible for my speech-acts performed upon you to permit, and continue permitting, a reply by you in terms of acts performed upon me; and so forth. If this is possible, the linguistic polity will have been preserved in the form of mutually perceived, intercommunicative strategies. Such seems to be the politics of the performative dialogue; we now need to look at theories whereby speech may be perceived as counter- and interperformative.

All speech, we have premissed, is performative in the sense that it does things to people. It redefines them in their own perceptions, in those of others and by restructuring the conceptual universes in which they are perceived. Given the premiss of intersubjectivity, it is important to realize, there can be no such thing as a purely self-defining speech-act. A recent book about revolt bears the title *The Right to Say We.*[7] Now clearly I cannot say 'we' without redistributing a number of other human beings among the categories 'we', 'you', and 'they'. To do this to people can have very considerable consequences for them, and these I perform by an act of my own. Liberation even, that image of such potency in the contemporary sensibility, involves an act of power over others: a speech-act by which I define myself is performed in another's universe and redefines him as well as me. Our language assigns us roles, either directly or indirectly; to reshape language so as to reshape myself is to reshape another's self, both by changing the ways in which I appear and perform in his universe and by changing the ways in which he can define himself. As our common universe becomes increasingly second-person and intersubjective, it is increasingly hard for me to redefine myself without committing some direct (but, alas, not necessarily second-person) attack on his definition of himself. The problem is that of affording him the means of counter-performance.

Henry Kariel's recent writings appear to me to travel some distance into this problem.[8] He develops very ingeniously – from a standpoint which I take to be radical – the concept of play as a means of countering the repressive tendencies of languages. The prevailing language structure assigns to us universes in which we play roles; it does so without consulting us and in ways which we may very well find repressive. But on the margins and at the buried roots of language, there is a rich field of ambiguities, absurdities, and contradictions awaiting our exploitation. By speech-acts, other acts of communication and by acts themselves considered as communications, we not merely expose these to the satiric eye but use them to liberate ourselves from the life styles imposed upon us. We act in ways consonant with language and yet unexpected; we reverse roles; we discover contradictions and negations; we set off resonances whose subversive tremors may be felt at the heart of the system; and we discover roles for ourselves in the teeth of the roles which language seeks to impose. This is the image of the clown as liberator; but there have been some remarkably sinister clowns in our time, and when the clown or the counter-culture becomes evil it is often because, in his enthusiasm for antinomian behavior, he has forgotten the unilateral and unlimited acts of power which antinomian actions may become when they are performed in and upon the lives of others. The polis is not the circus; a higher level of audience participation is guaranteed. I think, however, that Kariel's thesis provides an effective defense against this danger, though at a higher price than he may be willing to pay.

His strategy is an obviously effective means of dealing with a language universe conceived of in alien, impersonal, or third-person terms; as Other, as a system or power-structure in which I am not as free as I could be and other persons or groups, or impersonal institutions, are enabled by the language, to impose roles and universes upon me. I therefore set out to shake up, send up, and generally disconcert Them and It. Well and good; but the spectre of the clown as evil has to be invoked to raise the question of You. What am I doing to you and how may you respond? It is simply not enough that I invite, enjoin or oblige you to join my act and become We. You are inescapably the object of some of my acts, the subject of some of the changes I induce.

Kariel's concept of language, if I have not distorted it, is not unlike the one I have been using here. He recognizes both that it performs upon us by assigning us a distribution of authority and roles which go with that structure, and that it is a sedimentation of unintended as well as intended results and therefore always negatable, always the source of means of reversing the roles which it assigns. If it can always be screwed, it can always be penetrated; it consists of a tissue of closed contexts which can always in principle be rendered open. Unless – and this I find hard to reconcile with the concept of play or of language – some rigorous historical dialectic separates it absolutely into one dead crust and one living growth, the game can begin at any point and can be played. I am trying to play my way out of the role which language assigns me. This involves my assigning to you a role in the implementation of the language structure – whether that of ruler or of mediator, it will necessarily be that of manipulator – which may well be objectively justified; and my further assigning you a new role, consequent on my change of role, which is far more the creation of my freedom. You need to respond, since you cannot afford to accept inertly the roles I have assigned you. Let us further suppose that you are – as, indeed, I have defined you – more interested than I am in maintaining the existing structure of role ascription; it will actually be harder for you if you are not as I have assumed; and let us finally suppose that I am seeking to pen you up in that role as a first step to making you surrender it. What do you do now?

If we are talking the same language, and I am merely exploiting its content unintended by you, neither of us has the last word; there is not a last word. The game I am proposing is one that two can play. If I can discern unexpected possibilities in your language, you can discern others in mine; if I can perform in unexpected fashion the roles which language thrusts upon me, you can perform in ways I do not anticipate the roles which I am thrusting upon you. Let us certainly keep in mind here the differences between real and bogus revolutions; you may indeed be a ruler so far imprisoned in your role that you respond with precisely the degree of brutality I have expected of you. But it was of Brezhnev and Daley that Auden wrote, in *August 1968*: 'The ogre cannot master speech.' If you have not lost control of your own language, you can understand the games I am playing with it; and though I have seized the initiative and caught you off guard, it still gives you plenty of opportunity for counter-maneuver. And if you are in power, the language I am turning against you is still more your language than it is mine. By discerning a latent irony or absurdity in the role you have assigned me, I have reversed some language-game and sought to imprison you in a role assigned to you; but there should still be opportunity for you to discover ambiguities in the language by which I do this and to maneuver between the role I seek to fix on you and the roles which language otherwise makes available to you. There is a complex of role-ambiguities out of which you may answer me and I you. Frictions are back in the medium, and the comedy of strategies is on.

Kariel's sense of the absurdities inherent in language, then, seems to involve only an impure dialectic and to be wholly compatible with intelligent conservatism. It was, after all, Michael Oakeshott who defined political conversation as 'pursuing the intimations of a tradition of behaviour', and pursuing the intimations is very much what the clown and the counter-clown are doing. That the ruler may be seen as comedian, not ogre, is apparent to anyone who has lived in England and seen the extent to which comedy is used as an instrument of rule and of ruling-class adaptiveness; it can easily be overstated, but it is there. We had better remind ourselves of the truism that the conservative may be as disrespectful of rigid structures of authority as any radical; he knows the advantages of freedom of maneuver and does not propose to be imprisoned by the system he desires to maintain – that is now what he is maintaining it for. He will therefore play politics as a game with zest and appreciation; nor need it be a very clean game. If Creon succeeds in treating the whole thing as a joke, what happens to Antigone, for whom it is no joke at all? In some versions of the tale, she manages to insist on death for them both rather than let this happen; but suppose Creon puts the choice before her in exactly those terms?[9] The weapon of death is still available, but it is used on others as well as on herself. If she wants an ending in terms of finite values – of comedy and polity – it is her business to outwit Creon, not outdo him in authenticity; she can leave him with the option of accepting the result.[10]

I am enlarging the trusim that revolution is not a game for two players into the statement that the character of language as a two-way communication system is hard to reconcile with revolution as a one-way act of power. Therefore, the verbal strategy characteristic of the revolutionary is the reduction of You to a choice between We and Them, or even It. He justifies doing so on the grounds that They have for some time been saying You to him in such a way that They mean It when they say You. This may well be more or less true; it corresponds to recognizable experience; but it is difficult to eliminate the second person altogether from any shared language system. The unintended sediment sees to that. When rulers reduce men to things, or You to It, they do so by a kind of deliberate blindness, as when the Lord hardened Pharaoh's heart, but revolutionaries do it with their eyes open. Rulers do not much care about authenticity, but revolutionaries do; their search for it carries them to the point of saying We, but authenticity alone does not impel them to say You, and revolutions are notoriously bad at becoming polities or games for two players. The character of the language polity seems to indicate why this is so. Humpty Dumpty wanted power, but would matters have been any better if he had desired language that would have represented his intentions with absolute purity? We are humanized by language and by communication with each other in polity; but the medium, it seems, is necessarily impure.

NOTES

1 See J. G. A. Pocock, *Politics, Language and Time* (New York: Atheneum, 1971), chapter 2.
2 R. G. Collingwood, *The New Leviathan* (Oxford: Clarendon Press, 1942), p. 97.
3 Language from P. L. Berger and T. Luckmann, *The Social Construction of Reality* (New York: Doubleday, 1966).
4 Thomas Hobbes, *Leviathan* I (n.d.), p. 16.
5 Lewis Carroll, *Alice Through the Looking Glass* (n.d.), chapters 4 and 9.
6 The term 'performative' here is not used precisely as in J. L. Austin, *How To Do Things with Words* (New York: Oxford University Press, 1965); I am arguing that either a true/false statement or an Austinian performative may act upon speaker, hearer, or referent, and modify his circumstances – how to do things to people with words.
7 R. Zorza, *The Right To Say We* (New York: Praeger, 1970).
8 H. S. Kariel, *Open Systems: Arenas for Political Action* (Itasca Ill.: F. E. Peacock, 1969); H. S. Kariel, 'Expanding the political present', *American Political Science Review* 43 (1969), p. 3.
9 A literary and political exercise: *Creon: All right, go ahead and bury him; I'll fix it up somehow.* Complete the play from this point.
10 The comedic ending is, of course, compatible with Antigone's being wholly in earnest about her central value-judgement.

4

The Political Language of the Helping Professions*

MURRAY EDELMAN†

Hospital staff often deny or ignore the requests of angry mental patients because to grant them would 'reinforce deviant behavior'. Teachers sometimes use the same rationale to justify ignoring or punishing demanding students. The last two Presidents of the United States have declared on occasion that they would pay no attention to peace demonstrators who resort to irritating or allegedly illegal methods. We commonly regard the last as a political act and the first two as therapeutic; but all of them are easily perceived as either political or therapeutic. How they are classified depends upon the assumptions of the observer, not upon the behavior he is judging. Some psychologists reject the 'reinforcement of deviant behavior' rationale on the ground that it pays no attention to all the special cognitive and symbolizing abilities of the human mind, equating people with rats; they believe such treatment too easily ignores reasonable grounds for anger and depresses the self-esteem of people who already suffer from too little of it, contributing to further 'deviance', not to health. In this view the 'treatment' is self-serving political repression, rationalized as rehabilitative to salve the consciences of those in authority and of the public. Some psychiatrists, on the other hand, see political demonstrators or ghetto rioters as sick, calling for drugs or psychosurgery, not political negotiation, as the appropriate response; the Law Enforcement Assistance Administration has generously supported experiments based on the premiss.

*Murray Edelman, 'The Political Language of the Helping Professions', reprinted from *Politics and Society* 4 No. 3 (1974), pp. 295–310, by permission © Geron – X, Inc.

†This research was supported in part by funds granted to the Institute for Research on Poverty at the University of Wisconsin-Madison by the Office of Economic Opportunity pursuant to the Economic Opportunity Act of 1964. The opinions expressed are those of the author.

The language of 'reinforcement' and 'help' evokes in our minds a world in which the weak and the wayward need to be controlled for their own good. The language of 'authority' and 'repression' evokes a different reality, in which the rights of the powerless need to be protected against abuse by the powerful. Each linguistic form marshals public support for professional and governmental practices that have profound political consequences: for the status, the rights, and the freedom of professionals, of clients, and of the wider public as well; but we rarely have occasion to inhabit or examine both worlds at the same time.

Language is the distinctive characteristic of human beings. Without it we could not symbolize: reason, remember, anticipate, rationalize, distort, and evoke beliefs and perceptions about matters not immediately before us. With it we not only describe reality but create our own realities, which take forms that overlap with each other and may not be mutually consistent. When it suits us to see rationalization as reason, repression as help, distortion as creation, or the converse of any of these, language and mind can smoothly structure each other to do so. When it suits us to solve complicated problems of logic and mathematics, language and mind smoothly structure each other to do that as well. When the complicated problems involve social power and status, distortion and misperception are virtually certain to occur.

It is a commonplace of linguistic theory that language, thought, and action shape each other. Language is always an intrinsic part of some particular social situation; it is never an independent instrument or simply a tool for description. By naively perceiving it as a tool, we mask its profound part in creating social relationships and in evoking the roles and the 'selves' of those involved in the relationships.

Because the helping professions define other people's statuses (and their own), the special terms they employ to categorize clients and justify restrictions of their physical movements and of their moral and intellectual influence are especially revealing of the political functions language performs and of the multiple realities it helps create. Just as any single numeral evokes the whole number scheme in our minds, so a term, a syntactic form, or a metaphor with political connotations can evoke and justify a power hierarchy in the person who used it and in the groups that respond to it.

Social scientists, and a large segment of the public, have grown sensitive and allergic to agitational political rhetoric and to the ambiguities of such labels as 'democracy', 'communist', and 'law and order'. The most fundamental and long-lasting influences upon political beliefs flow, however, from language that is not perceived as political at all, but nonetheless structures perceptions of status, authority, merit, deviance, and the causes of social problems. Here is a level of politics, and analysis, that conventional political science rarely touches, but one that explains a great deal of the overt political maneuvering and control upon which people normally focus.[1]

The special language of the helping professions, which we are socialized to see as professional and as non-political, is a major example of this level of politics, though not the only one. Through devices I explore here, these professions create and reinforce popular beliefs about which kinds of people are worthy and which are unworthy: about who should be rewarded through governmental action and who controlled or repressed. Unexamined language and actions can help us understand more profoundly than legislative histories or administrative or judicial proceedings how we decide upon status, rewards, and controls for the wealthy, the poor, women, conformists, and non-conformists.

In this paper I examine such political uses of language in psychiatry, social work, psychiatric nursing, public school education, and law enforcement. My observations are based upon extensive (and depressing) reading in the textbooks and professional journals of these professions published in the last decade. I looked for covert as well as overt justifications for status differentials, power differentials, and authority. Once the subtle ways in which language serves power are recognized, the central function of language in all political interactions becomes clear, whether we call the interactions 'government' or 'professional'.

THERAPY AND POWER

To illustrate the subtle bearing of language on status and authority consider a common usage that staff, clients, and the general public all accept as descriptive of a purely professional process: the term 'therapy'. In the journals, textbooks and talk of the helping professions the term is repeatedly used as a suffix or qualifier. Mental patients do not hold dances; they have dance therapy. If they play volleyball, that is recreation therapy. If they engage in a group discussion, that is group therapy.

Even reading is 'bibliotherapy'; and the professional literature warns that it may be advisable to restrict, supervise, or forbid reading on some subjects, especially politics and psychiatry.

Because it is a polar example, such an assertion forces us to notice what we normally pass over. To label a common activity as though it were a medical one is to establish superior and subordinate roles, to make it clear who gives orders and who takes them, and to justify in advance the inhibitions placed upon the subordinate class. It does so without arousing resentment or resistance either in the subordinates or in outsiders sympathetic to them, for it super-imposes a political relationship upon a medical one while still depicting it as medical.

Though the linguistic evocation of the political system is subtle, that very fact frees the participants to act out their political roles blatantly for they see themselves as helping, not as repressing. In consequence assaults on people's freedom and dignity can be as polar and degrading as those typically occurring in authoritarian regimes, without qualms or protest by authorities, clients, or the public that hears about them. In this way a suffix or qualifier evokes a full blown political system. No doubt it does so for most profes-sionals who draw power from the system as persuasively and unobtrusively as it does for the clientele groups whom it helps induce to submit to authority and to accept the status of a person who must let others decide how he or she should behave.

To call explicit attention to the political connotations of a term for power, on the other hand, is to rally opposition rather than support. To label an authority relationship 'tyrannical' is an ex-hortation to oppose it, not a simple description. The chief function of any political term is to marshal public support or opposition. Some terms do so overtly, but the more potent ones, including those used by professionals, do so covertly, portraying a power relation-ship as a helping one. When the power of professionals over other people is at stake, the language employed implies that the profes-sional has ways to ascertain who are dangerous, sick, or inadequate; that he knows how to render them harmless, rehabilitate them, or both; and that his procedures for diagnosis and for treatment are too specialized for the lay public to understand or judge them. A patient with a sore throat is anxious for his doctor to exercise a certain amount of authority; but the diagnosis is easily checked, and the problem itself circumscribes the doctor's authority. When there is an allegation of mental illness, delinquency, or intellectual incapacity, neither the diagnosis nor the scope of authority is readily checked or limited, but its legitimacy is linguistically created and reinforced.

It is of course the ambiguity in the relationship, and the ambiva-lence in the professional and in the client, that gives the linguistic usage its flexibility and potency. That is always true of symbolic evocations, and it radically distinguishes such evocations from simple deception. Many clients want help, virtually all professionals think they are providing it, and sometimes they do so. Just as the helping seems manifest until it is self-consciously questioned, and then it becomes problematic, so the political relationship seems non-existent until it is self-consciously questioned, and then it becomes manifest.

The special language of the helping professions merges cognition and affect. The term 'mental illness' and the names for specific deviant behaviors encourage the observer and the actor to condense and confound several facets of his perception: helping the suffering sick person, repressing the dangerous non-conformist, sympathy for the former, fear of the latter, and so on. The terms carry all these connotations, and the actor-speaker-listener patterns them so as to utilize semantic ambiguity to cope with his ambivalence.

We normally fail to recognize this catalytic capacity of language because we think of linguistic terms and syntactical structures as signals rather than as symbols. If a word is a name for a specific thing or action, then terms like 'mental illness', 'delinquency prone', or 'schizophrenic' have narrowly circumscribed meanings. But if a word is a symbol that condenses and rearranges feelings, memories, perceptions, beliefs, and expectations, then it evokes a particular structuring of beliefs and emotions, a structuring that varies with people's social situations. Language as symbol catalyses a subjective world in which uncertainties are clarified and appropriate courses of action become clear. Yet this impressive process of symbolic creation is not self-conscious. On the contrary, our naive view holds that linguistic terms stand for particular objects or behaviors, and so we do not ordinarily recognize that elaborate cognitive structures are built upon them.

In the symbolic worlds evoked by the language of the helping professions speculations and verified fact readily merge with each other. Language dispels the uncertainty in speculation, changes facts to make them serve status distinctions, and reinforces ideology. The names for forms of mental illness, forms of delinquency and for educational capacities are the basic terms. Each of them normally involves a high degree of unreliability in diagnosis, in prognosis, and in the prescription of rehabilitative treatments; but also entail unambiguous constraints upon clients, especially their confinement and subjection to the staff and the rules of a prison, school, or hospital. The confinement and constraints are converted into liberating and altruistic acts by defining them as education, therapy, or rehabilitation and by other linguistic forms to be examined shortly. The arbitrariness and speculation in the diagnosis and the prognosis, on the other hand, are converted into clear and specific perceptions of the need for control. Regardless of the arbitrariness or technical unreliability of professional terms, their political utility is manifest; they marshal popular support for professional discretion, concentrating public attention upon procedures and rationlizing in advance any failures of the procedures to achieve their formal objectives.

Categorization is necessary to science and, indeed, to all perception. It is also a political tool, establishing status and power hierarchies. We ordinarily assume that a classification scheme is either scientific or political in character, but any category can serve either or both functions, depending upon the interests of those who employ it rather than upon anything inherent in the term. The name for a category therefore confuses the two functions, consigning people to high or low status and power while drawing legitimacy from its scientific status.

Any categorization scheme that consigns people to niches according to their actual or potential accomplishments or behavior is bound to be political, no matter what its scientific function is. IQ's; psychiatric labels; typologies of talent, skills, or knowledge; employment statuses; criminal statuses; personality types – all exemplify the point. Regardless of their validity and reliability (which are notoriously low), or their analytic uses, such classifications rank people and determine degrees of status and of influence. The categorizations of the helping professions are pristine examples of the functions, and many of these categories carry over into the wider society. Once established, a categorization defines what is relevant about the people who are labeled. It encourages others to seek out data and interpret developments so as to confirm the label and to ignore, discount, or reinterpret counter-evidence. As a civil rights lawyer recently noted, 'While psychiatrists get angry, patients get aggressive; nurses daydream, but patients withdraw.'[2] The eternal human search for meaning and for status can be counted on to fuel the interpretation.

The language of the helping professions reveals in an especially stark way that perception of the same act can range all the way from one pole to its opposite. Is an action punishment or is it help? The textbooks and psychiatric journals recommend actions that look like sadism to many and like therapy to many others: deprivation of food, bed, walks in the open air, visitors, mail, or telephone calls; solitary confinement; deprivation of reading or entertainment materials; immobilizing people by tying them into wet sheets and then exhibiting them to staff and other patients; other physical restraints on body movement; drugging the mind against the client's will; incarceration in locked wards; a range of public humiliations such as the prominent posting of alleged intentions to escape or commit suicide, the requirement of public confessions of misconduct or guilt, and public announcement of individual misdeeds and abnormalities.

The major psychiatric and nursing journals describe and prescribe all these practices, and more repressive ones, repeatedly. The May 1973 issue of *Psychiatry* tells of a psychiatric ward in which a sobbing patient was required to scrub a shower room floor repeatedly with a toothbrush while two 'psychiatric technicians' stood over her shouting directions, calling her stupid, and pouring dirty water on the floor.[3] Another recent professional article suggests withholding meals from non-compliant patients,[4] and a third recommends that cold wet sheet pack restraints be used more often, because they gratify the patient's dependency needs.[5]

To describe these practices in such everyday language evokes horror at the 'treatments' in a person who takes the description naively, without the conditioning to the professional perspective to which everyone has in some degree been exposed. In the professionals and those who accept their perspective, on the other hand, it is the *language* rather than the actions that evokes horror, for they have been socialized to see these things only as procedures, as *means* to achieve rehabilitation, not as acts inflicted upon human beings. Language is consequently perceived as a distortion if it depicts what is observably *done* to clients rather than what ends the professional thinks the client should read into them and what the professional himself reads into them.

The professional's reaction to language of this kind exemplifies the reaction of powerful people in general to accounts of their dealings with those over whom they hold authority. Because the necessary condition of willing submission to authority is a belief that submission benefits the subordinate, it is crucial to the powerful that descriptions of their treatment of others highlight the benefit and not the physical, psychological, or economic costs of submission, as an unadorned factual description does. The revenue service deprives people of money, almost always involuntarily; the military draft imposes involuntary servitude; thousands of other agents of the state deprive people of forms of freedom. Usually the rationale for such restraints is an ambiguous abstraction: national security, the public welfare, law and order. We do not experience or name these ambiguous and abstract objectives as any different from goals that consist of concrete benefits, such as traffic control and disease control. Linguistic ambiguity spreads the potent rationale of these latter types of benefits to justify far more severe constraints and deprivations (including death in war) in policy areas in which benefits are non-demonstrable and doubtless often non-existent. We experience as radical rhetoric any factual description of authoritative actions that does not call attention to their alleged benefits to all citizens or to some, and authorities typically characterize such descriptions as subversive, radical, or treasonous. They are indeed subversive of ready submission and of political support.

The point becomes vivid if we restate the actions described above from the professional's perspective: discouraging sick behavior and encouraging healthy behavior through the selective granting of rewards; the availability of seclusion, restraints, and closed wards to grant a patient a respite from interaction with others and from making decisions, and prevent harm to himself or others; enabling him to think about his behavior, to cope with his temptations to elope and succumb to depression, and to develop a sense of security; immobilizing the patient to calm him, satisfy his dependency needs, give him the extra nursing attention he values, and enable him to benefit from peer confrontation; placing limits on his acting out; and teaching him that the staff cares.

The two accounts describe the same phenomena, but they occur in phenomenologically different worlds. Notice that the professional terms carry connotations about both physical conditions and the desires of clients that depict constraints as non-restrictive. To speak of 'elopement' rather than 'escape', as psychiatrists and staff members do, is to evoke a picture of individual freedom to leave when one likes (as eloping couples do) rather than of the locks, iron bars, and bureaucratic prohibitions against voluntary departure that actually exist. To speak of 'seclusion' or 'quiet room' rather than solitary confinement is again to suggest voluntary and enjoyable retirement from others and to mask the fact that the patient is locked in against his will and typically resists and resents the incarceration. Such terms do in a craftsmanlike and non-obvious way what professionals also do directly to justify restrictions on inmates. They assert in textbooks, journals, and assurances to visitors that some patients feel more secure in locked wards and in locked rooms, that professionals know when this is the case, and that the patients' statements to the contrary cannot be taken at face value.

To speak of 'limits' is to mask the fact of punishment for misbehavior and to perceive the patient as inherently irrational, thereby diverting attention from the manifest frustrations and aggravations that come from bureaucratic restrictions and from consignment to the lowest and most powerless status in the institution.

Many clients come in time to use the professional's language and to adopt his perspective. To the staff, their adoption of the approved linguistic forms is evidence of insight and improvement. All clients probably do this in some degree, but for many the degree is so slight that the professional descriptions serve as irony or as mockery. They are repeatedly quoted ironically by students, patients, and prisoners.

In the institutions run by the helping professions established roles and their special language create a world with its own imperatives. To recognize the power of language and roles to reinforce each other in this special setting is to understand the frequency with which good men and women in the larger society support governments that mortify, harass, torture, and kill large numbers of their citizens. To the outsider such behavior signals sadism and self-serving evil, and it is impossible to identify with it. To the people who avidly act out their roles inside that special world, motives, actions, and consequences of acts are radically different. Theirs is a work of purification: of ridding the inherently or ideologically contaminated of their blight or of ridding the world of the contamination they embody.

It is no accident that governments intent on repression of liberties and lives are consistently puritanical, just as helping professionals exhibit few qualms about exterminating resistance to their therapies in people they have labelled dangerous and in need of help. To the inhabitants of other worlds the repression is a mask for naked power, but to those who wield authority, power is a means to serve the public good. Social scientists cannot explain such phenomena as long as they place the cause inside people's psyches rather than in the social evocation of roles. To attribute evil or merit to the psyche is a political act rather than a scientific one, for it justifies repression or exaltation, while minimizing observation. To explore phenomenological diversity in people's worlds and roles is to begin to recognize the full range of politics.

Class or status differences may also entail wide differences in the labelings of identical behaviors. The teacher's underachiever may be the epitome of the 'cool' student who refuses to 'brownnose'. The middle class's criminal or thief may be a 'political prisoner' to the black poor. Such labels with contrasting connotations occur when a deprived population sees the system as unresponsive to its needs and organized rebellion as impossible. In these circumstances only individual non-conformity remains as a way to maintain self-respect. To the deprived the non-conformity is a political act. To the beneficiaries of the system it is individual pathology. Each labels it accordingly.

The term 'juvenile delinquent' historically served the political function of forcing the assimilation of Catholic immigrants to the WASP culture of late nineteenth- and early twentieth-century America. This new category defined as 'criminal' youthful behaviors handled informally among the urban Catholics and not perceived by them as crime at all: staying out late, drinking, smoking, reading comic books, truancy, disobedience. Now, however, the definition of prevailing urban norms as 'delinquency' justified the authorities in getting the Irish children away from their 'bigoted' advisors, the priests.[6] The language of individual pathology was part of an effort to repress a distinctive culture and a religion, but the language that described it masked its political consequences while rationalizing it in terms of its motivation of salvaging youth from crime.

Some professionals reject the professional perspective, and all, no doubt, retain some skepticism about it and some ability to see things from the perspective of the client and the lay public. In these cases the ambivalence is typically resolved in more militant, decisive, and institutionalized forms than is true of ambivalent clients; for status, self-conception, and perhaps income hinge upon how it is resolved. In consequence professionals adopt radical therapy, existentialist, or Szaszian views, or they attack these dissidents as unprofessional and unscientific.

The lay public by and large adopts the professional perspective; for its major concern is to believe that others can be trusted to handle the problem, which is potentially threatening to them but not a part of their everyday lives. This public reaction is the politically crucial one, for it confers power upon professionals and legitimizes their norms for society generally. The public reaction, in turn, is a response to the language of the professionals and to the social milieu that gives that language its authoritative meaning. When status and self-concept are reciprocal for two groups, it is natural that one group's 'repression' should be another's 'therapy'. Through ambiguous language forms, professionals, clients, and outsiders manage to adjust to each other and to themselves and to establish and maintain status hierarchies.

PROFESSIONAL IMPERIALISM

The special language of the helping professions extends and en-
larges authority as well as defining and maintaining it. It accom-
plishes this by defining the deviance of one individual as necessarily
involving others as well, by seeing the absence of deviant behaviors
as evidence of *incipient* deviance, and by defining as deviant forms
of behaviour that laymen regard as normal.

Because man is a social animal, deviance by definition involves
others as well. In the helping professions this truism serves as a
reason to multiply the range of people over whom the professional
psychiatrist, school psychologist, social worker, or law enforcement officer has authority. The 'multi-problem family' needs
counseling or therapy as much as its emotionally disturbed member. The person who adopts a non-middle class norm needs help
even if she or he does not want it; and the professional has an
obligation to 'reach out' or engage in 'case finding'. These phrases
and approaches place a particular interpretation upon the sense in
which deviance is social in character; namely, that because other
people are involved, they also need the ministrations of the professional. By the same token they mask an alternative interpretation:
that it is the conditions of deviants' lives, their environments, and
their opportunities that primarily need change, not the state of
mind of their families and associates. Manifestly, both interpretations and approaches are appropriate. The professional interpretation, whatever its clinical uses, also serves the political function of
extending authority over those not yet subject to it and the more
far-reaching political function of shaping public perceptions so as
to mask the appropriateness of change in economic and social
institutions.

The more sweeping professional forays into alien territory rely
upon lack of evidence to prove the need for treatment. Consider
one of the favorite terms of social work literature: the 'pre-
delinquent'; or corresponding psychiatric terms, like the 'pre-
psychotic'. On their face such terms imply that the reference is to all
who have not yet misbehaved, and that is certainly one of their
connotations, one that would appear to give the professional *carte
blanche* to assert authority over everybody who has not yet committed a crime or displayed signs of disturbance.

Though they do permit a wide range of arbitrary action, the
terms usually have a considerably narrower connotation in practice, for social workers, teachers, psychiatrists, and law enforce-

ment officials apply them largely to the poor and usually to children. Affluent adults are often in fact 'pre-delinquent' or 'pre-psychotic'; but it is not actual behavior that governs the connotations of these terms, but rather the statistical chances for a group and the belief that poor children are high risks, especially if they come from broken homes. They are indeed high statistical risks: partly because their labeling as pre-delinquents and the extra surveillance are certain to yield a fair number of offenders, just as they would in a wealthy population; and partly because poverty does not encourage adherence to middle-class behaviour.

In a program to treat 'pre-delinquents' in a middle-class neighborhood of Cambridge-Somerville, Massachusetts, the 'treated' group more often became delinquent than a control group, due, apparently, to the effects on the labeled people of their stigmatization. In a similar experiment in a slum neighborhood this result did not appear, apparently due to the fact that the stigmatization was not significantly different from the demeaning labels routinely applied to slum residents.[7]

The term 'pre-delinquent' nonetheless focuses the mind of its user and of his audience upon the need for preventive surveillance and control and diverts the mind from the appropriateness of social change. The term also evokes public confidence in the professionals' ability to distinguish those who will commit crimes in the future from those who will not. Once again we have an illustration of the power of an unobtrusive symbol to evoke a structured world and to direct perception and norms accordingly.

Still another form of extension of authority through the pessimistic interpretation of normal behavior is exemplified in the psychiatric phrase, 'escape to health'. Here the linguistic term again draws its connotation from the disposition to interpret behavior according to the status of the person engaging in it. If a psychiatric patient shows no pathological symptoms, the professional can designate the phenomenon as 'escape to health', implying that the healthy behavior is itself a sign that the patient is still sick, possibly worse than before, but intent now on deceiving himself and the staff. The consequence is continued control over him or her.

The term epitomizes an attitude common to authorities who know or suspect that their charges would prefer to escape their supervision rather then 'behave themselves'. The student typed as a trouble-maker or unreliable excites as much suspicion when he is quiet as when he is active. Parole boards have their choice of interpreting an inmate's conformist prison behavior as reform or as cunning deception. Anxious public officials in all historical eras

have feared both passivity and peaceful demonstrations among the
discontented as the groundwork for rebellion. Always, there are
metaphoric phrases to focus such anxieties and arouse them in the
general public: underground subversion, plotting, the calm before
the storm, quiet desperation, escape to health. Always, they point
to an internal psychological state or a physical allegation not susceptible to empirical observation.

In the schools other phrases emphasize student non-actions, discount their observable actions, and so justify special staff controls
over them. Especially common are 'underachiever' and 'overachiever'. The former implies that the student is lazy, the latter that
he is neurotic. 'Overachiever' is an especially revealing case, for it
offers a rationale for treating achievement as deviance. The helping
professions are often suspicious of people who display talents
beyond the 'norm', as they must be in view of their veiled equation
of the norm with health. Textbooks in 'special education' and
'learning disabilities' group gifted or exceptionally able students
with the retarded and the emotionally disturbed as special students
and advocate separating these 'special' students from the normal
ones. They urge that the gifted be required to do extra work
('enrichment'). This may or may not mean they learn more or learn
faster. It certainly means that they are kept busy and so discouraged
either from making demands on the teacher's time or intelligence or
from pointing up the stultifying character of the curriculum
through restiveness or rebelliousness.

At least as common is the view that the poor require treatment
and control whether or not they display any pathological symptoms. Though this belief is manifestly political and class based, the
language social workers use to justify surveillance and regulation of
the poor is psychological in character. Here are some examples
from social work and psychiatric journals and textbooks.

Regarding a pre-school nursery in a slum area:[8]

> The children did not have any diagnosed pathology, but as a
> result of existing in an atmosphere of cultural deprivation,
> they were vulnerable to many psychosocial problems.

From an article in *Social Work* suggesting devices through which a
social caseworker can induce the poor to come for counseling or
treatment by deceiving them into thinking they are only accompanying their children, or only attending a party or social meeting:[9]

> cognitive deficiency ... broadly refers to the lacks many

people suffer in the normal development of their thinking processes. For the most part, though not exclusively, such deficits occur among the poor regardless of nationality or race.

The same article quotes a memorandum issued by the Family Services Association of Nassau County: 'Culturally deprived adults seem to be impaired in concepts of causality and time.'[10] This last sentence very likely means that the poor are likely to attribute their poverty to inadequate pay or unemployment rather than to personal defects (causality) and are not punctual in keeping appointments with caseworkers (time). It is bound to be based upon a limited set of observations that have powerful implications for the professional observer's own status and authority. The quotation is an example of one of the most common linguistic devices for connoting pathology from specific behaviors equally open to alternative interpretations that make them seem natural and normal. One of several concrete acts becomes a generalization about an 'impairment'. To those who do not know the basis for the generalization, it is *prima facie* scientific. To the professionals who have already been socialized into the view the generalization connotes, it is persuasive and profound. To those who meet neither of these conditions, it is a political exhortation rather than a scientific generalization. These people are inclined to treat it as problematic and controversial rather than as established by authoritative procedures.

Still another psychiatric convention legitimizes surveillance over people without symptoms: the inhibition against describing any former patient as cured. To use the word 'cured' is to demonstrate naivete and an unprofessional stance. The approved term in the professional literature is 'improved'.

Vacuous language serves several functions. Because it is a special vocabulary, it marks off the insiders from the outsiders and defines the former as authoritative and professional. It helps insiders to legitimize social and political biases. They are not prejudiced against the poor, but against cognitive deficiencies; not against women, but against impulsive-hysterics; not against political radicals, but against paranoids; not against homosexuals, but against deviants. They are not in favor of punishing, stigmatizing, humiliating, or imprisoning people, but rather of meeting dependency needs, security needs, and of rehabilitation.

It is not chance that the groups constrained by these rationales are also the groups repressed by society at large or that the 'treatment' consists of either restoring conformist behavior or removing political offenders from the sight, the consciences, and the career competition of the conventional. Those who become clients have experienced problems either because they have acted unconventionally or because they belong to a category (the young, the poor, women, blacks) whose behavior is largely assessed because of who they are rather than because of what they do. As long as they define their function as winning acceptance for deviants in the existing social structure, the helping professions can only promote conventionality. An alternative is to embrace an explicitly political role as well as a professional one: to promote change in the social structure and to promote the extermination of extant definitions of acceptable behaviors and acceptable social groups. Some helping professionals have adopted this role, fully or partially.

'HELPING' AS A POLITICAL SYMBOL

The ambiguity of 'helping' is pointed up when we examine the contrasting ways in which society 'helps' elites and non-elites. Subsidies from the public treasury to businessmen are not justified as help to individuals, but as promotion of a popularly supported goal: defense, agriculture, transportation, and so on. The abstractions are not personified in the people who get generous depletion allowances, cost-plus contracts, tax write-offs, or free government services. To see the expenditure as a subsidy to real people would portray it as a blatant inequity in public policy. The word 'help' is not used in this context, though these policies make people rich and substantially augment the wealth of the already rich. Nor is there a dependency relationship or a direct personal relationship between a recipient and a grantor with discretion to withhold benefits. The grantor wields no power over the administrators who carry out the law; for there are always legislators and executives eager to penalize bureaucrats who call attention to the subsidy aspect of the program; and some of the more co-operative administrators can look forward to lucrative employment in the industries they come to know as dispensers of governmental benefits.

When 'help' is given to the poor or the unconventional, a wholly different set of role relationships and benefits appears. Now it is the beneficiaries who are sharply personified and brought into focus. They are individuals living off the taxpayer or flouting conventionality. What they personify is poverty, delinquency, dependency, or other forms of deviance. They are in need of help, but help in money, in status, and in autonomy must be sharply limited so as to avoid malingering. One of the consistent characteristics of the 'helping' institutions is their care to *limit* forms of help that would make clients autonomous: money for the poor; liberating education and freedom for children of the poor, or for 'criminals'; physical and intellectual autonomy. The limit is enforced in practice while denied in rhetoric.

The 'help' for non-elite recipients of the largesse of the state that draws ready political support is control of their deviant tendencies: laziness, mental illness, criminality, non-conformity. They are taught to tolerate indignity and powerlessness when employed, poverty when unemployed, and the family and social stresses flowing from these conditions without unconventional modes of complaint or resistance and without making too many demands on society.

In at least one of the worlds elites and professionals create for themselves and for a wider public the help is real and the need for it is manifest. So manifest that it must be given even if it is not wanted. So manifest that failure to want to becomes evidence that it is needed and that it should be forced on recipients involuntarily and through incarceration if necessary.

When a helping relationship of this kind is established, it is likely to dominate the self-conception and the world view of those on both sides of the relationship. When a doctor sets a patient's broken arm, neither doctor nor patient lets the relationship significantly influence his self-conception or his view of his function in society. When a public official tests an applicant for a driver's license or a radio license, this relationship is also just one more among many for both parties. But the psychiatrist who defines a patient as psychopathic or paranoid, or the teacher who defines a student as a slow learner or a genius, creates a relationship that is far more fundamental and influential for both professional and client. It tells them both who they are and so fundamentally creates their social worlds that they resist evidence that the professional competence of the one or the stigmatizing or exalting label of the other may be unwarranted. For both, the label tends to become a self-fulfilling prophecy and sometimes immune to falsifying evidence.

In consequence the professional and the public official whose function it is to 'help' the inadequate, the powerless, or the deviant is willing and eager to play his role, equipped with a built-in reason to discount or reinterpret qualms, role conflicts, and disturbing facts. To comfort, to subsidize, to limit, to repress, to imprison, even to kill are all sometimes necessary to protect the client and society, and the conscientious professional or political authority plays his role to be true to himself.

60 *Murray Edelman*

As any society grows more frustrating and more alienating for a larger proportion of its inhabitants, more behaviors are inevitably labeled deviant and more people have good reason to experience themselves as unfulfilled and repressed. Such a society can survive, and maintain its frustrating institutions, only as long as it is possible to manipulate the discontented into conformity and docility and to isolate or incarcerate those who refuse to be 'rehabilitated'. The helping professions are the most effective contemporary agents of social conformity and isolation. In playing this political role they undergird the entire political structure, yet are largely spared from self-criticism, from political criticism, and even from political observation through a special symbolic language.

NOTES

1 I have examined some of the functions of political language in *The Symbolic Uses of Politics* (Urbana: University of Illinois, 1964), chapters 6, 7 and 8 and in *Politics As Symbolic Action* (Chicago: Markham, 1971), chapter 5.
2 Daniel Oran, 'Judges and Psychiatrists Lock Up Too Many People', *Psychology Today* 7 (August, 1973), p. 22.
3 D. L. Staunard, 'Ideological Conflict on a Psychiatric Ward', *Psychiatry* 36 (May, 1973), pp. 143–56.
4 Carl G. Carlson, Michael Hersen, and Richard M. Eisler, 'Token Economy Programs in the Treatment of Hospitalized Adult Psychiatric Patients', *Mental Health Digest* 4 (December, 1972), pp. 21–7.
5 Rose K. Kilgalen, 'Hydrotherapy – Is It All Washed Up?', *Journal of Psychiatric Nursing* 10 (November–December, 1972), pp. 3–7.
6 *Struggle for Justice*. Prepared for the American Friends Service Committee, Hill and Wang, 1971, p. 112.
7 Jackson Toby, 'An Evaluation of Early Identification and Intensive Treatment Programs for Predelinquents', *Social Problems* 13 (Fall, 1965), pp. 160–75; David B. Harris, 'On Differential Stigmatization for Predelinquents', *Social Problems* 15 (Spring, 1968), pp. 507–8.
8 Evelyn McElroy and Anita Narciso, 'Clinical Specialist in the Community Mental Health Program', *Journal of Psychiatric Nursing* 9 (January–February, 1971), p. 19.
9 Robert Sunley, 'New Dimensions in Reaching-out Casework', *Social Work* 13 (April, 1968), pp. 64–74.
10 Ibid., p. 73.

5
The Rhetoric of Hitler's 'Battle'*

KENNETH BURKE

The appearance of *Mein Kampf* in unexpurgated translation has called forth far too many vandalistic comments. There are other ways of burning books than on the pyre – and the favorite method of the hasty reviewer is to deprive himself and his readers by inattention. I maintain that it is thoroughly vandalistic for the reviewer to content himself with the mere inflicting of a few symbolic wounds upon this book and its author, of an intensity varying with the resources of the reviewer and the time at his disposal. Hitler's 'Battle' is exasperating, even nauseating. Yet the fact remains: If the reviewer but knocks off a few adverse attitudinizings and calls it a day, with a guaranty, in advance, that his article will have a favorable reception among the decent members of our population, he is contributing more to our gratification than to our enlightenment.

Here is the testament of a man who swung a great people into his wake. Let us watch it carefully; and let us watch it, not merely to discover some grounds for prophesying what political move is to follow Munich, and what move is to follow that move, etc.; let us try also to discover what kind of 'medicine' this medicine-man has concocted, that we may know, with greater accuracy, exactly what to guard against if we are to forestall the concocting of similar medicine in America.

Already, in many quarters of our country, we are 'beyond' the stage where we are being saved from Nazism by our *virtues*. And fascist integration is being staved off, rather, by the *conflicts among our vices*. Our vices cannot get together in a grand united front of prejudice; and the result of this frustration, if or until they succeed in surmounting it, speaks, as the Bible might say, 'in the name of' democracy. Hitler found a 'cure for what ails you', a 'snakeoil', that made such sinister unifying possible within his own nation. And he

*Kenneth Burke, 'The Rhetoric of Hitler's "Battle"', reprinted from *The Southern Review* 5 (1939–1940), pp. 1–21.

was helpful enough to put his cards face up on the table, that we might examine his hands. Let us, then, for God's sake, examine them. This book is the well of Nazi magic; crude magic, but effective. A people trained in pragmatism should want to inspect this magic.

I

Every movement that would recruit its followers from among many discordant and divergent bands, must have some spot toward which all roads lead. Each man may get there in his own way, but it must be the one unifying center of reference for all. Hitler considered this matter carefully, and decided that this center must be not merely a centralizing hub of *ideas*, but a Mecca geographically located towards which all eyes could turn at the appointed hours of prayer (or, in this case, the appointed hours of prayer-in-reverse, the hours of vituperation). So he selected Munich, as the *materialization* of his unifying panacea. As he puts it:[1]

> The geo-political importance of a center of a movement cannot be overrated. Only the presence of such a center and of a place, bathed in the magic of a Mecca or a Rome, can at length give a movement that force which is rooted in the inter unity and in the recognition of a head that represents this unity.

If a movement must have its Rome, it must also have its devil. For as Russell pointed out years ago, an important ingredient of unity in the Middle Ages (an ingredient that long did its unifying work despite the many factors driving towards disunity) was the symbol of a *common enemy*, the Prince of Evil himself. Men who can unite on nothing else can unite on the basis of a foe shared by all. Hitler himself states the case very succinctly:

> As a whole, and at all times, the efficiency of the truly national leader consists primarily in preventing the division of the attention of a people, and always in concentrating it on a single enemy. The more uniformly the fighting will of a people is put into action, the greater will be the magnetic force of the movement and the more powerful the impetus of the blow. It is part of the genius of a great leader to make adversaries of

different fields appear as always belonging to one category only, because to weak and unstable characters the knowledge that there are various enemies will lead only too easily to incipient doubts as to their own cause.

As soon as the wavering masses find themselves confronted with too many enemies, objectivity at once steps in, and the question is raised whether actually all the others are wrong and their own nation or their own movement alone is right.

Also with this comes the first paralysis of their own strength. Therefore, a number of essentially different enemies must always be regarded as one in such a way that in the opinion of the mass of one's own adherents the war is being waged against one enemy alone. This strengthens the belief in one's own cause and increases one's bitterness against the attacker.

As everyone knows, this policy was exemplified in his selection of an 'internationl' devil, the 'international Jew' (the Prince was international, universal, 'catholic'). This *materialization* of a religious pattern is, I think, one terrifically effective weapon of propaganda in a period where religion has been progressively weakened by many centuries of capitalist materialism. You need but go back to the sermonizing of centuries to be reminded that religion had a powerful enemy long before organized atheism came upon the scene. Religion is based upon the 'prosperity of poverty', upon the use of ways for converting our sufferings and handicaps into a good – but capitalism is based upon the prosperity of acquisitions, the only scheme of value, in fact, by which its proliferating store of gadgets could be sold, assuming for the moment that capitalism had not got so drastically in its own way that it can't sell its gadgets even after it has trained people to feel that human dignity, the 'higher standard of living', could be attained only by their vast private accumulation.

So, we have, as unifying step No. 1, the international devil materialized, in the visible, point-to-able form of people with a certain kind of 'blood', a burlesque of contemporary neo-positivism's ideal of meaning, which insists upon a *material* reference.

Once Hitler has thus essentialized his enemy, all 'proof' henceforth is automatic. If you point out the enormous amount of evidence to show that the Jewish worker is at odds with the 'international Jew stock exchange capitalist', Hitler replies with 100 per cent regularity: That is one more indication of the cunning with

which the 'Jewish plot' is being engineered. Or would you point to
'Aryans' who do the same as his conspiratorial Jews? Very well; it is
proof that the 'Aryan' has been 'seduced' by the Jew.

The sexual symbolism that runs through Hitler's book, lying in
wait to draw upon the responses of contemporary sexual values,
is easily characterized: Germany in dispersion is the 'dehorned
Siegfried'. The masses are 'feminine'. As such, they desire to be led
by a dominating male. This male, as orator, woos them – and,
when he has won them, he commands them. The rival male, the
villainous Jew, would on the contrary 'seduce' them. If he succeeds,
he poisons their blood by intermingling with them. Whereupon, by
purely associative connections of ideas, we are moved into attacks
upon syphilis, prostitution, incest, and other similar misfortunes,
which are introduced as a kind of 'musical' argument when he is
on the subject of 'blood-poisoning' by intermarriage or, in its
'spiritual' equivalent, by the infection of 'Jewish' ideas, such as
democracy.

The 'medicinal' appeal of the Jew as scapegoat operates from
another angle. The middle class contains, within the mind of each
member, a duality: its members simultaneously have a cult of
money and a detestation of this cult. When capitalism is going well,
this conflict is left more or less in abeyance. But when capitalism is
balked, it comes to the fore. Hence, there is 'medicine' for the
'Aryan' members of the middle class in the projective device of the
scapegoat, whereby the 'bad' features can be allocated to the 'devil',
and one can 'respect himself' by a distinction between 'good' capitalism and 'bad' capitalism, with those of a different lodge being the
vessels of the 'bad' capitalism. It is doubtless the 'relief' of this
solution that spared Hitler the necessity of explaining just how the
'Jewish plot' was to work out. Nowhere does this book, which is so
full of war plans, make the slightest attempt to explain the steps
whereby the triumph of 'Jewish Bolshevism', which destroys *all*
finance, will be the triumph of '*Jewish*' finance. Hitler well knows
the point at which his 'elucidations' should rely upon the lurid
alone.

The question arises, in those trying to gauge Hitler: Was his
selection of the Jew, as his unifying devil-function, a purely calcu-
lating act? Despite the quotation I have already given, I believe that
it was *not*. The vigor with which he utilized it, I think, derives from
a much more complex state of affairs. It seems that, when Hitler
went to Vienna, in a state close to total poverty, he genuinely
suffered. He lived among the impoverished; and he describes his
misery at the spectacle. He was *sensitive* to it; and his way

of manifesting this sensitiveness impresses me that he is, at this point, wholly genuine, as with his wincing at the broken family relationships caused by alcoholism, which he in turn relates to impoverishment. During this time he began his attempts at political theorizing; and his disturbance was considerably increased by the skill with which Marxists tied him into knots. One passage in particular gives you reason, reading between the lines, to believe that the dialecticians of the class struggle, in their skill at blasting his muddled speculations and making the problem of 'unity' too complex for his chauvinistic mind, put him into a state of uncertainty that was finally 'solved' by rage:

The more I argued with them, the more I got to know their dialectics. First they counted on the ignorance of the adversary; then, when there was no way out, they themselves pretended stupidity. If all this was of no avail, they refused to understand or they changed the subject when driven into a corner; they brought up truisms, but they immediately transferred their acceptance to quite different subjects, and, if attacked again, they gave way and pretended to know nothing exactly. Wherever one attacked one of these prophets, one's hands seized slimy jelly; it slipped through one's fingers only to collect again in the next moment. If one smote one of them so thoroughly that, with the bystanders watching, he could but agree, and if one thus thought he had advanced at least one step, one was greatly astonished the following day. The Jew did not in the least remember the day before, he continued to talk in the same old strain as if nothing had happened, and if indignantly confronted, he pretended to be astonished and could not remember anything except that his assertions had already been proved true the day before.

Often I was stunned.

One did not know what to admire more: their glibness of tongue or their skill in lying.

I gradually began to hate them.

At this point, I think, he is tracing the *spontaneous* rise of his anti-Semitism. He tells how, once he had discovered the 'cause' of the misery about him, he could *confront* it. Where he had had to avert his eyes, he could now *positively welcome* the scene. Here his drastic structure of *acceptance* was being formed. He tells of the 'internal happiness' that descended upon him.

This was the time in which the greatest change I was ever to
experience took place in me.

From a feeble cosmopolite I turned into a fanatical anti-
Semite. . . .

And thence we move, by one of those associational tricks which he
brings forth at all strategic moments, into a vision of the end of the
world – out of which in turn he emerges with his slogan: 'I am
acting in the sense of the Almighty Creator: *By warding off the
Jews I am fighting for the Lord's work*' [italics his].

He talks of this transition as a period of 'double life', a struggle of
'reason' and 'reality' against his 'heart'. It was as 'bitter' as it was
'blissful'. And finally, it was 'reason' that won! Which prompts us
to note that those who attack Hitlerism as a cult of the irrational
should emend their statements to this extent: irrational it is, but it is
carried on under the *slogan* of 'reason'. Similarly, his cult of war is
developed 'in the name of' humility, love, and peace. Judged on a
quantitative basis, Hitler's book certainly falls under the classification of hate. Its venom is everywhere, its charity is sparse. But the
rationalized family tree for this hate situates it in 'Aryan love'.
Some deep-probing German poets, whose work adumbrated the
Nazi movement, did gravitate towards thinking *in the name of* war,
irrationality, and hate. But Hitler was not among them. After all,
when it is so easy to draw a doctrine of war out of a doctrine of
peace, why should the astute politician do otherwise, particularly
when Hitler has slung together his doctrines without the slightest
effort at logical symmetry? Furthermore, church thinking always
got to its wars in Hitler's 'sounder' manner; and the patterns
of Hitler's thought are a bastardized or caricatured version of
religious thought.

I spoke of Hitler's fury at the dialectics of those who opposed
him when his structure was in the stage of scaffolding. From this we
may move to another tremendously important aspect of his theory:
his attack upon the *parliamentary*. For it is a major aspect of his
medicine, in its function as medicine for him personally and as
medicine for those who were later to identify themselves with him.

There is a problem in the parliament – and nowhere was this
problem more acutely in evidence than in the pre-war Vienna that
was to serve as Hitler's political schooling. The parliament, at its
best, is a 'babel' of voices. There is a wrangle of men representing
interests lying awkwardly on the bias across one another, sometimes opposing, sometimes vaguely divergent. Morton Prince's
psychiatric study of 'Miss Beauchamp', the case of a woman split

into several sub-personalities at odds with one another, variously combining under hypnosis, and frequently in turmoil, is the allegory of a democracy fallen upon evil days. The parliament of the Hapsburg Empire just prior to its collapse was an especially drastic instance of such disruption, such vocal diaspora, with movements that would reduce one to a disintegrated mass of fragments if he attempted to encompass the totality of its discordancies. So Hitler, suffering under the alienation of poverty and confusion, yearning for some integrative core, came to take this parliament as the basic symbol of all that he would move away from. He damned the tottering Hapsburg Empire as a 'State of Nationalities'. The many conflicting voices of the spokesmen of the many political blocs arose from the fact that various separationist movements of a nationalistic sort had arisen within a Catholic imperial structure formed prior to the nationalistic emphasis and slowly breaking apart under its development. So, you had this babel of voices; and, by the method of associative mergers, *using ideas as imagery*, it became tied up, in the Hitler rhetoric, with 'Babylon', Vienna as the city of poverty, prostitution, immorality, coalitions, half measures, incest, democracy (i.e., majority-rule leading to 'lack of personal responsibility'), death, internationalism, seduction, and anything else of thumbs-down sort the associative enterprise cared to add on this side of the balance.

Hitler's way of treating the parliamentary babel, I am sorry to say, was at one important point not much different from that of the customary editorial in our own newspapers. Every conflict among the parliamentary spokesmen represents a corresponding conflict among the material interests of the groups for whom they are speaking. But Hitler did not discuss the babel from this angle. He discussed it on a purely *symptomatic* basis. The strategy of our orthodox press, in thus ridiculing the cacophonous verbal output of Congress, is obvious: by thus centering attack upon the *symptoms* of business conflict, as they reveal themselves on the dial of political wrangling, and leaving the underlying cause, the business conflicts themselves, out of the case, they can gratify the very public they would otherwise alienate: namely, the businessmen who are the activating members of their reading public. Hitler, however, went them one better. For not only did he stress the purely *symptomatic* attack here. He proceeded to search for the 'cause'. And this 'cause' of course, he derived from his medicine, his racial theory by which he could give a non-economic interpretation of a phenomenon economically engendered.

Here again is where Hitler's corrupt use of religious patterns

comes to the fore. Church thought, being primarily concerned with
matters of the 'personality', with problems of moral betterment,
naturally, and I think rightly, stresses as a necessary feature, the act
of will upon the part of the individual. Hence its resistance to a
purely 'environmental' account of human ills. Hence its emphasis
upon the 'person'. Hence its proneness to seek a non-economic
explanation of economic ills. Hitler's proposal of a non-economic
'cause' for the disturbances thus had much to recommend it from
this angle. And, as a matter of fact, it was Lueger's Christian-Social
Party in Vienna that taught Hitler the tactics of tying up a program
of social betterment with an anti-Semitic 'unifier'. The two parties
he carefully studied at that time were this Catholic faction and
Schoenerer's Pan-German group. And his analysis of their attain-
ments and shortcomings, from the standpoint of demagogic efficacy, is an extremely astute piece of work, revealing how carefully
this man used the current situation in Vienna as an experimental
laboratory for the maturing of his plans.

His unification device, we may summarize, had the following
important features:

(1) Inborn dignity. In both religious and humanistic patterns
of thought, a 'natural born' dignity of man is stressed. And
this categorical dignity is considered to be an attribute of *all
men*, if they will but avail themselves of it, by right thinking
and right living. But Hitler gives this ennobling attitude an
ominous twist by his theories of race and nation, whereby the
'Aryan' is elevated above all others by the innate endowment
of his blood, while other 'races', in particular Jews and Neg-
roes, are innately inferior. This sinister secularized revision of
Christian theology thus puts the sense of dignity upon a
fighting basis, requiring the conquest of 'inferior races'. After
the defeat of Germany in the World War, there were especially strong emotional needs that this compensatory doctrine of
an *inborn* superiority could gratify.
(2) *Projection* device. The 'curative' process that comes with
the ability to hand over one's ills to a scapegoat, thereby
getting purification by dissociation. This was especially medicinal, since the sense of frustration leads to a self-questioning.
Hence if one can hand over his infirmities to a vessel, or
'cause', outside the self, one can battle an external enemy
instead of battling an enemy within. And the greater one's
internal inadequacies, the greater the amount of evils one can
load upon the back of 'the enemy'. This device

is furthermore given a semblance of reason because the individual properly realizes that he is not alone responsible for his condition. There *are* inimical factors in the scene itself. And he wants to have them 'placed', preferably in a way that would require a minimum change in the ways of thinking to which he has been accustomed. This was especially appealing to the middle class, who were encouraged to feel that they could conduct their businesses without any basic change whatever, once the businessmen of a different 'race' were eliminated.

(3) Symbolic rebirth. Another aspect of the two features already noted. The projective device of the scapegoat, coupled with the Hitlerite doctrine of inborn racial superiority, provides its followers with a 'positive' view of life. They can again get the feel of *moving forward*, towards a *goal* (a promissory feature of which Hitler makes much). In Hitler, as the group's prophet, such rebirth involved a symbolic change of lineage. Here, above all, we see Hitler giving a malign twist to a benign aspect of Christian thought. For whereas the Pope, in the familistic pattern of thought basic to the Church, stated that the Hebrew prophets were the *spiritual ancestors* of Christianity, Hitler uses this same mode of thinking in reverse. He renounces this 'ancestry' in a 'materialistic' way by voting himself and the members of his lodge a different 'blood stream' from that of the Jews.

(4) Commercial use. Hitler obviously here had something to sell – and it was but a question of time until he sold it (i.e., got financial backers for his movement). For it provided a *non-economic interpretation of economic ills*. As such, it served with maximum efficiency in deflecting the attention from the economic factors involved in modern conflict; hence by attacking 'Jew finance' instead of *finance*, it could stimulate an enthusiastic movement that left 'Aryan' finance in control.

Never once, throughout his book, does Hitler deviate from the above formula. Invariably, he ends his diatribes against contemporary economic ills by a shift into an insistence that we must get to the 'true' cause, which is centered in 'race'. The 'Aryan' is 'constructive'; the Jew is 'destructive'; and the 'Aryan', to continue his *construction*, must *destroy* the Jewish *destruction*. The Aryan, as the vessel of *love*, must *hate* the Jewish *hate*.

Perhaps the most enterprising use of his method is in his chapter 'The Causes of the Collapse', where he refuses to consider Germany's plight as in any basic way connected with the consequences of war. Economic factors, he insists, are 'only of second or even third importance', but 'political, ethical-moral, as well as factors of blood and race, are of the first importance'. His rhetorical steps are especially interesting here, in that he begins by seeming to flout the national susceptibilities: 'The military defeat of the German people is not an undeserved catastrophe, but rather a deserved punishment by eternal retribution.' He then proceeds to present the military collapse as but a 'consequence of moral poisoning, visible to all, the consequence of a decrease in the instinct of self-preservation . . . which had already begun to undermine the foundations of the people and the Reich many years before.' This moral decay derived from 'a sin against the blood and the degradation of the race', so its innerness was an outerness after all: the Jew, who thereupon gets saddled with a vast amalgamation of evils, among them being capitalism, democracy, pacifism, journalism, poor housing, modernism, big cities, loss of religion, half measures, ill health, and weaknesses of the monarch.

II

Hitler had here another important psychological ingredient to play upon. If a state is in economic collapse (and his theories, tentatively taking shape in pre-war Vienna, were but developed with greater efficiency in post-war Munich), you cannot possibly derive dignity from economic stability. Dignity must come first – and if you possess it, and implement it, from it may follow its economic counterpart. There is much justice to this line of reasoning, so far as it goes. A people in collapse, suffering under economic frustration and the defeat of nationalistic aspirations, with the very midrib of their integrative efforts (the army) in a state of dispersion, have little other than some 'spiritual' basis to which they could refer their nationalistic dignity. Hence, the categorical dignity of superior race was a perfect recipe for the situation.

Furthermore, you had the desire for unity, such as a discussion of class conflict, on the basis of conflicting interests, could not satisfy. The yearning for unity is so great that people are always willing to meet you halfway if you will give it to them by fiat, by flat statement, regardless of the facts. Hence, Hitler consistently refused to consider internal political conflict on the basis of conflicting interests. Here again, he could draw upon a religious pattern, by insisting upon a *personal* statement of the relation between classes, the relation between leaders and followers, each group in its way fulfilling the same commonalty of interests, as the soldiers and captains of an army share a common interest in victory. People so dislike the idea of internal division that, where there is a real internal division, their dislike can easily be turned against the man or group who would so much as *name* it, let alone proposing to act upon it. Their natural and justified resentment against internal division itself, is turned against the diagnostician who states it as a *fact*. This diagnostician, it is felt, is the *cause* of the disunity he named.

Cutting in from another angle, therefore, we note how two sets of equations were built up, with Hitler combining or coalescing *ideas* the way a poet combines or coalesces *images*. On the one side, were the ideas, or images, of disunity, centering in the parliamentary wrangle of the Hapsburg 'State of Nationalities'. This was offered as the antithesis of German nationality, which was presented in the curative imagery of unity, focused upon the glories of the Prussian Reich, with its Mecca now moved to 'folkish' Munich. For though Hitler at first attacked the many 'folkish' movements, with their hankerings after a kind of Wagnerian mythology of Germanic origins, he subsequently took 'folkish' as a basic word by which to conjure. It was, after all, another non-economic basis of reference. At first we find him objecting to 'those who drift about with the word "folkish" on their caps', and asserting that 'such a Babel of opinions cannot serve as the basis of a political fighting movement'. But later he seems to have realized, as he well should, that its vagueness was a major point in its favor. So it was incorporated in the grand coalition of his ideational imagery, or imagistic ideation; and chapter XI ends with the vision of 'a State which represents not a mechanism of economic considerations and interests, alien to the people, but a folkish organism'.

So, as against the disunity equations, already listed briefly in our discussions of his attacks upon the parliamentary, we get a contrary purifying set; the wrangle of the parliamentary is to be stilled by the giving of *one* voice to the whole people, this to be the 'inner voice' of Hitler, made uniform throughout the German boundaries, as leader and people were completely identified with each other. In sum: Hitler's inner voice, equals leader-people identification, equals unity, equals Reich, equals the Mecca of Munich, equals plow, equals sword, equals work, equals war, equals army as midrib, equals responsibility (the personal responsibility of the absolute ruler), equals sacrifice, equals the theory of 'German democracy' (the free popular choice of the leader, who then accepts the respon-

sibility, and demands absolute obedience in exchange for his sacrifice), equals love (with the masses as feminine), equals idealism,
equals obedience to nature, equals race, nation.

And, of course, the two keystones of these opposite equations
were Aryan 'heroism' and 'sacrifice' vs. Jewish 'cunning' and 'arrogance'. Here again we get an astounding caricature of religious
thought. For Hitler presents the concept of 'Aryan' superiority, of
all ways, in terms of 'Aryan humility'. This 'humility' is extracted
by a very delicate process that requires, I am afraid, considerable
'goodwill' on the part of the reader who would follow it.

The Church, we may recall, had proclaimed an integral relationship between Divine Law and Natural Law. Natural Law was
the expression of the Will of God. Thus, in the Middle Ages, it was
a result of natural law, working through tradition, that some people were serfs and other people nobles. And every good member of
the Church was 'obedient' to this law. Everybody resigned himself
to it. Hence, the serf resigned himself to his poverty, and the noble
resigned himself to his riches. The monarch resigned himself to his
position as representative of the people. And at times the Church-
men resigned themselves to the need of trying to represent the
people instead. And the pattern was made symmetrical by the
consideration that each traditional 'right' had its corresponding
'obligations'. Similarly, the Aryan doctrine is a doctrine of resigna-
tion, hence of humility. It is in accordance with the laws of nature
that the 'Aryan blood' is superior to all other bloods. Also, the 'law
of the survival of the fittest' is God's law, working through natural
law. Hence, if the Aryan blood has been vested with the awful
responsibility of its inborn superiority, the bearers of this 'culture-
creating' blood must resign themselves to struggle in behalf of its
triumph. Otherwise, the laws of God have been disobeyed, with
human decadence as a result. We must fight, he says, in order to
'deserve to be alive'. The Aryan 'obeys' nature. It is only 'Jewish
arrogance' that thinks of 'conquering' nature by democratic ideals
of equality.

This picture has some nice distinctions worth following. The
major virtue of the Aryan race was its instinct for self-preservation
(in obedience to natural law). But the major vice of the Jew was his
instinct for self-preservation; for, if he did not have this instinct to a
maximum degree, he would not be the 'perfect' enemy – that is, he
wouldn't be strong enough to account for the ubiquitousness and
omnipotence of his conspiracy in destroying the world to become
its master.

How, then, are we to distinguish between the benign instinct of self-preservation at the roots of Aryanism, and the malign instinct of self-preservation at the roots of Semitism? We shall distinguish thus: The Aryan self-preservation is based upon *sacrifice*, the sacrifice of the individual to the group, hence, militarism, army discipline, and one big company union. But Jewish self-preservation is based upon individualism, which attains its cunning ends by the exploitation of peace. How, then, can such arrant individualists concoct the world-wide plot? By the help of their 'herd instinct'. By their sheer 'herd instinct' individualists can band together for a common end. They have no real solidarity, but unite opportunistically to seduce the Aryan. Still, that brings up another technical problem. For we have been hearing much about the importance of the *person*. We have been told how, by the 'law of the survival of the fittest', there is a sifting of people on the basis of their individual capacities. We even have a special chapter of pure Aryanism: 'The strong Man is Mightiest Alone.' Hence, another distinction is necessary: The Jew represents individualism; the Aryan represents 'super-individualism'.

I had thought, when coming upon the 'Strong Man is Mightiest Alone' chapter, that I was going to find Hitler at his weakest. Instead, I found him at his strongest. (I am not referring to *quality*, but to *demagogic effectiveness*.) For the chapter is not at all, as you might infer from the title, done in a 'rise of Adolph Hitler' manner. Instead, it deals with the Nazis' gradual absorption of the many disrelated 'folkish' groups. And it is managed throughout by means of a spontaneous identification between leader and people. Hence, the Strong Man's 'aloneness' is presented as a *public* attribute, in terms of tactics for the struggle against the *Party's* dismemberment under the pressure of rival saviors. There is no explicit talk of Hitler at all. And it is simply *taken for granted* that *his* leadership is the norm, and all other leaderships the abnorm. There is no 'philosophy of the superman', in Nietzschean cast. Instead, Hitler's blandishments so integrate leader and people, commingling them so inextricably, that the politician does not even present himself as candidate. Somehow, the battle is over already, the decision has been made. 'German democracy' had chosen. And the deployments of politics are, you might say, the chartings of Hitler's private mind translated into the vocabulary of nationalistic events. He says *what he thought* in terms of *what parties did*.

Here, I think, we see the distinguishing quality of Hitler's method as an instrument of persuasion, with reference to the question whether Hitler is sincere or deliberate, whether his vision of the omnipotent conspirator has the drastic honesty of paranoia or the sheer shrewdness of a demogogue trained in Realpolitik of the Machiavellian sort. Must we choose? Or may we not, rather, replace the 'either-or' with a 'both-and'? Have we not by now offered grounds enough for our contention that Hitler's sinister powers of persuasion derive from the fact that he spontaneously evolved his 'cure-all' in response to inner necessities?

III

So much, then, was 'spontaneous'. It was further channelized into the anti-Semitic pattern by the incentives he derived from the Catholic Christian-Social Party in Vienna itself. Add, now, the step into *criticism*. Not criticism in the 'parliamentary' sense of doubt, of hearkening to the opposition and attempting to mature a policy in the light of counter-policies; but the 'unified' kind of criticism that simply seeks for conscious ways of making one's position more 'efficient', more thoroughly itself. This is the kind of criticism at which Hitler was an adept. As a result, he could *spontaneously* turn to a scapegoat mechanism, and he could, by conscious planning, perfect the symmetry of the solution towards which he had spontaneously turned.

This is the meaning of Hitler's diatribes against 'objectivity'. 'Objectivity' is interference-criticism. What Hitler wanted was the kind of criticism that would be a pure and simple coefficient of power, enabling him to go most effectively in the direction he had chosen. And the 'inner voice' of which he speaks would henceforth dictate to him the greatest amount of realism, as regards the tactics of efficiency. For instance, having decided that the masses required certainty, and simple certainty, quite as he did himself, he later worked out a 25-point program as the platform of his National Socialist German Workers Party. And he resolutely refused to change one single item in this program, even for purposes of 'improvement'. He felt that the *fixity* of the platform was more important for propagandistic purposes than any revision of his slogans could be, even though the revisions in themselves had much to be said in their favor. The astounding thing is that, although such an attitude gave good cause to doubt the Hitlerite promises, he could explicitly explain his tactics in his book and still employ them without loss of effectiveness.

Hitler also tells of his technique in speaking, once the Nazi party had become effectively organized, and had its army of guards, or bouncers, to maltreat hecklers and throw them from the hall. He would, he recounts, fill his speech with *provocative* remarks, whereat his bouncers would promptly swoop down in flying formation, with swinging fists, upon anyone whom these provocative remarks provoked to answer. The efficiency of Hitlerism is the efficiency of the one voice, implemented throughout a total organization. The trinity of government which he finally offers is: *popularity* of the leader, *force* to back the popularity, and popularity and force maintained together long enough to become backed by a *tradition*.

Freud has given us a succinct paragraph that bears upon the spontaneous aspect of Hitler's persecution mania. (A persecution mania, I should add, different from the pure product in that it was constructed of *public* materials; all the ingredients Hitler stirred into his brew were already rife, with spokemen and bands of followers, before Hitler 'took them over'. Both the pre-war and post-war periods were dotted with saviors, of nationalistic and 'folkish' cast. This proliferation was analogous to the swarm of barter schemes and currency-tinkering that burst loose upon the United States after the crash of 1929. Also, the commercial availability of Hitler's politics was, in a low sense of the term, a *public* qualification, removing it from the realm of 'pure' paranoia, where the sufferer develops a wholly *private* structure of interpretations.)

I cite from Freud's *Totem and Taboo*:

> Another trait in the attitude of primitive races towards their rulers recalls a mechanism which is universally present in mental disturbances, and is openly revealed in the so-called delusions of persecution. Here the importance of a particular person is extraordinarily heightened and his omnipotence is raised to the improbable in order to make it easier to attribute to him responsibility for everything painful which happens to the patient. Savages really do not act differently towards their rulers when they ascribe to them power over rain and shine, wind or weather, and then dethrone them or kill them because nature has disappointed their expectation of a good hunt or a ripe harvest. The prototype which the paranoiac reconstructs in his persecution mania, is found in the relation of the child to its father. Such omnipotence is regularly attributed to the father in the imagination of the son, and distrust of the father has been shown to be intimately connected with the heightened esteem for him. When a paranoiac names a person of his acquaintance as his 'persecutor', he thereby elevates him to

the paternal succession and brings him under conditions which enable him to make him responsible for all the misfortune which he experiences.

I have already proposed my modifications of this account when discussing the symbolic change of lineage connected with Hitler's project for a 'new way of life'. He is voting himself a new identity (something contrary to the wrangles of the Hapsburg Babylon, a soothing national unity); whereupon the vessels of the old identity (essentialized in the 'bloodstream' of 'spiritual ancestors', the Hebrew prophets) become a 'bad' father, i.e., the persecutor. It is not hard to see how, when his enmity becomes implemented by the backing of an organization, the role of 'persecutor' is transformed into the role of persecuted, as he sets out with his like-minded band to 'destroy the destroyer'.

Were Hitler simply a poet, he might have written a work with an anti-Semitic turn, and let it go at that. But Hitler, who began as a student of painting, and later shifted to architecture, himself treats his political activities as an extension of his artistic ambitions. He remained, in his own eyes, an 'architect', building a 'folkish' state that was to match, in political materials, the 'folkish' architecture of Munich.

We might consider the matter this way (still trying, that is, to make precise the relationship between the drastically sincere and the deliberately scheming): Do we not know of many authors who seem, as they turn from the role of citizen to the role of spokesman, to leave one room and enter another? Or who has not, on occasion, talked with a man in private conversation, and then been almost startled at the transformation this man undergoes when addressing a public audience? And I know persons today, who shift from the writing of items in the class of academic, philosophic speculation to items of political pamphleteering, and whose entire style and method change with this change of role. In their academic manner, they are cautious, painstaking, eager to present all significant aspects of the case they are considering; but when they turn to political pamphleteering, they hammer forth with vituperation, they systematically misrepresent the position of their opponent, they go into a kind of political trance, in which, during its throes, they throb like a locomotive; and behold, a moment later, the mediumistic state is abandoned, and they are the most moderate of men.

Now, one will find few pages in Hitler that one could call 'moderate'. But there are many pages in which he gauges resistances and opportunities with the 'rationality' of a skilled advertising man planning a new sales campaign. Politics, he says, must be sold like soap — and soap is not sold in a trance. But he did have the experience of his trance, in the 'exaltation' of his anti-Semitism. And later, as he became a successful orator (he insists that revolutions are made solely by the power of the spoken word), he had this 'poetic' role to draw upon, plus the great relief it provided as a way of slipping from the burdens of logical analysis into the pure 'spirituality' of vituperative prophecy. What more natural, therefore, than that a man so insistent upon unification would integrate this mood with his less ecstatic moments, particularly when he had found the followers and the backers that put a price, both spiritual and material, upon such unification?

Once this happy 'unity' is under way, one has a 'logic' for the development of a method. One knows when to 'spiritualize' a material issue, and when to 'materialize' a spiritual one. Thus, when it is a matter of materialistic interests that cause a conflict between employer and employee, Hitler here disdainfully shifts to a high moral plane. He is 'above' such low concerns. Everything becomes a matter of 'sacrifice' and 'personality'. It becomes crass to treat employers and employees as different *classes* with a corresponding difference in the classification of their interests. Instead, relations between employer and employee must be on the 'personal' basis of leader and follower, and 'whatever may have a divisive effect in national life should be given a unifying effect through the army.' When talking of national rivalries, however, he makes a very shrewd materialistic gauging of Britain and France with relation to Germany. France, he says, desires the 'Balkanization of Germany' (i.e., its breakup into separationist movements — the 'disunity' theme again) in order to maintain commercial hegemony on the Continent. But Britain desires the 'Balkanization of *Europe*', hence would favor a fairly strong and unified Germany, to use as a counterweight against French hegemony. *German* nationality, however, is unified by the *spiritual* quality of Aryanism (that would produce the national organization via the Party) while this in turn is *materialized* in the myth of the bloodstream.

IV

What are we to learn from Hitler's book? For one thing, I believe that he has shown, to a very disturbing degree, the power of repetition. Every circular advertising a Nazi meeting had, at the bottom, two slogans: 'Jews not admitted' and 'War victims free'. And the substance of Nazi propaganda was built about these two 'complementary' themes. He describes the power of spectacle; insists that mass meetings are the fundamental way of giving the individual the sense of being protectively surrounded by a movement, the sense of 'community'. He also drops one wise hint that I wish the American authorities would take in treating Nazi gatherings. He says that the presence of a special Nazi guard, in Nazi uniforms, was of great importance in building up, among the followers, a tendency to place the center of authority in the Nazi party. I believe that we should take him at his word here, but use the advice in reverse, by insisting that, where Nazi meetings are to be permitted, they be policed by the constituted authorities alone, and that uniformed Nazi guards to enforce the law be prohibited.

But is it possible that an equally important feature of appeal was not so much in the repetitiousness *per se*, but in the fact that, by means of it, Hitler provided a 'world view' for people who had previously seen the world but piecemeal? Did not much of his lure derive, once more, from the *bad* filling of a *good* need? Are not those who insist upon a purely *planless* working of the market asking people to accept far too slovenly a scheme of human purpose, a slovenly scheme that can be accepted so long as it operates with a fair degree of satisfaction, but becomes abhorrent to the victims of its disarray? Are they not then psychologically ready for a rationale, *any* rationale, if it but offer them some specious 'universal' explanation? Hence, I doubt whether the appeal was in the sloganizing element alone (particularly as even slogans can only be hammered home, in speech after speech, and two or three hours at a stretch, by endless *variations* on the themes). And Hitler himself somewhat justifies my interpretation by laying so much stress upon the *half measures* of the middle-class politicians, and the contrasting *certainty* of his own methods. He was not offering people a *rival* world view; rather, he was offering a world view to people who had no other to pit against it.

As for the basic Nazi trick: the 'curative' unification by a fictitious devil-function, gradually made convincing by the sloganizing repetitiousness of standard advertising technique – the opposition must be as unwearying in the attack upon it. It may well be that people, in their human frailty, require an enemy as well as a goal. Very well: Hitlerism itself has provided us with such an enemy – and the clear example of its operation is guaranty that we have, in Hitler and all he stands for, no purely fictitious 'devil-function' made to look like a world menace by rhetorical blandishments, but a reality whose ominousness is clarified by the record of its conduct to date. In selecting his brand of doctrine as our 'scapegoat', and in tracking down its equivalents in America, we shall be at the very center of accuracy. The Nazis themselves have made the task of clarification easier. Add to them Japan and Italy, and you have *case histories* of fascism for those who might find it more difficult to approach an understanding of its imperialistic drives by a strictly economic explanation.

But above all, I believe, we must make it apparent that Hitler appeals by relying upon a bastardization of fundamentally religious patterns of thought. In this, if properly presented, there is no slight to religion. There is nothing in religion proper that requires a fascist state. There is much in religion, when misused, that does lead to a fascist state. There is a Latin proverb, '*Corruptio optimi pessima*', the corruption of the best is the worst. And it is the corruptors of religion who are a major menace to the world today, in giving the profound patterns of religious thought a crude and sinister distortion.

Our job, then, our Anti-Hitler Battle, is to find all available ways of making the Hitlerite distortions of religion apparent, in order that politicians of his kind in America be unable to perform a similar swindle. The desire for unity is genuine and admirable. The desire for national unity, in the present state of the world, is genuine and admirable. But this unity, if attained on a deceptive basis, by emotional trickeries that shift our criticism from the accurate locus of our troubles, is no unity at all. For, even if we are among those who happen to be 'Aryans', we solve no problems even for ourselves by such solutions, since the factors pressing towards calamity remain. Thus, in Germany, after all the upheaval, we see nothing beyond a drive for ever more and more upheaval, precisely because the 'new way of life' was no new way, but the dismally oldest way of sheer deception – hence, after all the 'change', the factors driving towards unrest are left intact, and even strengthened. True, the Germans had the resentment of a lost war to increase their susceptibility to Hitler's rhetoric. But in a wider sense, it has repeatedly been observed, the whole world lost the war – and the accumulating ills of the capitalist order were but accelerated in their movement towards confusion. Hence, here too there are the resentments that go with frustration of men's ability to work and earn. At that point, a certain kind of industrial or financial monopolist may, annoyed by the contrary views of parliament, wish for the momentary peace of one voice, amplified by social organization, with all the others not merely quieted, but given the quietus. So he might, under Nazi promptings, be tempted to back a group of gangsters who, on becoming the political rulers of the state, would protect him against the necessary demands of the workers. His gangsters, then, would be his insurance against his workers. But who would be his insurance against his gangsters?

NOTE

1 The quotations are from the Reynal & Hitchcock edition.

6

Language and Nihilism: Nietzsche's Critique of Epistemology*

TRACY B. STRONG†

'So you are saying that human agreement decides what is true and what is false?' – It is what human beings *say* that is true and false; and they agree in the *language* they use. That is not agreement in opinions, but in forms of life.

Ludwig Wittgenstein,
Philosophical Investigations, p. 241

That language both gives us a world and at the same time necessarily poses (usually unrecognized) limits to that world may now be considered a generally recognized principle of linguistics and the philosophy of language.[1] Much less attention, however, has been paid to precisely the sort of world which a particular language surrounds us with. Generally speaking, the effects of seeing and being in the world in the particular manner which a given language engenders have gone unattended to.

The main exceptions to this general disregard have in the twentieth century fallen into two groups with no apparent links to each other. On the one hand, there is the school of anthropological linguistics associated with the writings of Edward Sapir and Benjamin L. Whorf.[2] Their thesis is now well known: they posit a close relationship between the structure of a language and the conceptual categories which govern the behavior of native speakers of that language. In Whorf's famous example, the Hopi who do not make categorical distinctions between time and space in the subject–

*Tracy B. Strong, 'Language and Nihilism: Nietzsche's Critique of Epistemology', reprinted from *Theory and Society*, 3 (Summer, 1976), pp. 239–63, by permission © Tracy B. Strong.
†Adapted from a chapter in the author's *Friedrich Nietzsche and the Politics of Transfiguration*, published by the University of California Press.

object relationship understand the world in a manner better suited
to the findings of the physics of relativity. Westerners, who do make
such distinctions, are linguistically better suited to the paradigm of
classical mechanics.

Both Whorf and Sapir have come under much, often fully justified criticism. This criticism has centred around the rather simplistic
picture they tend to present of the relation between language and
'reality'.[3] This is perhaps not the place to explore this relationship
in full detail, nor the shortcomings of this school of anthropology.
Suffice it to note that Whorf and Sapir and those associated with
them do make two interesting and central claims: first, that the
world of language and the world of categories are to a great degree
co-terminous, and second, that there is no way in which one can get
outside the perceptual set which a language enforces upon its
speaker, except by speaking another language.

In the other group, the schools of philosophy associated with
'ordinary language' or 'Oxford' philosophy and with the writings
of Ludwig Wittgenstein have developed very sophisticated understandings of the relations between words and the world, and of the
constraints and freedom that a language as a whole puts on a
speaker.[4] Here again I cannot replay the debates and claims which
swirl about these disciplines. Suffice it to summarize the claims of
this philosophy with the words of Stanley Cavell:[5]

> In proceeding from ordinary language . . . one is in a frame of
> mind in which it seems (1) that one can as appropriately or
> truly be said to be looking at the world as looking at lan-
> guage: (2) that one is seeking necessary truths 'about' the
> world (or 'about' language) and therefore cannot be satisfied
> with anything I, at least, would recognize as a description of
> how people in fact talk – one might say that one is seeking one
> kind of explanation of *why* people speak as they do; and even
> (3) that one is not finally interested *at all* in how 'other' people
> talk, but in determining where and why one wishes, or hesi-
> tates, to use a particular expression oneself.

The thought of Friedrich Nietzsche on language is a combination
of both of these approaches. He is concerned with the anthropology
of our lives and languages and how they relate to each other; he
attempts to analyze in a systematic manner the resonances and
concatenations of meaning which language must contain. His
claims are perhaps far more detailed than those of Whorf and Sapir,
and more radical than those of the philosophers who proceed from

ordinary language. Though his writings on this topic have not attracted much focused attention,[6] and though they are scattered throughout his philosophical enterprise, they do form a coherent and comprehensive analysis of both the past and future nature and development of the languages and life of Europe and the West.

For Nietzsche, humans are caught both *by* the phantasmic fetishes their language creates, and *in* that world which their language engenders, maintains and is engendered by. The thrust of Nietzsche's analysis goes very deep here. As we shall see, it is not just that human beings are enchained by their language: such a facile romanticism would make liberation simply a question of breaking loose. For Nietzsche, it is not that we are bound by our language, but that we are in effect defined by our chains. Without the fetters of our language, so to speak, there would be nothing and no one at all. The choice for Nietzsche is not prison or freedom, but limitation of the chaos or not being.

Nietzsche is very radical here. He argues at length against the Kantian position that self-critical rationality provides a fulcrum potentially not subject to the distortion of our conceptual apparatus.[7] Even self-critical reason cannot deal with the nightmare of our world, for, in Nietzsche's view, it too is part of the tide of nihilism which increasingly engulfs us all and all our actions. I should note here that the radicalness of this position has not gone unnoticed, nor unchallenged. Jürgen Habermas, for instance, goes after this aspect of Nietzsche in two long chapters of his *Knowledge and Human Interests*. He claims that Nietzsche's critique of language and rationality fails in its mark, in that Nietzsche's understanding of epistemology remains in a dialectical way fatally tied to positivism. I shall try to show that this is a false characterization of Nietzsche's position; it is, however, certainly true that Habermas has identified the key element in Nietzsche's diagnosis of the crisis of the bourgeois spirit which might cause severe problems for the project of liberation which Habermas envisages. If everything that we can do or say or think, if the very stuff of ourselves in the world is all indelibly colored by the same tincture of nihilism, then all attempts at liberation or escape must also manifest this stain. The more one tries to escape the chains which bind one in, the more imprisoned one becomes, for what appear as the tools of freedom will in fact only increase the strength of that which holds us prisoner.

I do not in this essay intend to enter into extensive *widersagen* with Habermas's specific claims.[8] I do hope to set out in as forceful detail as possible Nietzsche's understanding of knowledge in order to demonstrate that his discussion is more powerful than Habermas makes it out to be and more coherent than Whorf's and Sapir's. If in the process he seems to draw close to an anthropologically conceived understanding of Wittgenstein, I shall not be too disturbed.

LANGUAGE AND REALITY

Nietzsche's discussion of language falls into two main categories, that of language *per se* and that of Western languages (Indo-European tongues) in particular.[9] Even if Nietzsche occasionally talks about each of these in the same paragraph or even the same breath, it is important to keep them separate so as not to conclude that his antagonism towards certain aspects of our language also be construed as a hostility towards language in general. I propose in this section then to give an account of what Nietzsche has to say about the general architectonics of language, about what one is doing when one speaks.

In the first book of *Human, all-too-human* Nietzsche notes that language creates 'another world of its own from which this world is looked at and that this creation provides humans with a fulcrum by which they think to master the first'. 'We think,' Nietzsche continues, 'that it is really in language that we have knowledge of the world.'[10] His argument is that language provides the point from which a necessitating regularity can be constructed. The regularities which are our life are engendered and supported in language.

For Nieztsche, then, language serves a double function. On the one hand it is the means by which we construct the world. The categories which we use must necessarily correspond to the shape and structure of the world as it appears to us and as we are in it. Indeed, it would be surprising if our categories of thought and action did not make manifest possibilities of coherent and recurrent perceptions of the world. For, if there were not language, then one really wouldn't know what to say about the world: the point is both Palissian and profound and does not more than repeat Wittgenstein's aphorism which serves as an epigraph to this essay. The second function of language which Nietzsche sees will then be complementary to the first. Language makes the world present, and in doing so it also provides men with the tools by which they must deal with the world.

Language and the world then form a sort of circle. Now there is nothing particularly wrong, nor does Nietzsche claim that there is, with the fact that language interaction with the world moves in a sort of more or less well closed circle. There is certainly no need to presuppose that it might be anything else. But for Nietzsche there are two sorts of circles, the first a healthy assertion of the eternal presence of an activity (for instance, the skill which makes improvisation sound like thought-out music),[11] the other a neurotic and compulsive repetition of an activity which one can not desist from. The danger with language even in general is that it tends to fall into the second category. Since language works so well for men (or at least well enough), they tend to think of it as merely providing sign posts for 'naturally' valid concepts. Hence, if men try to make sense of their activity (which they must necessarily do in language) they will think either real and natural that which is the result of their own activity (something Marx was later to call fetishism and Freud totemization) or else come up with the solipsistic regress of 'knowing that we know because we know that we know because . . .' Such a quest presupposes a stopping point in a realm which could not be shaped by language and which would not be co-terminous with language. Yet it must be clear that if there be such a grounding, there can, by definition be nothing to be said about it, nor could it be found.[12] The point is simply this: implicit in the attempt to find or uncover a rationale for life and activity must be the presupposition that the language necessarily used is appropriate to that which is sought. Yet that which is sought here must, as even Kant was forced to admit, not be subject to the general architectonic of language and hence cannot be directly known. Nietzsche, in the face of claims such as Kant's, can no more admit the existence of a world which, though unknowable, would provide a firm foundation for the fulcrum of language, than he could think of God as still providing an answer to the problem of the value of life and truth.

I should immediately emphasize two points here about Nietzsche's critique so as to prevent potential misunderstandings. First, Nietzsche is not 'opposed' to language (whatever that might mean). It is, of course, true that a number of people and schools reacted to the Kantian discovery of the limits of thought and reason by standing the Königsberg philosopher on his head. Instead of searching for truth in the transcendental realm, or assuming its pure existence, many thought that truth might be found in that of which we could not speak: in silence, mystery, intuition, in the wisdom of emotion, of blood and soil and the homeland.[13] Just as men could not speak accurately of the sphere of theoretical reason, similarly there would be no words for this 'home' world. Instead of the transcendental world, the 'home of Being' now became the problem. Such a position is already implicit in the early German romantic tradition, in poets such as Hölderlin, and underlies much of the work of Fichte and Schelling and finds its modern culmination, in my understanding, in the work of Martin Heidegger.[14] Nietzsche, however, must reject any such tendency. That there is only practical reason means precisely that: *only*. For though language 'is built on the most naive of prejudices . . . [we] cease to think if we do not wish to do it under the constraint of language'.[15]

Secondly, it is entirely possible that a 'new' language might be constructed, if one means by new a previously unemployed series of interrelated concepts which pictures the world anew. It is apparent from the unpublished notes that Nietzsche had dreams of either removing from language those qualities which he saw as the message and herald of nihilism (e.g., the subject–object distinction, see below), and, even more radically, of revolutionizing discourse into a new language which would rest on a radically different grammar.[16] The meaning and the feasibility of such a product cannot be dealt with here. Most important, though, is the realization that Nietzsche is no more opposed to language than he is to 'truth'. Rather men need to understand what they are doing when they speak (of truth, for instance); that this understanding be destructive to the illusions one might have held, Nietzsche understood and encouraged.

Finally, it is true that Nietzsche saw the world as undergoing a new set of experiences for which it had not yet the words. Given the ultimate unity of language and life which he sees, it follows that since men as yet have no words for what is happening to them, they will generally be unable to formulate any knowledge of what is happening to them. Nietzsche sees himself as providing the first attempts at dealing with what he thinks will be the coming experiences of Europeans over the next two centuries. 'Let us imagine,' he proposes in *Ecce Homo*, '. . . a book which speaks of nothing but events which lie altogether beyond the possibility of any frequent or even rare experience – that is, the first language for a new series of experiences. In that case, simply nothing will be heard, but there will be the acoustic illusion that where nothing is heard, nothing is there.'[17] If the problem of modern men is, as Nietzsche argued in the *Birth of Tragedy*, that they are too 'theoretical', I must understand by this that they do not live their experiences, that they have no words for them, no manner to make them exist for themselves. But to achieve a reintegration of words and the world will first require breaking the hold language has on men. The practical disjuncture between words and life is not the result of the simple misuse of words; it is inherent in the natural operation of the language. In the early essay, *On Words and Music*, Nietzsche investigates the analogies between music and speech which had already formed the basis of the *Birth of Tragedy*. He writes: 'In the multiplicity of languages the fact at once manifests itself that word and thing do not necessarily coincide with one another, but that the word is a symbol. But what does the word symbolize? Most certainly only conceptions, be they conscious ones, or, as in the greater number of the cases, unconscious; for how could a word-symbol correspond to that innermost nature of which we and the world are images? Only as a conception do we know that kernel . . .'[18] Nietzsche soon abandons the notion of the 'kernel of existence', or what he calls, in the word preparatory for the *Birth of Tragedy*, the *Urein*.[19] It is nevertheless possible to extract a number of Nietzsche's more permanent views about the general structure of language from the passage.

First, language and words do not themselves respond to 'reality', but to a set of conceptualizations which make a certain type of survival possible. Language is used 'like a spider web to capture what we need to know'.[20] And, as we talk about the world, so must it be; an at least partial effect feedback must exist. But, the 'reality to which they [words] correspond is in fact already a human invented reality.' Thus investigation of the structure of language will lay bare part of the genealogy which makes our world what it is for us. 'We are constantly led astray by words and concepts,' writes Nietzsche in the *Wanderer and his Shadow*, and are induced to think of things as other than they are, as separated, indivisible, existing in the absolute. *Language contains a hidden philosophical mythology*.[21] This mythology is the formulation of some particular event such that it appears to acquire a universal and absolute sense; this event is to be uncovered. Nietzsche shares such a goal of unmasking with Freud and Marx.

Second, the mythology prevents people from seeing language as a problem in itself, since it continually will tend to present to men the same things as problems. If there were to be a totally new set of experiences, then, as Nietzsche notes above, they would remain unknown; men would not have the words for them. The reverse presumably also follows: if we continue using the words and language we have, there will never be a 'totally new' set of experiences; in fact, we will be prevented from recognizing them as such, by virtue of our continued use of the same language. We are 'caught in a picture' – one might say a family portrait. Nietzsche recognizes

this potentially neurotic repetition with exactly the same term that
Wittgenstein was later to make famous. He writes: 'The strange
family resemblance of all Indian, German and Greek philosophizing is explained easily enough. Where there is kinship of languages,
it cannot but happen, due to the common philosophy of grammar –
I mean due to the unconscious domination by similar grammatical
functions – that everything is prepared from the outset for a similar
development and sequence of philosophical systems . . .'[22] In a
sense, the focus on language allows Nietzsche to bring Hegel back
to earth: language provides a set of plebeian *Weltgeister* which
establish the recurrent and recognizable developmental patterns in
the world around us. Without language, without the ability to
formulate the world, all would appear as it does to an infant, the
play and chaos of an unending river which is never twice the same.

Finally, as there is no agreement among languages as to what
constitutes 'reality', there is no language which might on some scale
be rated more 'correct' than any other. Such a scale would be like a
Ding an sich in epistemology; it would imply the existence of a
world which affects men and about which they could by definition
know nothing. This is again the criticism that Nietzsche levels at the
sphere of theoretical reason. The mind, however, Nietzsche remarks, constantly seeks to persuade itself of the contrary. It is a
'mask of dissimulation' and 'seeks to celebrate its Saturnalia where
there would be a happy union of word and world'.[23] The imagery is
drawn from Hegel; but, whereas Hegel believed such a union
possible in principle and in time, for Nietzsche, once again, the
mind is only seeking to persuade itself that the world it knows is the
one true world.

THE MORALITY OF LANGUAGE

By now it should be apparent that Nietzsche ascribes to language a
sense at least as broad as does Wittgenstein in the *Investigations*.
For both writers a language is very much an expressable way of
doing things and of going about one's business. It does not simply
mean the uttering of words used to describe life; such would imply
too great a separation of language from the world, and would repeat
the error that Nietzsche understands to occur in the division of the
world into 'real' and 'apparent'. A language describes and is (part
of) a form of life, a fussily coherent way of doing things. It is not
intended to cover all possibilities – that would make it perfect; it
rather blurs out at the edges. Thus 'words are acoustical signs for
concepts; concepts, however, are more or less definite sign images

for often recurring and associated sensations, for groups of sensations. To understand one another, it is not enough that one uses the
same words; one also has to use the same words for the same
species of internal experiences; in the end one has to have one's
experiences in common [*gemein*].'[24]

Here again Nietzsche refuses a simple nominalism or relativism.
As he also argues about morality and truth, things are not just what
men make of them; there can be no such separation between doer
and deed. Errors are not due to a false or improper creation, but
rather reside in the whole context. Men are in fact 'caught in error';
no one has a necessary right to his or her own opinions. The
'mistakes' we are led by language to make are 'mistakes' for the
whole form of life that we are. They are caused by accepting what
we see – what the language presents to us – as real. In other words,
they are caused by accepting as 'real' a distinction (already implicit
in language) between man and the world. 'It is no different in this
case than with the movement of the sun'; writes Nietzsche in the
Twilight of the Idols, 'there our eye is a constant advocate of error,
here it is our language'. We have projected the world with a
distorted lens, yet the vision is taken as real. Nietzsche continues:
'Indeed nothing has yet possessed a more naive power of persuasion
than the error concerning being [*Sein*] . . . After all, every word we
say and every sentence we speak is in its favor . . . Reason in
language – Oh! what an old deceptive female she is: I am afraid that
we shall not be rid of our belief in God because we still have faith in
grammar.'[25]

The link of the belief in God and the faith in grammar shows that
Nietzsche does not hold that the belief in God was simply a mistake, or deluded pure foolishness; such Voltairiana is far too easy
and superficial a criticism. Nor does he assume that because the
belief in God is 'mere illusion', a simple announcement might lift
this burden off the shoulders of contemporary man. Rather he is
suggesting that the structure of culture is synergistic; a change in
one part of it will necessarily eventually show up in other parts.
Such a perspective would be fundamentally conservative – it is
normally identified in Western thought with Edmund Burke –
except for the fact that Nietzsche wishes to encourage such change.
God is dead: so much has been announced and slowly and inexor-
ably the structure of language must respond to this news. Men will
continue, in Nietzsche's angry accusation, to live on in the 'shadows of the dead God', still influenced and controlled by the
left-over effects of such a belief. The gradual approach of the 'great
noon' signifies for Nietzsche that time when all shadows disappear;

he has, for instance, only cold contempt for a writer like George
Eliot who, while proclaiming herself an agnostic, still retains fundamentally Christian moral principles.[26] In effect, Nietzsche has
taken the statement that 'God is truth' in a chillingly literal fashion.
The long process by which men effectuated the murder of God does
not stop with the single announcement of the death of the divinity
in the famous aphorism about the 'Marketplace' in the *Gay Science*. The death of God is simply a signal point in a long process
whose ultimate conclusion is the destruction of the foundations of
truth itself. As truth becomes, in Nietzsche's understanding, increasingly impossible, so also must all die that depended on it, in
particular here the language which made it possible and which was
a part of it. The language will not survive if that which makes
it possible perishes; it too is one of those great things about
which Nietzsche notes in the *Genealogy* that they 'perish of
their own accord by an act of self-cancellation: so that law of life
decrees . . .'[27]

Nietzsche is here asserting that over the passage of time and
through the evolution of its own logic of transformation, the relation of language to the world can become highly problematic. Our
time is one of these, as was, one suspects also for Nietzsche, the
Germany before Luther's Bible. We are no longer able to talk about
what is happening to us. By Nietzsche's view of language, this
historical fact is also a problem of language and of our language in
particular. By seeing language as a problem, and by making its
status questionable, Nietzsche can deal appropriately and effectively with a time when a society has been forced into moral behavior
patterns which do not admit of expression within the moral logic of
the language.[28] For instance, in an example which Nietzsche would
have understood perfectly, George Orwell evolved the language of
Newspeak for the world of *1984*. It is not important here whether
or not one person can so consciously evolve a language. What is
more significant is Orwell's warning and contention, shared by
Nietzsche, that there may be worlds and times when it would be
necessary, if such action were possible, to develop a form of discourse which rendered morally compatible acts and concepts
which by our present understanding are antithetical. The society of
Oceania required that Love and Hate, War and Peace be synony-
mous: it was necessary there to be able to say them both with no
feeling of moral contradiction. For such purposes, one needed a
language with which to talk of them. Newspeak was to be the
language which fulfilled the necessities of the society: it expressed
that which was becoming a socio-political fact. That Orwell's vi-

sion is no more imagination and that Nietzsche's diagnosis is not fanciful should be obvious by a short reflection on the Army major who had to 'destroy the village in order to save it' or the high officials able to maintain in the face of publication of previously secret documents on the development of Vietnam war policy that there was no deceit practiced on the American people. For Nietzsche, words do not mean what one *wants* them to mean, they mean what the speakers *need* to have them mean if their position and integrity is to be preserved.

Language is involved in making things the same for people, in their commonality and communality. It is also therefore a means of enforcing a common behavior on individuals. But what it does enforce is *a* common behavior. Nietzsche is analyzing the effects of a language on behavior, but there is no reason to assume that he is *attacking* anything more than the particular forms of a communality which a particular language happens to enforce. He does not, after all, attack in the same way the community which was the Greek polis, nor the culture that was the *Iliad*. If our language develops in response to our needs, it is, for Nietzsche *our* language and *our* needs which must be called to the genealogical bar of judgement. Nietzsche understood as well as anyone after Rousseau the tremendous inertia of language. Already in the early essay on *Richard Wagner in Bayreuth*, Nietzsche writes that language now separates men from each other while denying them the knowledge of their divorce. 'Man can no longer make his misery known to others by means of language; thus he cannot really express himself anymore . . .: language has gradually become a force which drives humanity where it least wishes to go. . . . The results of this inability to communicate is that the creations of common action . . . all bear the stamp of mutual non-comprehension.'[29]

That which was supposed to bring men together now separates them: instead of life, men have in their language merely the accoutrements of a hollow idol. The genealogical investigation of language reveals to Nietzsche those structures which give us our particular way of being together. His dissection is an anatomy of what has slowly evolved as European society.

THE STRUCTURE OF OUR LANGUAGE

In Nietzsche's thought, there is, then, no attempt to reject language in favor of something else, intuition, for instance, or emotion, or blind advocacy and adherence to any of the solutions which have formed most of the political history of the twentieth century. For there is nothing wrong in general with dividing up the world into 'fictitious' categories; indeed, that humans do so is the very source of their particular being, pose and definition.[30] Nietzsche certainly does not say that any manner is as good as any other, however, even if all manners be errors. Suppose even, though, that as Nietzsche says, 'We will not be rid of our belief in God until we have abandoned our faith in grammar.' Is this necessarily so bad that humans should spend other than philosophical time worrying about it? Why should we not be content to rest, uncomfortably perhaps, 'in the shadows of the dead God', since, as Nietzsche repeatedly assures us, there is, in fact, no permanent resting place for 'truth'.

The problem however is that our language will not let us rest. Matters may have been different with Homeric Greek, but in Nietzsche's understanding, the particular structure of our manner of conceptualizing the world will never allow us peace. Instead we are pushed even onwards, not towards a possible or even hidden goal, but towards nothing at all. Our situation is a bit as if an early Calvinist had suddenly come to the realization that the *Deus absconditus* had been annihilated, yet was unable to stop acting like a Calvinist.[31] To understand why, we must now investigate the particular needs which our language serves, the particular beliefs which our forms of life require. We must investigate, so to speak, what our language makes seem natural to us.

That Nietsche finds the key to the epistemology of contemporary nihilism in the categories which Western men use and formulate is hardly open to doubt. He calls them the 'basic cause [*Ursache*] of nihilism' and suggests that through them men measure 'the worth of the world in categories which [are] founded on a purely imaginary world.'[32] What then are these categories which Nietzsche suggests originate in the requirements of our very nature?

The first category of epistemology[33] which Nietzsche considers is the 'subject–object' distinction. It is also probably the most important.[34] In practical terms, it allows men to separate the 'dancer from the dance', the person from his acts. Consider what is implied in making the distinction. Nietzsche sees the separation of a person from his acts as analogous to the distinction of the 'real' and 'apparent' worlds. The actor, if considerable apart from his action, assumes the role of the 'real' world. The action in question is held to be a conditioned part of the actor; the actor acquires a permanence which is not allocated to the action. Judgements therefore can be made about him independently of his action proper. The

actor is thus reified into an entity which has conceptual and potentially moral independence of his acts. He is so to speak, taken
outside the world and is then dealt with in terms of those idealized
categories which language so appropriately provides for such occasions. Thus, for Nietzsche, 'popular moralizing divorces strength
from the manifestation of strength, as if there were beneath the
strong a stratum of indifference able to manifest its strength or not.
This reads the action out of the actor – it places the emphasis on the
perpetrator of the action and presumes that he might have done
otherwise. An actor can thus be seen as responsible for his supposed
choice, but in fact *'der Täter ist bloss zur Tat hinzugedichtet'*. ('The
actor is merely a fiction added to the deed.') Obvious examples of
this general practice are sentences as 'the lightning flashed', 'a force
moved the object'. Such propositions are referred to by Nietzsche as
a *Tun-Tun*, in that they state the same event twice, once as subject
and once as object, and presume some meaningful relation between
them. Much energy can be expended on the investigation of this
so-called relationship, but for Nietzsche *'Das Tun ist alles.'* ('The
action of doing is all'.)[35]

When combined with the general architectonic features of language, the subject–object distinction produces particularly unfortunate consequences. The first appears to be an over-valuation of
consciousness. The actor acquires an ability to separate himself
from his acts; in turn, this allows him to reflect upon himself.
Consciousness makes man *qua* subject a prime mover in his own
right; it tends to fix a supposed correctness on whatever reflexive
conclusions the subject may arrive at. The subject becomes, Nietzsche says, 'a unity, a being', [36] and the conclusions consciousness
arrives at are given unquestioned status. For Nietzsche, this has two
important consequences. In the first place, it makes it difficult to
take into account the possibility that consciousness, even self-
consciousness, might, to use the metaphor which Freud was later to
make famous, merely be the 'tip of the iceberg'. The tip of an
iceberg is not significantly different material than that which lies
under the water: it is merely more visible to creatures which live
above the water. So also, consciousness would not, in this understanding, be qualitatively separable from non-consciousness, but
men would imagine that the two would somehow be different since
they experience them differently.

The second general consequence is an imperative towards a-
historicity. For Nietzsche, the 'hereditary failure' of philosophers is
due to a tendency to start with an assumption of the assumed
permanence of contemporary man. 'In an involuntary fashion man

appears as an *aeterna veritas* . . .' By unquestioned acceptance of the permanence of the products of reflexive self-consciousness, philosophers are able to ignore the effects of historical change on the *nature* of the subject. They are then led to see the 'last four thousand years as eternal', ignoring that there are no 'eternal facts and thus there are no eternal truths'.[37] For Nietzsche, like much of the rest of the world of ideality the subject–object distinction is an attempt to avoid dealing with the historicity or givenness of humanity.

It must be emphasized that Nietzsche is not saying that there is no such thing as human nature; rather he asserts that that which has been called human nature is transitory. The present episode seems to be over two thousand years.[38] In other words, what we take as permanent – human nature – is, in Nietzsche's understanding, finally coming to an end. There is probably nothing which will replace it: what overwhelms in Nietzsche is his consciousness of standing at the dusky end of a long era, with a less and less positive answer to the question 'what is living and what is dead in world history'.

There is then in Nietzsche a final extraordinary modesty about himself and his kind. One tends to overlook this because of the titles such as 'Why I am so Wise', 'Why I Write Such Good Books', which divide his autobiography. He is, however, simply refusing to allow man to be the measure of all things: wisest he finds those men whom he praises for 'going under', for their recognition that they are a dying breed. While Nietzsche is nothing if not serious, he does not take *himself* seriously and can accept that at the end of over two thousand years of western culture he and all that he has represented is coming to and end.

After the subject–object distinction, a second epistemological premiss is that of free will. In the notes prepared for the drafting of the second volume of *Human, all-too-human*, Nietzsche writes that 'speech is the way to the belief in the freedom of the will.'[39] His reasoning seems to be this. To speak of free will, it must be apparent that the action of willing makes a perceptible and more or less predictable difference in the world. If no change is made, or if the change is random, if, for instance when a person decided to go home, he found that for no apparent reason he sometimes made it and sometimes found himself a quantum leap next door, it would make no sense to speak of 'free will'. Free will then depends on the consistency of perception of that portion of the world which is not affected by willing. Since perceptions are predominantly formalized and given existence through language, it is, in Nietzsche's understanding, through language that the world is structured such that the operation of the will may be visible. Without language, there would be no facts, and without 'facts' men would not know what they do.[40]

The escape from a world of an Heraclitean, undifferentiated river of existence thus finds its 'surest grounds' in 'words and concepts'. Through the conceptualization inherent in speech, the 'raging spring torrent' is transfixed as a frozen river and traversed by bridges. Actions can have results, and willing consequences, which men are able to describe in terms that others will understand; the bridges enable humans to ignore the river, as long as it remains more or less frozen. Nietzsche continues on: 'The belief in the freedom of the will . . . has in speech its greatest evangelist and prophet.[41]

It is important not to mistake the thrust of Nietzsche's conceit about the river and the bridges. The image reappears again in *Zarathustra* and serves to indicate Nietzsche's contention that as long as it is *possible* to believe in free will (as long as the river is frozen) men will not only do so, but will insist that there 'really is' free will, here again refusing to acknowledge their own radical historicity. The doctrine of free will thus contributes to the evasions originally made possible by the subject–object distinction. Men tend to think, since they 'are' free that no necessary historical or epistemological chains bind them. If one does not *feel* tied to a certain form of perception, then all that is perceived tends to confirm the belief that men are, in fact, free. As Nietzsche says, 'we do not feel the delimitation as limit' (*Grenze als Grenze*),[42] and are led to accept as all of experience that which is delineated by our epistemological requirements. Even though, as Nietzsche writes in the second volume of *Human, all-too-human*, 'each word is a prejudice' and affects spiritual freedom, men feel free, since the world they encounter is one which to a considerable degree has elaborated the requirements of their form of life. For Nietzsche, humans have walled themselves into a world of their own making and have told themselves that they are still free; that their consciousness of the borders as barriers has vanished does not detract from the fact that it is not the only possible world.[43]

Freedom of the will becomes a manner of justifying a certain form of life and of asserting the legitimacy of that, and only that, over which this form of life has sway. It is thus a way of preserving a certain pattern of domination and of enforcing a legitimacy for a certain set of horizons, without it ever appearing necessary to seek justification for that enforcement. 'The doctrine of free will is a cunning method of preserving the credibility of the *ego-cogito*. Freedom of the will – that is the expression of a complex state of delight of the person exercising volition . . . What happens here is what happens in every well constructed commonwealth: namely that the governing class identifies itself with the success of the commonwealth.'[44]

The political reference is not 'just' a metaphor. In a 'happy commonwealth', the questions which would threaten the basis of its existence do not get asked; they are walled out, beyond the 'horizons'. They remain outside because the class which defines the commonwealth (in the sense that the *aristoi* define an aristocracy and the *demos* a democracy) is identified with that which makes the commonwealth what it is. Just as there is no reason to call the freedom of the will into question when will produces results with the unquestioned clockwork of a propelled billiard ball striking another, so also there is no reason to call into question the defining function of the 'governing classes' as long as the commonwealth meets with success, as long as the will of that class leads to results, as long as the words we use to define our world enable us to deal with that world. Should failures become the order of the day, then doubts will arise, horizons be questioned and grounds will have to be sought. Until then, the politics of the situation will be happy.

Here again a note of warning is appropriate. Nietzsche thinks the doctrine of the freedom of the will to be at best a useful descriptive fiction; he is not thereby arguing for its opposite. He does not want to say that humans are really 'not free', nor that freedom lies elsewhere. He understands full well that one cannot reject one side of a dialectical proposition in favor of the other: rather his argument rests on the understanding that men are never so separate from the world that they might be in a position – epistemological or physical – to ultimately have or not have free will. Such a thought would require 'more than Munchhausen's audacity, to pull oneself up and into existence by the hair out of the swamps of nothingness'. Once we have gotten rid of the 'boorish simplicitly' of this doctrine, both sides of the dialectic must disappear. To do otherwise would amount to a 'misuse of cause and effect'.[45]

The discussion of free will evolves naturally for Nietzsche into a consideration of a third epistemological prejudice which Nietzsche sees as blighting our life. This is the sequencing of activity into cause and effect, another version of the atomizing process noted in the previous section. Were there an intellect who saw the flux of events as a continuum and not a series of distinguished parts, the concept of cause and effect, indeed, of all conditionality, could not exist for him. In Nietzsche's reasoning (here derivative of Hume), that one can imagine such a state, if not actually put oneself into it, indicates that it would be 'ludicrously immodest' to behave as if the only legitimate manner of viewing the world were the cause-effect sequence which appears so naturally our own.[46] This categorization is then another ruse, best preserved and operationalized in language. It keeps the world limited and comprehensible. 'The separation of the "doer" from the "deed" of the event from some-one who produces events, of the process from something that is not a process but enduring as substance, thing, body, soul, etc. . . . – the attempt to comprehend an event as a sort of shifting and place changing on the part of a being of something constant: this ancient mythology established the belief in "cause and effect", after it had found a firm form in the function of language and grammar,'[47] Here again men are reading 'the unfamiliar back into the familiar',[48] and deriving from that act a feeling of power, security, comfort and satisfaction.

Nietzsche's critique of causality is then not so much directed at the question of the existence of causality, as against the notion. That causality was not a fact, in the sense that a chair or a moun-tain might be, had been firmly established by Hume. Kant, who was much concerned with Hume's argument, had pursued this line and shown, as Nietzsche sees it, not only that causality was a process of the mind and could not therefore inhere in events themselves, but had also delineated the realm in which causality could provide a useful and heuristic tool.[49]

So far Nietzsche is in agreement with Kant, but he sees him as also attempting to deal with the consequences of this limitation by positing a *Kausalitäts-Sinn*, yet another *ad hoc* 'explanation'. Nietzsche here can pursue his radical critique of Kant. 'One is surprised,' he exclaims sardonically, 'one is disturbed, one desires something familiar to hold on to – as soon as we are shown something old in something new, we are calmed. The supposed instinct of causality is only a fear of the unfamiliar and the attempt to discover something known – a search not for causes, but for the familiar.'[50] Again Nietzsche sees that Kant analyzed correctly but was keep from the logical conclusion of his analysis by the desire to retain a foundation for what his sense told him to be true. To this effect Kant discovers the 'sense of causality'. It is not that this concept is not useful, Nietzsche argues, but that there is no reason to deduce the reality of a concept from its usefulness.

In all three of these epistemological prejudices, Nietzsche's analy-sis tries to show a common tendency, namely the over-valuation and absolutizing of the ego (the human self). In conscious opposition to Descartes he writes in *Beyond Good and Evil*: 'When I analyze the process that is expressed in the sentence "I think", I find a whole series of daring assertions that would be difficult, perhaps impossible, to prove: for example, that it is I that thinks, that thinking is an operation and an activity on the part of a being who is thought of as a cause, that there is an "I", finally that it is already determined what is to be described as thought – that I *know* what thinking is.'[51] Thus, by making language a problem, we can see that Nietzsche is driven back to a position where *men themselves become the problem*. For Nietzsche, even man himself ('human nature') cannot provide a firm rock on which one might ground an accurate epistemology. In an important section of *Twilight of the Idols* he writes: 'People have believed at all times that they knew what a cause is; but whence our faith that we had such knowledge? . . . We believed ourselves to be causal in the act of willing: we thought that here at least we caught causality in the act. Nor did anyone doubt that the antecedents of such an act, its causes, were to be sought in consciousness and would be found there once sought – as "motives": else one would not have been free and responsible for it. Finally who would have denied that thought is caused, that the ego causes the thought?'[52] For Nietzsche, no explanation is achieved by tracing 'effects' back to some 'cause'. The source of the problem and the area of investigation should properly be human beings themselves.

Nietzsche's epistemological investigations on these matters can then be seen as a radicalization of what Kant posed as the 'problem of metaphysics', that men continue to seek that which their reason makes it impossible for them to achieve. Kant had thought that this applied to the use of reason and had sought to show that the limits of knowledge were in fact the definition of knowledge itself and in no ways at fault with knowledge. Nietzsche accepts much of this, but makes the limits of knowledge a definition of what it means to be human, all-too-human. Thus for him no more is metaphysics the 'queen of the sciences'; Kant's attempted rejuvenation of that 'outcast and forsaken maiden' fails and now the 'path to fundamental problems' must be understood to lie in psychology, in what leads men to pursue truth and meaning in the manner that they do.[53] Humans must deal with themselves as the source of problems, and this self is understood by Nietzsche to be only an historically specific necessity.

THE METAPHORICAL BASIS OF LIFE

Our language then repeats, in a sort of neurotic compulsion, our history and our selves to us. Language pulls together and is the world: this language, our world. The very ability to give names – to extend the control of language over the world – must then be a masterly trait, for it consists of saying what the world is.[54] To name is to define and bring under control; the allocation of names creates the world in the image of he who names. Such creations are properly termed meta-phors, they are artefacts which *carry* an intellectual process *beyond* the mind into the world.

Here Nietzsche's analysis is remarkably close to that of Marx and Freud. Both Freud and Marx develop the concept of fetishism; for both a man-made object is endowed by its human creator with a power and a right to control. The creation becomes a 'natural' force and turns back on its own creator. In *Totem and Taboo*, a primal band of brothers, after killing and devouring a sexually dominating father, only to see the cycle of mastership and slavery repeated as one of them emerged as a new father, finds it necessary to take Fatherhood out of the world and render it inaccessible. Thus was born God, religion, and civilization. For Marx, men mix their labor with nature in order to create an object which is then bought and sold as a commodity on the market, convinced that it is in the order of things that commodities be bought for a price other than the value of the labor with which they created it. In both cases, that which is a human creation is taken to be something wonderful and inaccessibly out of control.

Nietzsche's word for the results of this process is *idol*; it is his conviction of their twilight that informs the destructive side of his writing. As early as the essay *On Truth and Lie in the Extra-Moral Sense* (1873), he had begun to work out the process by which idols come to be consecrated. Truth is conceived of as metaphor. But, as Nietzsche notes in the *Gay Science*, 'unspeakably more depends on what things are called, than on what they are. The reputation, the name and appearance, . . . each being in origin most frequently an error and arbitrariness, thrown over things like a garment, and quite foreign to their essence [*Wesen*] and even to their exterior, have gradually by belief therein and growth from generation to generation, so to speak, grown on to things and into things and have become its very body.'[55] The metaphors which first lie on our life like a light cloak become an iron cage. That which enabled men to make the world rich to themselves – men need these imagined worlds[56] – is gradually 'enhanced, transposed, and embellished poetically and rhetorically and after long use seems firm, canonical, and obligatory to a people: truths are illusions about which one has forgotten that this is what they are; metaphors which are worn out and without sensuous power; coins which have lost their picture, and now only matter as metal, no longer as coins.'[57]

LANGUAGE AND NIHILISM

It is important to remember here that though the logic of fetishism or idolatry wears out the metaphors which serve as the foundation of life, Nietzsche in no way thinks that, having realized this, we will simply be able to do without them. In the first place, as we have seen, survival itself requires such illusions and metaphors; without them there would 'have long ago been nothing more (of mankind)'.[58] And in the second place, there is no way to simply abolish them, by some epistemological fiat. One would be a 'fool' to think that 'it would be enough here to refer to this (shabby) origin and this nebulous veil of illusion, in order to annihilate that which virtually passes for the world, namely so called "reality"'.[59] It is perfectly true that we live in a world which at one point was to a great degree of our own making, but to say that the world is therefore 'only' an illusion is accurate only if one accepts that without this illusion there would have been no world. For Nietzsche, there is no 'real' world underlying this one, no Sleeping Beauty to be awakened by a single epistemological kiss.

Nietzsche cannot then simply be content to *expose* the fact that men 'alone have devised cause, sequence, for-each-other, relativity, constraint, number, law, freedom, motive and purpose', and have mixed and projected this symbol-world into things as if it existed in itself. However we have to do this, or something like it. 'Suppose,' he writes, 'we have finally reached the conclusion that there is nothing good or evil in itself; but rather that these are qualities of the soul, which lead us to cover with such words things both inside and outside us. We have taken back the predicates from things; or we have at least recollected that we merely lent the things these predicates. *Let us be careful that this insight does not cause us to loose the faculty of lending* and that at the same time we do not become wealthier and more avaricious.'[60] We have seen however that the structures of our particular language, our particular epistemological prejudices, make it apparently impossible that we should find any way out from the fly bottle of this particular world.

What then is to be done? Nietzsche's ultimate answer requires an analysis of much more than epistemology and especially of eternal return. It is possible, though, to give some preliminary indications. Nietzsche finds that men have thought that they always possessed consciousness. Since it has not been in the past much of a problem, they have not given themselves much trouble in its acquisition. In particular, no attempt was made to acquire a given *kind* of consciousness, for they merely allowed that which was around to determine theirs, assuming it, perhaps, to be the only possibility. Thus, writes Nietzsche, 'it is an entirely new problem just dawning on the human eye and hardly yet plainly recognizable – to embody knowledge in ourselves and make it instinctive, a problem which is only seen by those who have grasped the fact that hitherto our errors alone have been embodied in us, and that all our consciousness is relative to errors.'[61] Two preliminary indications appear in this statement. First, it seems that the problem that Nietzsche sees facing humanity will be that of 'embodying' knowledge and 'making it instinctive'. He had already argued in the second of the *Untimely Meditations* that our present 'nature' had itself been acquired through precisely such an embodiment. How this is to proceed occupies much of Nietzsche's entire work thereafter. Secondly, it appears that there is some structure inherent in the way that men have approached the world which has led them to develop a life composed only of errors. Again in the essay *On the Use and Disadvantage of History for Life*, Nietzsche finds that 'our whole being is divided into an inner and outer side . . .; we suffer from the *malady of words* and have no trust in any feeling not stamped with its special word. . . . This life is sick and must be healed.'[62]

Sickness of the understanding results from the fact that the present structure of our thought leads us to approach knowledge and truth in a manner such that we can never be content. All searches for causes, for subjects and so forth, are for Nietzsche moral searches in the sense that they attempt to uncover who or what is responsible for things being as they are. Knowledge itself is in its essence a *'regressus in infinitum'*,[63] ultimately a moral ideology which men engage themselves in order better to survive.

The search for such responsibility is ultimately fueled by a moral imperative. The search operates in our consciousness, and thus cannot refrain from applying the same moral energy to consciousness itself. In an important passage dated 10 June 1887, as if he had finally gotten something right, Nietzsche notes: 'But among the forces cultivated by morality was truthfulness: this, one eventually turned against morality, discovered its teleology, its prejudiced [*interessiert*] perspective, and now the recognition of this long incarnate [*eingefleischt*] mendacity that one despairs getting rid of, becomes a stimulant. Now we discover in ourselves needs implanted by a long understanding of morality – which now appears to us as needs for untruth; on the other hand, these needs are those on which the values for which we endure life seem to hang. This antagonism – not to esteem what we know and not to be allowed any longer to value whose lies we would tell ourselves – results in a process of dissolution.'[64] Thus for Nietzsche, the *desire to found knowledge on truth*, itself made necessary and encouraged by the epistemological categories of our language, *results in a gradual undermining of that which might serve as the basis for truth*.

The will to truth carries a perverse necrophilia. If life is in fact appearance, and there is no 'truth' to be ultimately reached, the defense of the will to truth is the assertion of the ultimate validity of a man-made perspective, without there being in fact any reason why 'truth' should be sought or preferred. To affirm truth as an ultimate standard is to tie oneself to exhaustion and indeed Nietzsche is led to speculate, as Freud was also later to, if there did not lie in the will to truth a 'concealed will to death'.[65]

What then is the epistemology of nihilism? The hidden linguistic imperatives of the categories which men now live under force them towards nothingness. The end state of this process is nihilism, itself the final development of all morality, to which men arrive, in Nietzsche's understanding, *when they find both that there is no truth and that they should continue to seek it*. The will to truth drives men even further into the void: that they now recognize it as void is no help. As Nietzsche notes at the very end of the *Genealogy of Morals*, 'man would rather will the void, than be void of will'. Here then is the position we arrive at: the present structure of human life forces men to continue searching for that which their understanding tells them is not to be found. Such is the epistemology of nihilism.

Nietzsche seems then to leave an irresoluble dilemma. The search for liberation from the oppressions and chains of bourgeois society, itself but the latest manifestation of the genealogy of the West, forces a recognition that as an individual one cannot escape society, for that which structures society also structures the self. In fact, everything that one might do in such an attempt at liberation is itself imbued with that from which one is seeking to escape. So the attempt to free oneself results merely in a reinforcement of one's fetters. Our way of being in the world makes us seek freedom, the search binds us all the more to that which we would escape and we find both that we cannot achieve freedom nor desist from searching.

Nietzsche's understanding is not dissimilar from Marx's in its analysis of the discontents of bourgeois civilization. But whereas the logic of dialectical history permits revolution, the logic of the genealogical does not. For Nietzsche, bourgeois men are driven only into the void and the cunning of history is reduced to an empty laugh. In dynamics, Nietzsche's view resembles that which Freud depicts in *Civilization and its Discontents*, but Nietzsche's understanding seems much more detailed and complex than does Freud's. Finally in Nietzsche's discovery of our anthropology by the proceeding from our language, Nietzsche's enterprise presages that of Wittgenstein. Contrary to Wittgenstein though, Nietzsche thinks that the compulsions of our language reveal radical and incurable sickness in Western humans. Wittgenstein had hoped for a physician to cure the 'sickness of our understanding'; Nietzsche ultimately requires 'transfiguration'. A 'transfigured life' would be one which was not 'human, all-too-human', *übermenschlich*, with a 'new' nature. But what this might mean is already too far afield.

NOTES

1 The *locus classicus* is F. de Saussure, *Cours de linguistique générale*. See for a general discussion J. J. Katz, *The Philosophy of Language* (New York, 1966) and the material cited below.

2 See E. Sapir, *Language* (New York, 1921) and B. L. Whorf, *Language Thought and Reality* (Cambridge, Mass., 1964), esp. 'Language and Logic', pp. 233–45. A specific link between Nietzsche and the Whorf is drawn in H. Wein, 'Métaphysique et anti-métaphysique', *Revue de métaphysique et de morale*, 4 (1958), pp. 285–411.

3 The best known, if not best, article here is Max Black, 'Linguistic Relativity: the views of Benjamin LeeWhorf', *Philosophical Review*, 68 (1969), pp. 228–38. More important seems to me Claude Lévi-Strauss, *Structural Anthropology* (Garden City, 1967), pp. 66–95, who argues that Whorf makes an illegitimate move between the structure of language and behavior proper, rather than the *structure* of behavior.

4 See Ludwig Wittgenstein, *Philosophical Investigations* (New York, 1958); J. L. Austin, *Philosophical Papers* (Oxford, 1961). The strongest and most sympathetic reading here is Hanna Fenichel Pitkin, *Wittgenstein and Justice* (Berkeley and Los Angeles, 1972).

5 Stanley Cavell, *Must We Mean What We Say?* (New York, 1969), pp. 98–9.

6 See Erich Heller, 'Nietzsche and Wittgenstein', *Encounters*, ed. S. Spender (New York, 1961) and Stanley Cavell, 'Existentialism and Analytical Philosophy', *Daedalus* (Summer, 1964).

7 See Bernard Bueb, *Nietzsches Kritik der praktischen Vernunft* (Stuttgart, 1970).

8 But see the excellent Monika Funke, *Ideologiekritik und ihre Ideologie bei Nietzsche* (Stuttgart-Bad Connstatt, 1974).

9 Nietzsche's position thus bears certain relationships with Noam Chomsky's hypothesis that all languages share a common structure, relationships acquired through their mutual indebtedness to Kant.

10 I have used the following key for citations from Nietzsche:

EH	*Ecce Homo*	
FW	*Die fröhliche Wissenschaft*	The Gay Science
GD	*Götzendämmerung*	Twilight of the Idols
GM	*Zur Genealogie der Moral*	On the Genealogy of Morals
GT	*Die Geburt der Tragödie*	The Birth of Tragedy
JGB	*Jenseits von Gut und Böse*	Beyond Good and Evil
M	*Morgenröte*	Dawn of Day
MAM	*Menschliches, Allzumenschliches*	Human, all-too-human
RWB	*Richard Wagner in Bayreuth*	Richard Wagner in Bayreuth
WL	*Über Wahrheit und Lüge im aussermoralischen Sinn*	On Truth and Lies in the Extra-moral sense
WM	*Der Wille zur Macht*	The Will to Power
WS	*Der Wanderer und sein Schatten*	The Wanderer and his Shadow (part 2, Vol. II, MAM)
ZA	*Also Sprach Zarathustra*	Thus Spoke Zarathustra

Citations from Nietzsche are given by the above key and the relevant internal subdivisions. Except where noted I have also given a volume and page citation to *Werke in drei Bänden*, herausgegeben von Karl Schlechta (München: Carl Hansver Verlag, 1954). Thus JGB 23, II 587 is Beyond Good and Evil, paragraph 23, Schlechta edition, volume II, page 587. I have worked from the German but have not hesitated to inform myself and borrow from Walter Kaufmann's excellent translations.

The citation in this footnote is MAM i 11, II 453; see also the interesting discussion in Bernard Pautrat, *Versions du Soleil: figures et système de Nietzsche* (Paris, 1971), pp. 156–265.

11 FW 303.

12 This is the source of the problems which swirl about Kant's notion of the thing in itself. See Stanley Cavell, *The Senses of Walden* (New York, 1972), esp. p. 104 for an interesting if cryptic discussion. See also Wittgenstein, *Philosophical Investigations*, # 127–33.

13 Cf. Stanley Rosen, 'Nihilism', in J. Edie, ed. *New Essays in Phenomenology* (Chicago, 1964), pp. 151–8; see also his *Nihilism: A Philosophical Essay* (New Haven, 1969), esp. pp. xiii–xx.

14 See especially his *On the Way to Language* (New York, 1970), pp. 1–57. Such an interpretation of Nietzsche has been done by Pierre Klossowski, *Nietzsche et le cercle vicieux* (Paris, 1969). Pautrat (*Ver-*

sions du Soleil, pp. 358–61) also thinks that this is what Nietzsche is trying to do, but thinks it impossible.

15 III 862 (WM 522).

16 M. Heidegger, *Nietzsche* (Pfullingen, 1961), vol. II, p. 378, argues that Nietzsche thinks that all notions of the transcendental derive from the subject–object distinction. Arthur Danto, *Nietzsche as Philosopher* (New York, 1968) has argued the same from the point of view of analytical philosophy. See also his 'Semantical Theory and the Logical Limits of Nihilism', in Edie, *New Essays in Phenomenology*, pp. 159–76.

17 EH *Why I Write Such Good Books*, 1, II, 1100.

18 This essay is not included in the Schlechta edition. See 'On Words and Music', *The Complete Works of Friedrich Nietzsche*, ed. O. Levy, Vol. II, pp. 30–1. See Wittgenstein *Philosophical Investigations*, # 301.

19 GT *Attempt at a Self Critique, passim*, esp. 3 and 7, I II and 17.

20 Friedrich Nietzsche, *Die Unschuld des Werdens*, herausgegeben von A. Bäumler (Stuttgart, 1956), Vol. II, p. 41.

21 WS 11, 1, 879.

22 JGB 20, II 584. See his proposal at the end of the first essay of GM for a prize to be offered to the best essay on the question 'What light does linguistics and especially the study of etymology throw on the history of the evolution of moral concepts?'

23 WL 2, III 320 (my italics); See G. W. F. Hegel, *The Phenomenology of Mind* (London, 1966), p. 105.

24 JGB 268, II 740.

25 GD Reason in Philosophy 5, II 960. On truth as a woman see JGB preface, II 565.

26 GD Skirmishes 5, II, 993.

27 GM iii 27, II 898–99.

28 I have sought to do a particular investigation of this in my 'Civil Disobedience and Legitimacy', forthcoming.

29 RWB 5, I, 387.

30 See HL 10, I 284.

31 This is the situation which Max Weber describes at the end of *The Protestant Ethic and the Spirit of Capitalism*. On the relations of Nietzsche and Weber, see Robert Eden, *Political Leadership and Philosophical Praxis: A Study of Weber and Nietzsche* (Ph.D. Dissertation, Harvard Univ., 1974).

32 III 678 (WM 12).

33 There is a rather harsh debate raging among Nietzsche scholars as to whether or not Nietzsche 'had' an epistemology. K. Jaspers (*Nietzsche: An Introduction to his Philosophical Activity*) and K. Schlechta (*Der Fall Nietzsche*) maintain that he did not. They argue that since no 'true' knowledge is possible that there can be no real epistemology. Against this Arthur Danto, *Nietzsche as Philosopher*, and E. R. Dodds ('Appendix' to his edition of the *Gorgias*) try to show that Nietzsche had a coherent epistemology which Danto refers to as non-cognitivism. The

problem with Danto's conclusion is that, as K. R. Fischer points out in his review (*Journal of Philosophy*, LXIV, 18, pp. 564–9), it depends on the presumption that the reason that Nietzsche did not formulate this epistemology is that he never got around to it. Danto sees himself as reconstructing what Nietzsche could/would/should have done, but never asks himself why Nietzsche did not. In addition, Danto's approach is suspect on two other grounds; as Kaufmann points out he (a) finds no difference between those works Nietzsche saw to press and those assembled by his editors and (b) often uses truncated citations. See Kaufmann's edition of GM p. 22. Both schools though, retain the notion that the only way to discuss epistemology is in a 'pure' Kantian sense whereas Nietzsche argues for many epistemologies.

34 See Heidegger, *Nietzsche*, Vol. II, p. 378.

35 GM i 13, II 789–90. See Whorf, *Language, Thought and Reality*, p. 243, for a discussion of such examples. These considerations make it difficult to hold with Walter Kaufmann that Nietzsche's conception of the will to power resembles Shakespeare's in *Measure for Measure*, when Isabella asserts:

> O, it is excellent to have a giant's strength; but it is tyrannous to use it like a giant.   *Lucio*: That's well said.

I have added the line for Lucio; the context, in my reading, casts some doubt on Shakespeare's intention. In any case it is not Nietzsche's position, but there can be no doubt that Kaufmann thinks it to be. In his *Shakespeare to Existentialism*, p. 249: 'This is Nietzsche in a nutshell.' For an elaboration of these problems see John Silber, 'Being and Doing', *Chicago Law Review* (Autumn, 1967), pp. 47–91; S. Freud, 'Criminality from a Sense of Guilt', *Collected Papers IV* (London, 1953), pp. 341–4 and Za, *The Pale Criminal*, II pp. 303–5.

36 III 733 (WM 529).

37 MAM i 2, I 448.

38 F. Nietzsche, *Werke* (Leipzig: Naumann, 1898), Vol. XII, p. 129.

39 F. Nietzsche, *Werke*, herausgegeben von G. Colli und M. Montinari (Berlin: Gruyter, 1967ff), Vol. IV, p. 305.

40 MAM i 18, I 460.

41 WS 11, i 878.

42 III 862 (WM 522).

43 WS 55, I 903; cf. Ibid. 10, I 878; see also EH *Why I Write Such Good Books*, 1, II 1100.

44 JGB 19, 582.

45 JGB 21, II 585.

46 FW 374, II 249–50; cf. FW 112, II 119–20.

47 III 490 (WM 631).

48 GD *The Four Great Errors*, 5, II 975.

49 See FW 357, II 225–9.

50 III 768 (WM 550).

51 JGB 16, II 580.

52 GD *The Four Great Errors*, 3, II 973.

53 JGB 23, II 587. See I. Kant, *Critique of Pure Reason* (New York, 1957), pp. 7–8.

54 On naming and prohibitions on naming in Nietzsche see Pautrat, *Versions du Soleil*, pp. 235 ff.

55 FW 58, II 77–8.

56 See III 542 (WM 517).

57 WL i, III 314.

58 FW 11, II 44.

59 FW 58, II 78.

60 M 210, I 1161 (my italics).

61 FW 11, II 44.

62 HL 10, I 281 (my italics).

63 III 491 (WM 575).

64 III 852 (WM 5). Kaufmann (as well as Heidegger) refuses to take Nietzsche's biological language seriously. Thus in his translation he is led to use the figurative 'inveterate' for *eingefleischt*, which looses the physiological possibilities of 'incarnate'.

65 FW 344, II 207.

7

The Order of Discourse*

MICHEL FOUCAULT†

I

I wish I could have slipped surreptitiously into this discourse which I must present today, and into the ones I shall have to give here, perhaps for many years to come. I should have preferred to be enveloped by speech, and carried away well beyond all possible beginnings, rather than have to begin it myself. I should have preferred to become aware that a nameless voice was already speaking long before me, so that I should only have needed to join in, to continue the sentence it had started and lodge myself, without really being noticed, in its interstices, as if it had signalled to me by pausing, for an instant, in suspense. Thus there would be no beginning, and instead of being the one from whom discourse proceeded, I should be at the mercy of its chance unfolding, a slender gap, the point of its possible disappearance.

I should have liked there to be a voice behind me which had begun to speak a very long time before, doubling in advance everything I am going to say, a voice which would say: 'You must go on, I can't go on, you must go on, I'll go on, you must say words, as long as there are any, until they find me, until they say me, strange pain, strange sin, you must go on, perhaps it's done already, perhaps they have said me already, perhaps they have carried me to the threshold of my story, before the door that opens on my story, that would surprise me, if it opens.'[1]

I think a good many people have a similar desire to be freed from the obligation to begin, a similar desire to be on the other side of discourse from the outset, without having to consider from the outside what might be strange, frightening, and perhaps maleficent about it. To this very common wish, the institution's reply is ironic, since it solemnizes beginnings, surrounds them with a circle of

*Michel Foucault, 'The Order of Discourse', reprinted from Robert Young ed. *Untying The Text* (Boston and London: Routledge & Kegan Paul, 1981), pp. 51–77), by permission © Routledge & Kegan Paul.
†Inaugural Lecture at the Collège de France, 2 December 1970.

attention and silence, and imposes ritualized forms on them, as if to make them more easily recognizable from a distance.

Desire says: 'I should not like to have to enter this risky order of discourse; I should not like to be involved in its peremptoriness and decisiveness; I should like it to be all around me like a calm, deep transparence, infinitely open, where others would fit in with my expectations, and from which truths would emerge one by one; I should only have to let myself be carried, within it and by it, like a happy wreck.' The institution replies: 'You should not be afraid of beginnings; we are all here in order to show you that discourse belongs to the order of laws, that we have long been looking after its appearances; that a place has been made ready for it, a place which honours it but disarms it; and that if discourse may sometimes have some power, nevertheless it is from us and us alone that it gets it.'

But perhaps this institution and this desire are nothing but two contrary replies to the same anxiety: anxiety about what discourse is in its material reality as a thing pronounced or written; anxiety about this transitory existence which admittedly is destined to be effaced, but according to a time-scale which is not ours; anxiety at feeling beneath this activity (despite its greyness and ordinariness) powers and dangers that are hard to imagine; anxiety at suspecting the struggles, victories, injuries, dominations and enslavements, through so many words even though long usage has worn away their roughness.

What, then, is so perilous in the fact that people speak, and that their discourse proliferates to infinity? Where is the danger in that?

II

Here is the hypothesis which I would like to put forward tonight in order to fix the terrain – or perhaps the very provisional theatre – of the work I am doing: that in every society the production of discourse is at once controlled, selected, organized and redistributed by a certain number of procedures whose role is to ward off its powers and dangers, to gain mastery over its chance events, to evade its ponderous, formidable materiality.

In a society like ours, the procedures of exclusion are well known. The most obvious and familiar is the prohibition. We know quite well that we do not have the right to say everything, that we cannot speak of just anything in any circumstances whatever, and that not everyone has the right to speak of anything whatever. In the taboo on the object of speech, and the ritual of the circumstances of speech, and the privileged or exclusive right of the speaking subject, we have the play of three types of prohibition which intersect, reinforce or compensate for each other, forming a complex grid which changes constantly. I will merely note that at the present time the regions where the grid is tightest, where the black squares are most numerous, are those of sexuality and politics; as if discourse, far from being that transparent or neutral element in which sexuality is disarmed and politics pacified, is in fact one of the places where sexuality and politics exercise in a privileged way some of their most formidable powers. It does not matter that discourse appears to be of little account, because the prohibitions that surround it very soon reveal its link with desire and with power. There is nothing surprising about that, since, as psychoanalysis has shown, discourse is not simply that which manifests (or hides) desire – it is also the object of desire; and since, as history constantly teaches us, discourse is not simply that which translates struggles or systems of domination, but is the thing for which and by which there is struggle, discourse is the power which is to be seized.

There exists in our society another principle of exclusion, not another prohibition but a division and a rejection. I refer to the opposition between reason and madness.[2] Since the depths of the Middle Ages, the madman has been the one whose discourse cannot have the same currency as others. His word may be considered null and void, having neither truth nor importance, worthless as evidence in law, inadmissible in the authentification of deeds or contracts, incapable even of bringing about the trans-substantiation of bread into body at Mass. On the other hand, strange powers not held by any other may be attributed to the madman's speech: the power of uttering a hidden truth, of telling the future, of seeing in all naivety what the others' wisdom cannot perceive. It is curious to note that for centuries in Europe the speech of the madman was either not heard at all or else taken for the word of truth. It either fell into the void, being rejected as soon as it was proffered, or else people deciphered in it a rationality, naive or crafty, which they regarded as more rational than that of the sane. In any event, whether excluded, or secretly invested with reason, the madman's speech, strictly, did not exist. It was through his words that his madness was recognized; they were the place where the division between reason and madness was exercised, but they were never recorded or listened to. No doctor before the end of the eighteenth century had ever thought of finding out what was said, or how and why it was said, in this speech which nonetheless determined the difference. This whole immense discourse of the madman was taken for mere noise, and he was only symbolically allowed to speak, in the theatre, where he would step forward, disarmed and reconciled, because there he played the role of truth in a mask.

You will tell me that all this is finished today or is coming to an end; that the madman's speech is no longer on the other side of the divide; that it is no longer null and void; on the contrary, it puts us on the alert; that we now look for a meaning in it, for the outline or the ruins of some *oeuvre*; and that we have even gone so far as to come across this speech of madness in what we articulate ourselves, in that slight stumbling by which we lose track of what we are saying. But all this attention to the speech of madness does not prove that the old division is no longer operative. You have only to think of the whole framework of knowledge through which we decipher that speech, and of the whole network of institutions which permit someone – a doctor or a psychoanalyst – to listen to it, and which at the same time permit the patient to bring along his poor words or, in desperation, to withhold them. You have only to think of all this to become suspicious that the division, far from being effaced, is working differently, along other lines, through new institutions, and with effects that are not at all the same. And even if the doctor's role were only that of lending an ear to a speech that is free at last, he still does this listening in the context of the same division. He is listening to a discourse which is invested with desire, and which – for its greater exaltation or its greater anguish – thinks it is loaded with terrible powers. If the silence of reason is required for the curing of monsters, it is enough for that silence to be on the alert, and it is in this that the division remains.

It is perhaps risky to consider the opposition between true and false as a third system of exclusion, along with those just mentioned. How could one reasonably compare the constraint of truth with divisions like those, which are arbitrary to start with or which at least are organized around historical contingencies; which are not only modifiable but in perpetual displacement; which are supported by a whole system of institutions which impose them and renew them; and which act in a constraining and sometimes violent way?

Certainly, when viewed from the level of a proposition, on the inside of a discourse, the division between true and false is neither arbitrary nor modifiable nor institutional nor violent. But when we view things on a different scale, when we ask the question of what this will to truth has been and constantly is, across our discourses,

Michel Foucault

this will to truth which has crossed so many centuries of our history; what is, in its very general form, the type of division which governs our will to know (*notre volonté de savoir*), then what we see taking shape is perhaps something like a system of exclusion, a historical, modifiable, and institutionally constraining system.

There is no doubt that this division is historically constituted. For the Greek poets of the sixth century BC, the true discourse (in the strong and valorized sense of the word), the discourse which inspired respect and terror, and to which one had to submit because it ruled, was the one pronounced by men who spoke as of right and according to the required ritual; the discourse which dispensed justice and gave everyone his share; the discourse which in prophesying the future not only announced what was going to happen but helped to make it happen, carrying men's minds along with it and thus weaving itself into the fabric of destiny. Yet already a century later the highest truth no longer resided in what discourse was or did, but in what it said: a day came when truth was displaced from the ritualized, efficacious and just act of enunciation, towards the utterance itself, its meaning, its form, its object, its relation to its reference. Between Hesiod and Plato a certain division was established, separating true discourse from false discourse: a new division because henceforth the true discourse is no longer precious and desirable, since it is no longer the one linked to the exercise of power. The sophist is banished.

This historical division probably gave our will to know its general form. However, it has never stopped shifting: sometimes the great mutations in scientific thought can perhaps be read as the consequences of a discovery, but they can also be read as the appearance of new forms in the will to truth. There is doubtless a will to truth in the nineteenth century which differs from the will to know characteristic of Classical culture in the forms it deploys, in the domains of objects to which it addresses itself, and in the techniques on which it is based. To go back a little further: at the turn of the sixteenth century (and particularly in England), there appeared a will to know which, anticipating its actual contents, sketched out schemas of possible, observable, measurable, classifiable objects; a will to know which imposed on the knowing subject, and in some sense prior to all experience, a certain position, a certain gaze and a certain function (to see rather than to read, to verify rather than to make commentaries on); a will to know which was prescribed (but in a more general manner than by any specific instrument) by the technical level where knowledges had to be invested in order to be verifiable and useful. It was just as if, starting from the great Platonic division, the will to truth had its own history, which is not that of constraining truths: the history of the range of objects to be known, of the functions and positions of the knowing subject, of the material, technical, and instrumental investments of knowledge.

This will to truth, like the other systems of exclusion, rests on an institutional support: it is both reinforced and renewed by whole strata of practices, such as pedagogy, of course; and the system of books, publishing, libraries; learned societies in the past and laboratories now. But it is also renewed, no doubt more profoundly, by the way in which knowledge is put to work, valorized, distributed, and in a sense attributed, in a society. Let us recall at this point, and only symbolically, the old Greek principle: though arithmetic may well be the concern of democratic cities, because it teaches about the relations of equality, geometry alone must be taught in oligarchies, since it demonstrates the proportions within inequality.

Finally, I believe that this will to truth – leaning in this way on a support and an institutional distribution – tends to exert a sort of pressure and something like a power of constraint (I am still speaking of our own society) on other discourses. I am thinking of the way in which for centuries Western literature sought to ground itself on the natural, the *vraisemblable*, on sincerity, on science as well – in short, on 'true' discourse. I am thinking likewise of the manner in which economic practices, codified as precepts or recipes and ultimately as morality, have sought since the sixteenth century to ground themselves, rationalize themselves, and justify themselves in a theory of wealth and production. I am also thinking of the way in which a body as prescriptive as the penal system sought its bases or its justification, at first of course in a theory of justice, then, since the nineteenth century, in a sociological, psychological, medical, and psychiatric knowledge: it is as if even the word of the law could no longer be authorized, in our society, except by a discourse of truth.

Of the three great systems of exclusion which forge discourse – the forbidden speech, the division of madness and the will to truth, I have spoken of the third at greatest length. The fact is that it is towards this third system that the other two have been drifting constantly for centuries. The third system increasingly attempts to assimilate the others, both in order to modify them and to provide them with a foundation. The first two are constantly becoming more fragile and more uncertain, to the extent that they are now invaded by the will to truth, which for its part constantly grows stronger, deeper, and more implacable

And yet we speak of the will to truth no doubt least of all. It is as if, for us, the will to truth and its vicissitudes were masked by truth itself in its necessary unfolding. The reason is perhaps this: although since the Greeks 'true' discourse is no longer the discourse that answers to the demands of desire, or the discourse which exercises power, what is at stake in the will to truth, in the will to utter this 'true' discourse, if not desire and power? 'True' discourse, freed from desire and power by the necessity of its form, cannot recognize the will to truth which pervades it;[3] and the will to truth, having imposed itself on us for a very long time, is such that the truth it wants cannot fail to mask it.

Thus all that appears to our eyes is a truth conceived as a richness, a fecundity, a gentle and insidiously universal force, and in contrast we are unaware of the will to truth, that prodigious machinery designed to exclude. All those who, from time to time in our history, have tried to dodge this will to truth and to put it into question against truth, at the very point where truth undertakes to justify the prohibition and to define madness, all of them, from Nietzsche to Artaud and Bataille, must now serve as the (no doubt lofty) signs for our daily work.

III

There are, of course, many other procedures for controlling and delimiting discourse. Those of which I have spoken up to now operate in a sense from the exterior. They function as systems of exclusion. They have to do with the part of discourse which puts power and desire at stake.

I believe we can isolate another group: internal procedures, since discourses themselves exercise their own control; procedures which function rather as principles of classification, of ordering, of distribution, as if this time another dimension of discourse had to be mastered: that of events and chance.

In the first place, commentary. I suppose – but without being very certain – that there is scarcely a society without its major narratives, which are recounted, repeated, and varied; formulae, texts, and ritualized sets of discourses which are recited in well-defined circumstances; things said once and preserved because it is suspected that behind them there is a secret or a treasure. In short, we may suspect that there is in all societies, with great consistency, a kind of gradation among discourses: those which are said in the ordinary course of days and exchanges, and which vanish as soon as they have been pronounced; and those which give rise to a certain number of new speech-acts which take them up, transform them or speak of them, in short, those discourses which, over and above their formulation, are said indefinitely, remain said, and are to be said again. We know them in our own cultural system: they are religious or juridical texts, but also those texts (curious ones, when we consider their status) which are called 'literary'; and to a certain extent, scientific texts.

This differentiation is certainly neither stable, nor constant, nor absolute. There is not, on the one side, the category of fundamental or creative discourses, given for all time, and on the other, the mass of discourses which repeat, gloss, and comment. Plenty of major texts become blurred and disappear, and sometimes commentaries move into the primary position. But though its points of application may change, the function remains; and the principle of a differentiation is continuously put back in play. The radical effacement of this gradation can only ever be play, utopia, or anguish. The Borges-style play of a commentary which is nothing but the solemn and expected reappearance word for word of the text that is commented on; or the play of a criticism that would speak forever of a work which does not exist. The lyrical dream of a discourse which is reborn absolutely new and innocent at every point, and which reappears constantly in all freshness, derived from things, feelings or thoughts. The anguish of that patient of Janet's for whom the least utterance was gospel truth, concealing inexhaustible treasures of meaning and worthy to be repeated, re-commenced, and commented on indefinitely: 'When I think,' he would say when reading or listening, 'when I think of this sentence which like the others will go off into eternity, and which I have perhaps not yet fully understood.'[4]

But who can fail to see that this would be to annul one of the terms of the relation each time, and not to do away with the relation itself? It is a relation which is constantly changing with time; which takes multiple and divergent forms in a given epoch. The juridical exegesis is very different from the religious commentary (and this has been the case for a very long time). One and the same literary work can give rise simultaneously to very distinct types of discourse: the *Odyssey* as a primary text is repeated, in the same period, in the translation by Bérard, and in the endless *explications de texte*, and in Joyce's *Ulysses*.

For the moment I want to do no more than indicate that, in what is broadly called commentary, the hierarchy between primary and secondary text plays two roles which are in solidarity with each other. On the one hand it allows the (endless) construction of new discourses: the dominance of the primary text, its permanence, its status as a discourse which can always be re-actualized, the multiple or hidden meaning with which it is credited, the essential reticence and richness which is attributed to it, all this is the basis for an open possibility of speaking. But on the other hand the commentary's only role, whatever the techniques used, is to say at last what was silently articulated 'beyond', in the text. By a paradox which it always displaces but never escapes, the commentary must say for the first time what had, nonetheless, already been said, and must tirelessly repeat what had, however, never been said. The infinite rippling of commentaries is worked from the inside by the dream of a repetition in disguise: at its horizon there is perhaps nothing but what was at its point of departure – mere recitation. Commentary exorcizes the chance element of discourse by giving it its due; it allows us to say something other than the text itself, but on condition that it is the text itself which is said, and in a sense completed. The open multiplicity, the element of chance, are transferred, by the principle of commentary, from what might risk being said, on to the number, the form, the mask, and the circumstances of the repetition. The new thing here lies not in what is said but in the event of its return.

I believe there exists another principle of rarefaction of a discourse, complementary to the first, to a certain extent: the author. Not, of course, in the sense of the speaking individual who pronounced or wrote a text, but in the sense of a principle of grouping of discourses, conceived as the unity and origin of their meanings, as the focus of their coherence. This principle is not everywhere at work, nor in a constant manner: there exist all around us plenty of discourses which circulate without deriving their meaning or their efficacity from an author to whom they could be attributed: everyday remarks, which are effaced immediately; decrees or contracts which require signatories but no author; technical instructions which are transmitted anonymously. But in the domains where it is the rule to attribute things to an author – literature, philosophy, science – it is quite evident that this attribution does not always play the same role. In the order of scientific discourse, it was indispensable, during the Middle Ages, that a text should be attributed to an author, since this was an index of truthfulness. A proposition was considered as drawing

even its scientific value from its author. Since the seventeenth
century, this function has steadily been eroded in scientific
discourse: it now functions only to give a name to a theorem, an
effect, an example, a syndrome. On the other hand, in the order of
literary discourse, starting from the same epoch, the function of the
author has steadily grown stronger: all those tales, poems, dramas
or comedies which were allowed to circulate in the Middle Ages in
at least a relative anonymity are now asked (and obliged to say)
where they come from, who wrote them. The author is asked to
account for the unity of the texts which are placed under his name.
He is asked to reveal or at least carry authentification of the hidden
meaning which traverses them. He is asked to connect them to his
lived experiences, to the real history which saw their birth. The
author is what gives the disturbing language of fiction its unities, its
nodes of coherence, its insertion in the real.

I know that I will be told: 'But you are speaking there of the
author as he is reinvented after the event by criticism, after he is
dead and there is nothing left except for a tangled mass of scrib-
blings; in those circumstances a little order surely has to be introduced into all that, by imagining a project, a coherence, a thematic
structure that is demanded of the consciousness or the life of an
author who is indeed perhaps a trifle fictitious. But that does not
mean he did not exist, this real author, who bursts into the midst of
all these worn-out words, bringing to them his genius or his
disorder.'[5]

It would of course, be absurd to deny the existence of the individual who writes and invents. But I believe that – at least since a
certain epoch – the individual who sets out to write a text on the
horizon of which a possible *oeuvre* is prowling, takes upon himself
the function of the author: what he writes and what he does not write,
what he sketches out, even by way of provisional drafts, as an outline of the *oeuvre*, and what he lets fall by way of commonplace
remarks – this whole play of differences is prescribed by the author-
function, as he receives it from his epoch, or as he modifies it in his
turn. He may well overturn the traditional image of the author;
nevertheless, it is from some new author-position that he will cut
out, from everything he could say and from all that he does say
every day at any moment, the still trembling outline of his *oeuvre*.

The commentary-principle limits the chance-element in discourse
by the play of an identity which would take the form of repetition
and sameness. The author-principle limits the same element of
chance by the play of an identity which has the form of individuality and the self.

We must also recognize another principle of limitation in what is called, not sciences but 'disciplines': a principle which is itself relative and mobile; which permits construction, but within narrow confines.

The organization of disciplines is just as much opposed to the principle of commentary as to that of the author. It is opposed to the principle of the author because a discipline is defined by a domain of objects, a set of methods, a corpus of propositions considered to be true, a play of rules and definitions, of techniques and instruments: all this constitutes a sort of anonymous system at the disposal of anyone who wants to or is able to use it, without their meaning or validity being linked to the one who happened to be their inventor. But the principle of a discipline is also opposed to that of commentary: in a discipline, unlike a commentary, what is supposed at the outset is not a meaning which has to be rediscovered, nor an identity which has to be repeated, but the requisites for the construction of new statements. For there to be a discipline, there must be the possibility of formulating new propositions, *ad infinitum*.

But there is more; there is more, no doubt, in order for there to be less: a discipline is not the sum of all that can be truthfully said about something; it is not even the set of all that can be accepted about the same data in virtue of some principle of coherence or systematicity. Medicine is not constituted by the total of what can be truthfully said about illness; botany cannot be defined by the sum of all the truths concerning plants. There are two reasons for this: first of all, botany and medicine are made up of errors as well as truths, like any other discipline – errors which are not residues or foreign bodies but which have positive functions, a historical efficacity, and a role that is often indissociable from that of the truths. And besides, for a proposition to belong to botany or pathology, it has to fulfil certain conditions, in a sense stricter and more complex than pure and simple truth: but in any case, other conditions. It must address itself to a determinate plane of objects: from the end of the seventeenth century, for example, for a proposition to be 'botanical' it had to deal with the visible structure of the plant, the system of its close and distant resemblances or the mechanism of its fluids; it could no longer retain its symbolic value, as was the case in the sixteenth century, nor the set of virtues and properties which were accorded to it in antiquity. But without belonging to a discipline, a proposition must use conceptual or technical instruments of a well-defined type; from the nineteenth century, a proposition was no longer medical – it fell 'outside medicine' and acquired the status of an individual phantasm or popular imagery – if it used notions that were at the same time metaphorical, qualitative, and substantial (like those of engorgement, of overheated liquids or of dried-out solids). In contrast it could and had to make use of notions that were equally metaphorical but based on another model, a functional and physiological one (that of the irritation, inflammation, or degeneration of the tissues). Still further: in order to be part of a discipline, a proposition has to be able to be inscribed on a certain type of theoretical horizon: suffice it to recall that the search for the primitive language, which was a perfectly acceptable theme up to the eighteenth century, was sufficient, in the second half of the nineteenth century, to make any discourse fall into – I hesitate to say error – chimera and reverie, into pure and simple linguistic monstrosity.

Within its own limits, each discipline recognizes true and false propositions; but it pushes back a whole teratology of knowledge beyond its margins. The exterior of a science is both more and less populated than is often believed: there is of course immediate experience, the imaginary themes which endlessly carry and renew immemorial beliefs; but perhaps there are no errors in the strict sense, for error can only arise and be decided inside a definite practice; on the other hand, there are monsters on the prowl whose form changes with the history of knowledge. In short, a proposition must fulfil complex and heavy requirements to be able to belong to the grouping of a discipline; before it can be called true or false, it must be 'in the true', as Canguilhem would say.

People have often wondered how the botanists or biologists of the nineteenth century managed not to see that what Mendel was saying was true. But it was because Mendel was speaking of objects, applying methods, and placing himself on a theoretical horizon which were alien to the biology of his time. Naudin, before him, had of course posited the thesis that hereditary traits are discrete; yet, no matter how new or strange this principle was, it was able to fit into the discourse of biology, at least as an enigma. What Mendel did was to constitute the hereditary trait as an absolutely new biological object, thanks to a kind of filtering which had never been used before: he detached the trait from the species, and from the sex which transmits it; the field in which he observed it being the infinitely open series of the generations, where it appears and disappears according to statistical regularities. This was a new object which called for new conceptual instruments and new theoretical foundations. Mendel spoke the truth, but he was not 'within the true' of the biological discourse of his time: it was not according to such rules that biological objects and concepts were formed. It needed a complete change of scale, the deployment of a whole new range of objects in biology for Mendel to enter into the true and for his propositions to appear (in large measure) correct. Mendel was a true monster, which meant that science could not speak of him; whereas about thirty years earlier, at the height of the nineteenth century, Scheiden, for example, who denied plant sexuality, but in accordance with the rules of biological discourse, was merely formulating a disciplined error.

It is always possible that one might speak the truth in the space of a wild exteriority, but one is 'in the true' only by obeying the rules of a discursive 'policing' which one has to reactivate in each of one's discourses.

The discipline is a principle of control over the production of discourse. The discipline fixes limits for discourse by the action of an identity which takes the form of a permanent re-actuation of the rules.

We are accustomed to see in an author's fecundity, in the multiplicity of the commentaries, and in the development of a discipline so many infinite resources for the creation of discourses. Perhaps so, but they are nonetheless principles of constraint; it is very likely impossible to account for their positive and multiplicatory role if we do not take into consideration their restrictive and constraining function.

IV

There is, I believe, a third group of procedures which permit the control of discourses. This time it is not a matter of mastering their powers or averting the unpredictability of their appearance, but of determining the condition of their application, of imposing a certain number of rules on the individuals who hold them, and thus of not permitting everyone to have access to them. There is a rarefaction, this time, of the speaking subjects; none shall enter the order of discourse if he does not satisfy certain requirements or if he is not, from the outset, qualified to do so. To be more precise: not all the regions of discourse are equally open and penetrable; some of them are largely forbidden (they are differentiated and differentiating), while others seem to be almost open to all winds and put at the disposal of every speaking subject, without prior restrictions.

In this regard I should like to recount an anecdote which is so beautiful that one trembles at the thought that it might be true. It gathers into a single figure all the constraints of discourse: those which limit its powers, those which master its aleatory appearances, those which carry out the selection among speaking subjects. At the beginning of the seventeenth century, the Shogun heard tell that the Europeans' superiority in matters of navigation, commerce, politics, and military skill was due to their knowledge of mathematics. He desired to get hold of so precious a knowledge. As he had been told of an English sailor who possessed the secret of these miraculous discourses, he summoned him to his palace and kept him there. Alone with him, he took lessons. He learned mathematics. He retained power, and lived to a great old age. It was not until the nineteenth century that there were Japanese mathematicians. But the anecdote does not stop there: it has its European side too. The story has it that this English sailor, Will Adams, was an autodidact, a carpenter who had learnt geometry in the course of working in a shipyard. Should we see this story as the expression of one of the great myths of European culture? The universal communication of knowledge and the infinite free exchange of discourses in Europe, against the monopolized and secret knowledge of Oriental tyranny?

This idea, of course, does not stand up to examination. Exchange and communication are positive figures working inside complex systems of restriction, and probably would not be able to function independently of them. The most superficial and visible of these systems of restriction is constituted by what can be gathered under the name of ritual. Ritual defines the qualification which must be possessed by individuals who speak (and who must occupy suchand-such a position and formulate such-and-such a type of statement, in the play of a dialogue, of interrogation or recitation); it defines the gestures, behaviour, circumstances, and the whole set of signs which must accompany discourse; finally, it fixes the supposed or imposed efficacy of the words, their effect on those to whom they are addressed, and the limits of their constraining value. Religious, judicial, therapeutic, and in large measure also political discourses can scarcely be dissociated from this deployment of a ritual which determines both the particular properties and the stipulated roles of the speaking subjects.

A somewhat different way of functioning is that of the 'societies of discourse', which function to preserve or produce discourses, but in order to make them circulate in a closed space, distributing them only according to strict rules, and without the holders being dispossessed by this distribution. An archaic model for this is provided by the groups of rhapsodists who possessed the knowledge of the poems to be recited or potentially to be varied and transformed. But though the object of this knowledge was after all a ritual recitation, the knowledge was protected, defended and preserved within a definite group by the often very complex exercises of memory which it implied. To pass an apprenticeship in it allowed one to enter both a group and a secret which the act of recitation showed but did not divulge; the roles of speaker and listener were not interchangeable.

There are hardly any such 'societies of discourse' now, with their ambiguous play of the secret and its divulgation. But this should not deceive us: even in the order of 'true' discourse, even in the order of discourse that is published and free from all ritual, there are still forms of appropriation of secrets, and non-interchangeable roles. It may well be that the act of writing as it is institutionalized today, in the book, the publishing-system and the person of the writer, takes place in a 'society of discourse', which though diffuse is certainly constraining. The difference between the writer and any other speaking or writing subject (a difference constantly stressed by the writer himself), the intransitive nature (according to him) of his discourse, the fundamental singularity which he has been ascribing for so long to 'writing', the dissymmetry that is asserted between 'creation' and any use of the linguistic system – all this shows the existence of a certain 'society of discourse', and tends moreover to bring back its play of practices. But there are many others still, functioning according to entirely different schemas of exclusivity and disclosure: e.g., technical or scientific secrets, or the forms of diffusion and circulation of medical discourse, or those who have appropriated the discourse of politics or economics.

At first glance, the 'doctrines' (religious, political, philosophical) seem to constitute the reverse of a 'society of discourse', in which the number of speaking individuals tended to be limited even if it was not fixed; between those individuals, the discourse could circulate and be transmitted. Doctrine, on the contrary, tends to be diffused, and it is by the holding in common of one and the same discursive ensemble that individuals (as many as one cares to imagine) define their reciprocal allegiance. In appearance, the only prerequisite is the recognition of the same truths and the acceptance of a certain rule of (more or less flexible) conformity with the validated discourses. If doctrines were nothing more than this, they would not be so very different from scientific disciplines, and the discursive control would apply only to the form or the content of the statement, not to the speaking subject. But doctrinal allegiance puts in question both the statement and the speaking subject, the one by the other. It puts the speaking subject in question through and on the basis of the statement, as is proved by the procedures of exclusion and the mechanisms of rejection which come into action when a speaking subject has formulated one or several unassimilable statements; heresy and orthodoxy do not derive from a fanatical exaggeration of the doctrinal mechanisms, but rather belong fundamentally to them. And conversely the doctrine puts the statements in question on the basis of the speaking subjects, to the extent that the doctrine always stands as the sign, manifestation and instrument of a prior adherence to a class, a social status, a race, a nationality, an interest, a revolt, a resistance or an acceptance. Doctrine binds individuals to certain types of enunciation and consequently forbids them all others; but it uses, in return, certain types of enunciation to bind individuals amongst themselves, and to differentiate them by that very fact from all others. Doctrine brings about a double subjection: of the speaking subjects to discourses, and of discourses to the (at least virtual) group of speaking individuals.

On a much broader scale, we are obliged to recognize large cleavages in what might be called the social appropriation of discourses. Although education may well be, by right, the instrument thanks to which any individual in a society like ours can have access to any kind of discourse whatever, this does not prevent it from following, as is well known, in its distribution, in what it allows and what it prevents, the lines marked out by social distances, oppositions and struggles. Any system of education is a political way of maintaining or modifying the appropriation of discourses, along with the knowledges and powers which they carry.

I am well aware that it is very abstract to separate speech-rituals, societies of discourse, doctrinal groups and social appropriations, as I have just done. Most of the time, they are linked to each other and constitute kinds of great edifices which ensure the distribution of speaking subjects into the different types of discourse and the appropriation of discourses to certain categories of subject. Let us say, in a word, that those are the major procedures of subjection used by discourse. What, after all, is an education system, other than a ritualization of speech, a qualification and a fixing of the roles for speaking subjects, the constitution of a doctrinal group, however diffuse, a distribution and an appropriation of discourse with its powers and knowledges? What is *écriture* (the writing of the 'writers') other than a similar system of subjection, which perhaps takes slightly different forms, but forms whose main rhythms are analogous? Does not the judicial system, does not the

institutional system of medicine likewise constitute, in some of their
aspects at least, similar systems of subjection of and by discourse?

V

I wonder whether a certain number of themes in philosophy have
not come to correspond to these activities of limitation and exclusion, and perhaps also to reinforce them.

They correspond to them first of all by proposing an ideal truth
as the law of discourse and an immanent rationality as the principle
of their unfolding, and they re-introduce an ethic of knowledge,
which promises to give the truth only to the desire for truth itself
and only to the power of thinking it.

Then they reinforce the limitations and exclusions by a denial of
the specific reality of discourse in general.

Ever since the sophists' tricks and influence were excluded and
since their paradoxes have been more or less safely muzzled, it
seems that Western thought has taken care to ensure that discourse
should occupy the smallest possible space between thought and
speech. Western thought seems to have made sure that the act of
discoursing should appear to be no more than a certain bridging
(*apport*) between thinking and speaking – a thought dressed in its
signs and made visible by means of words, or conversely the very
structures of language put into action and producing a meaning-
effect.

This very ancient elision of the reality of discourse in philosophical thought has taken many forms in the course of history. We
have seen it again quite recently in the guise of several familiar
themes.

Perhaps the idea of the founding subject is a way of eliding the
reality of discourse. The founding subject, indeed, is given the task
of directly animating the empty forms of language with his aims; it
is he who in moving through the density and inertia of empty things
grasps by intuition the meaning lying deposited within them; it is
likewise the founding subject who founds horizons of meaning
beyond time which history will henceforth only have to elucidate
and where propositions, sciences and deductive ensembles will find
their ultimate grounding. In his relation to meaning, the founding
subject has at his disposal signs, marks, traces, letters. But he does
not need to pass via the singular instance of discourse in order to
manifest them.

The opposing theme, that of originating experience, plays an analogous role. It supposes that at the very basis of experience, even before it could be grasped in the form of a *cogito*, there were prior significations – in a sense, already said – wandering around in the world, arranging it all around us and opening it up from the outset to a sort of primitive recognition. Thus a primordial complicity with the world is supposed to be the foundation of our possibility of speaking of it, in it, of indicating it and naming it, of judging it and ultimately of knowing it in the form of truth. If there is discourse, then, what can it legitimately be other than a discreet reading? Things are already murmuring meaning which our language has only to pick up; and this language, right from its most rudimentary project, was already speaking to us of a being of which it is like the skeleton.

The idea of universal mediation is yet another way, I believe, of eliding the reality of discourse, and despite appearances to the contrary. For it would seem at first glance that by rediscovering everywhere the movement of a *logos* which elevates particularities to the status of concepts and allows immediate consciousness to unfurl in the end the whole rationality of the world, one puts discourse itself at the centre of one's speculation. But this *logos*, in fact, is only a discourse that has already been held, or rather it is things themselves, and events, which imperceptibly turn themselves into discourse as they unfold the secret of their own essence. Thus discourse is little more than the gleaming of a truth in the process of being born to its own gaze; and when everything finally can take the form of discourse, when everything can be said and when discourse can be spoken about everything, it is because all things, having manifested and exchanged their meaning, can go back into the silent interiority of their consciousness of self.

Thus in a philosophy of the founding subject, in a philosophy of originary experience, and in a philosophy of universal mediation alike, discourse is no more than a play, of writing in the first case, of reading in the second, and of exchange in the third, and this exchange, this reading, this writing never put anything at stake except signs. In this way, discourse is annulled in its reality and put at the disposal of the signifier.

What civilization has ever appeared to be more respectful of discourse than ours? Where has it ever been more honoured, or better honoured? Where has it ever been, seemingly, more radically liberated from its constraints, and universalized? Yet is seems to me that beneath this apparent veneration of discourse, under this apparent logophilia, a certain fear is hidden. It is just as if prohibitions, barriers, thresholds and limits had been set up in order to master, at

least partly, the great proliferation of discourse, in order to remove
from its richness the most dangerous part, and in order to organize
its disorder according to figures which dodge what is most uncontrollable about it. It is as if we had tried to efface all trace of its
irruption into the activity of thought and language. No doubt there
is in our society, and, I imagine, in all others, but following a
different outline and different rhythms, a profound logophobia, a
sort of mute terror against these events, against this mass of things
said, against the surging-up of all these statements, against all that
could be violent, discontinuous, pugnacious, disorderly as well, and
perilous about them – against this great incessant and disordered
buzzing of discourse.

And if we want to – I would not say, efface this fear, but –
analyse it in its conditions, its action and its effect, we must, I
believe, resolve to take three decisions which our thinking today
tends to resist and which correspond to the three groups of functions which I have just mentioned: we must call into question our
will to truth, restore to discourse its character as an event, and
finally throw off the sovereignty of the signifier.

VI

These are the tasks, or rather some of the themes, which govern the
work I should like to do here in the coming years. We can see at
once certain methodological requirements which they imply.

First of all, a principle of reversal: where tradition sees the source
of discourses, the principle of their swarming abundance and of
their continuity, in those figures which seem to play a positive role,
e.g., those of the author, the discipline, the will to truth, we must
rather recognize the negative action of a cutting-up and a rarefaction of discourse.

But once we have noticed these principles of rarefaction, once we
have ceased to consider them as a fundamental and creative instance, what do we discover underneath them? Must we admit the
virtual plenitude of a world of uninterrupted discourses? This is
where we have to bring other methodological principles into play.

A principle of discontinuity, then: the fact that there are systems
of rarefaction does not mean that beneath them or beyond them
there reigns a vast unlimited discourse, continuous and silent,
which is quelled and repressed by them, and which we have the task
of raising up by restoring the power of speech to it. We must not
imagine that there is a great unsaid or a great unthought which runs

throughout the world and intertwines with all its forms and all its events, and which we would have to articulate or to think at last. Discourses must be treated as discontinuous practices, which cross each other, are sometimes juxtaposed with one another, but can just as well exclude or be unaware of each other.

A principle of specificity: we must not resolve discourse into a play of pre-existing significations; we must not imagine that the world turns towards us a legible face which we would have only to decipher; the world is not the accomplice of our knowledge; there is no prediscursive providence which disposes the world in our favour. We must conceive discourse as a violence which we do to things, or in any case as a practice which we impose on them; and it is in this practice that the events of discourse find the principle of their regularity.

The fourth rule is that of exteriority: we must not go from discourse towards its interior, hidden nucleus, towards the heart of a thought or a signification supposed to be manifested in it; but, on the basis of discourse itself, its appearance and its regularity, go towards its external conditions of possibility, towards what gives rise to the aleatory series of these events, and fixes its limits.

Four notions, then, must serve as the regulating principle of the analysis: the event, the series, the regularity, the condition of possibility. Term for term we find the notion of event opposed to that of creation, series opposed to unity, regularity opposed to originality, and condition of possibility opposed to signification. These other four notions (signification, originality, unity, creation) have in a general way dominated the traditional history of ideas, where by common agreement one sought the point of creation, the unity of a work, an epoch or a theme, the mark of individual originality, and the infinite treasure of buried significations.

I will add only two remarks. One concerns history. It is often entered to the credit of contemporary history that it removed the privileges once accorded to the singular event and revealed the structures of longer duration. That is so. However, I am not sure that the work of these historians was exactly done in this direction. Or rather I do not think there is an inverse ratio between noticing the event and analysing the long durations. On the contrary, it seems to be by pushing to its extreme the fine grain of the event, by stretching the resolution-power of historical analysis as far as official price-lists (*les mercuriales*), title deeds, parish registers, harbour archives examined year by year and week by week, that these historians saw – beyond the battles, decrees, dynasties or assemblies – the outline of massive phenomena with a range of a hundred or many hundreds of years. History as practised today does not turn away from events; on the contrary, it is constantly enlarging their field, discovering new layers of them, shallower or deeper. It is constantly isolating new sets of them, in which they are sometimes numerous, dense and interchangeable, sometimes rare and decisive: from the almost daily variations in price to inflations over a hundred years. But the important thing is that history does not consider an event without defining the series of which it is part, without specifying the mode of analysis from which that series derives, without seeking to find out the regularity of phenomena and the limits of probability of their emergence, without inquiring into the variations, bends and angles of the graph, without wanting to determine the conditions on which they depend. Of course, history has for a long time no longer sought to understand events by the action of causes and effects in the formless unity of a great becoming, vaguely homogeneous or ruthlessly hierarchized; but this change was not made in order to rediscover prior structures, alien and hostile to the event. It was made in order to establish diverse series, intertwined and often divergent but not autonomous, which enable us to circumscribe the 'place' of the event, the margins of its chance variability, and the conditions of its appearance.

The fundamental notions which we now require are no longer those of consciousness and continuity (with their correlative problems of freedom and causality), nor any longer those of sign and structure. They are those of the event and the series, along with the play of the notions which are linked to them: regularity, dimension of chance (*aléa*), discontinuity, dependence, transformation; it is by means of a set of notions like this that my projected analysis of discourses is articulated, not on the traditional thematics which the philosophers of yesterday still take for 'living' history, but on the effective work of historians.

Yet it is also in this regard that this analysis poses philosophical, or theoretical, problems, and very likely formidable ones. If discourses must be treated first of all as sets of discursive events, what status must be given to that notion of event which was so rarely taken into consideration by philosophers? Naturally the event is neither substance nor accident, neither quality nor process; the event is not of the order of bodies. And yet it is not something immaterial either; it is always at the level of materiality that it takes effect, that it is effect; it has its locus and it consists in the relation, the coexistence, the dispersion, the overlapping, the accumulation, and the selection of material elements. It is not the act or the property of a body; it is produced as an effect of, and within, a dispersion of matter. Let us say that the philosophy of the event should move in the at first sight paradoxical direction of a materialism of the incorporeal.

Furthermore, if discursive events must be treated along the lines of homogeneous series which, however, are discontinuous in relation to each other, what status must be given to this discontinuity? It is of course not a matter of the succession of instants in time, nor of the plurality of different thinking subjects. It is a question of caesurae which break up the instant and disperse the subject into a plurality of possible positions and functions. This kind of discontinuity strikes and invalidates the smallest units that were traditionally recognized and which are the hardest to contest: the instant and the subject. Beneath them, and independently of them, we must conceive relations between these discontinuous series which are not of the order of succession (or simultaneity) within one (or several) consciousnesses; we must elaborate – outside of the philosophies of the subject and of time – a theory of discontinuous systematicities. Finally, though it is true that these discontinuous discursive series each have, within certain limits, their regularity, it is undoubtedly no longer possible to establish links of mechanical causality or of ideal necessity between the elements which constitute them. We must accept the introduction of the *aléa* as a category in the production of events. There once more we feel the absence of a theory enabling us to think the relations between chance and thought.

The result is that the narrow gap which is to be set to work in the history of ideas, and which consists of dealing not with the representations which might be behind discourse, but with discourses as regular and distinct series of events – this narrow gap looks, I'm afraid, like a small (and perhaps odious) piece of machinery which would enable us to introduce chance, the discontinuous, and materiality at the very roots of thought. This is a triple peril which a certain form of history tries to exorcize by narrating the continuous unravelling of an ideal necessity. They are three notions that should allow us to connect the history of systems of thought to the practice of historians. And they are three directions which the work of theoretical elaboration will have to follow.

VII

The analyses which I propose to make, following these principles and making this horizon my line of reference, will fall into two sets.

On the one hand the 'critical' section, which will put into practice the principle of reversal: trying to grasp the forms of exclusion, of limitation, of appropriation of which I was speaking just now; showing how they are formed, in response to what needs, how they have been modified and displaced, what constraint they have effectively exerted, to what extent they have been evaded. On the other hand there is the 'genealogical' set, which puts the other three principles to work: how did series of discourses come to be formed, across the grain of, in spite of, or with the aid of these systems of constraints; what was the specific norm of each one, and what were their conditions of appearance, growth, variation.

First, the critical set. A first group of analyses might deal with what I have designated as functions of exclusion. I formerly studied one of them, in respect of one determinate period: the divide between madness and reason in the classical epoch. Later, I might try to analyse a system of prohibition of language, the one concerning sexuality from the sixteenth to the nineteenth century. The aim would be to see not how this interdiction has been progressively and fortunately effaced, but how it has been displaced and re-articulated from a practice of confession in which the forbidden behaviour was named, classified, hierarchized in the most explicit way, up to the appearance, at first very timid and belated, of sexual thematics in nineteenth-century medicine and psychiatry; of course these are still only somewhat symbolic orientation-points, but one could already wager that the rhythms are not the ones we think, and the prohibitions have not always occupied the place that we imagine.

In the immediate future, I should like to apply myself to the third system of exclusion; this I envisage in two ways. On the one hand, I want to try to discover how this choice of truth, inside which we are caught but which we ceaselessly renew, was made – but also how it was repeated, renewed, and displaced. I will consider first the epoch of the Sophists at its beginning, with Socrates, or at least with Platonic philosophy, to see how efficacious discourse, ritual discourse, discourse loaded with powers and perils, gradually came to conform to a division between true and false discourse. Then I will consider the turn of the sixteenth century, at the time when there appears, especially in England, a science of the gaze, of observation of the established fact, a certain natural philosophy, no doubt inseparable from the setting-up of new political structures, and, inseparable too, from religious ideology; this was without a doubt a new form of the will to know. Finally, the third orientation-point will be the beginning of the nineteenth century, with its great acts that founded modern science, the formation of an industrial society and the positivist ideology which accompanied it. These will be my three cross-sections in the morphology of our will to know, three stages of our philistinism.

I would also like to take up the same question again, but from a quite different angle: to measure the effect of a discourse with scientific claims – a medical, psychiatric, and also sociological discourse – on that set of practices and prescriptive discourses constituted by the penal system. The starting point and basic material for this analysis will be the study of psychiatric expertise and its role in penal practices.

Still looking at it from this critical perspective, but at another level, the procedures of limitation of discourses should be analysed. I indicated several of these just now: the principle of the author, of commentary, of the discipline. A certain number of studies can be envisaged from this perspective. I am thinking, for example, of an analysis of the history of medicine from the sixteenth to the nineteenth century. The objective would be not so much to pinpoint the discoveries made or the concepts put to work, but to grasp how, in the construction of medical discourse, and also in the whole institution that supports, transmits and reinforces it, the principle of the author, of the commentary, and of the discipline were used. The analysis would seek to find out how the principle of the great author operated: Hippocrates and Galen, of course, but also Paracelsus, Sydenham, or Boerhaave. It would seek to find out how the practice of the aphorism and the commentary were carried on, even late into the nineteenth century, and how they gradually gave place to the practice of the case, of the collection of cases, of the clinical apprenticeship using a concrete case. It would seek to discover, finally, according to what model medicine tried to constitute itself as a discipline, leaning at first on natural history, then on anatomy and biology.

One could also consider the way in which literary criticism and literary history in the eighteenth and nineteenth centuries constituted the person of the author and the figure of the *oeuvre*, using, modifying, and displacing the procedures of religious exegesis, biblical criticism, hagiography, historical or legendary 'lives', autobiography, and memoirs. One day we will also have to study the role played by Freud in psychoanalytic knowledge, which is surely very different from that of Newton in physics (and of all founders of disciplines), and also very different from the role that can be played by an author in the field of philosophical discourse (even if, like Kant, he is at the origin of a different way of philosophizing).

So there are some projects for the critical side of the task, for the analysis of the instances of discursive control. As for the genealogical aspect, it will concern the effective formation of discourse either within the limits of this control, or outside them, or more often on both sides of the boundary at once. The critical task will be to analyse the processes of rarefaction, but also of regrouping and unification of discourses; genealogy will study their formation, at once dispersed, discontinuous, and regular. In truth these two tasks are never completely separable: there are not, on one side, the forms of rejection, exclusion, regrouping and attribution, and then on the other side, at a deeper level, the spontaneous surging-up of discourses which, immediately before or after their manifestation, are submitted to selection and control. The regular formation of discourse can incorporate the procedures of control, in certain conditions and to a certain extent (that is what happens, for instance, when a discipline takes on the form and status of a scientific discourse); and conversely the figures of control can take shape within a discursive formation (as is the case with literary criticism as the discourse that constitutes the author): so much so that any critical task, putting in question the instances of control, must at the same time analyse the discursive regularities through which they are formed; and any genealogical description must take into account the limits which operate in real formations. The difference between the critical and the genealogical enterprise is not so much a difference of object or domain, but of point of attack, perspective, and delimitation.

Earlier on I mentioned one possible study, that of the taboos which affect the discourse of sexuality. It would be difficult, and in any case abstract, to carry out this study without analysing at the same time the sets of discourses – literary, religious or ethical, biological or medical, juridical too – where sexuality is discussed, and where it is named, described, metaphorized, explained, judged. We are very far from having constituted a unitary and regular discourse of sexuality; perhaps we never will, and perhaps it is not in this direction that we are going. No matter. The taboos do not have the same form and do not function in that same way in literary discourse and in medical discourse, in that of psychiatry or in that of the direction of conscience. Conversely, these different discursive regularities do not have the same way of reinforcing, evading, or displacing the taboos. So the study can be done only according to pluralities of series in which there are taboos at work which are at least partly different in each.

One could also consider the series of discourses which in the sixteenth and seventeenth centuries dealt with wealth and poverty, money, production, commerce. We are dealing there with sets of very heterogeneous statements, formulated by the rich and the poor, the learned and the ignorant, protestants and catholics, officers of the king, traders or moralists. Each one has its own form of regularity, likewise its own systems of constraint. None of them exactly prefigures that other form of discursive regularity which will later take on the air of a discipline and which will be called 'the analysis of wealth', then 'political economy'. Yet it is on the basis of this series that a new regularity was formed, taking up or excluding, justifying or brushing aside this one or that one of their utterances.

We can also conceive of a study which would deal with the discourses concerning heredity, such as we can find them, up to the beginning of the twentieth century, scattered and dispersed through various disciplines, observations, techniques and formulae. The task would then be to show by what play of articulation these series in the end recomposed themselves, in the epistemologically coherent and institutionally recognized figure of genetics. This is the work that has just been done by François Jacob with a brilliance and an erudition which could not be equalled.

Thus the critical and the genealogical descriptions must alternate, and complement each other, each supporting the other by turns. The critical portion of the analysis applies to the systems that envelop discourse, and tries to identify and grasp these principles of sanctioning, exclusion, and scarcity of discourse. Let us say, playing on words, that it practises a studied casualness. The genealogical portion, on the other hand, applies to the series where discourse is effectively formed: it tries to grasp it in its power of affirmation, by which I mean not so much a power which would be opposed to that of denying, but rather the power to constitute domains of objects, in respect of which one can affirm or deny true or false propositions. Let us call these domains of objects positivities, and let us say, again playing on words, that if the critical style is that of studious casualness, the genealogical mood will be that of a happy positivism.

In any event, one thing at least has to be emphasized: discourse analysis understood like this does not reveal the universality of a meaning, but brings to light the action of imposed scarcity, with a fundamental power of affirmation. Scarcity and affirmation; ultimately, scarcity *of* affirmation, and not the continuous generosity of meaning, and not the monarchy of the signifier.

And now, let those with gaps in the vocabulary say – if they find the term more convenient than meaningful – that all this is structuralism.

VIII

I know that but for the aid of certain models and supports I would not have been able to undertake these researches which I have tried to sketch out for you. I believe I am greatly indebted to Georges Dumézl, since it was he who urged me to work, at an age when I still thought that to write was a pleasure. But I also owe a great deal to his work. May he forgive me if I have stretched the meaning or departed from the rigour of those texts which are his and which dominate us today. It was he who taught me to analyse the internal economy of a discourse in a manner quite different from the methods of traditional exegesis or linguistic formalism. It was he who taught me to observe the system of functional correlations between discourses by the play of comparisons from one to the other. It was he who taught me how to describe the transformations of a discourse and its relations to institutions. If I have tried to apply this method to discourses quite different from legendary or mythical narratives, it was probably because I had in front of me the works of the historians of science, especially Georges Canguilhem. It is to him that I owe the insight that the history of science is not necessarily caught in an alternative: either to chronicle discoveries or to describe the ideas and opinions that border science on the side of its indeterminate genesis or on the side of its later expulsions, but that it was possible and necessary to write the history of science as a set of theoretical models and conceptual instruments which is both coherent and transformable.

But I consider that my greatest debt is to Jean Hyppolite. I am well aware that in the eyes of many his work belongs under the aegis of Hegel, and that our entire epoch, whether in logic or epistemology, whether in Marx or Nietzsche, is trying to escape from Hegel: and what I have tried to say just now about discourse is very unfaithful to the Hegelian *logos*.

But to make a real escape from Hegel presupposes an exact appreciation of what it costs to detach ourselves from him. It presupposes a knowledge of how close Hegel has come to us, perhaps insidiously. It presupposes a knowledge of what is still Hegelian in that which allows us to think against Hegel; and an ability to gauge how much our resources against him are perhaps still a ruse which he is using against us, and at the end of which he is waiting for us, immobile and elsewhere.

If so many of us are indebted to Jean Hyppolite, it is because he tirelessly explored, for us and ahead of us, this path by which one gets away from Hegel, establishes a distance, and by which one ends up being drawn back to him, but otherwise, and then constrained to leave him once again.

First of all Jean Hyppolite took the trouble to give a presence to the great and somewhat ghostly shadow of Hegel which had been on the prowl since the nineteenth century and with which people used to wrestle obscurely. It was by means of a translation (of the 'Phenomenology of Mind') that he gave Hegel this presence. And the proof that Hegel himself is well and truly present in this French text is the fact that even Germans have consulted it so as to understand better what, for a moment at least, was going on in the German version.

Jean Hyppolite sought and followed all the ways out of this text, as if his concern was: can we still philosophize where Hegel is no longer possible? Can a philosophy still exist and yet not be Hegelian? Are the non-Hegelian elements in our thought also necessarily non-philosophical? And is the anti-philosophical necessarily non-Hegelian? So that he was not merely trying to give a meticulous historical description of this presence of Hegel: he wanted to make it into one of modernity's schemata of experience (is it possible to think science, history, politics and everyday suffering in the Hegelian mode?); and conversely he wanted to make our modernity the test of Hegelianism and thereby of philosophy. For him the relation to Hegel was the site of an experiment, a confrontation from which he was never sure that philosophy would emerge victorious. He did not use the Hegelian system as a reassuring universe; he saw in it the extreme risk taken by philosophy.

Hence, I believe, the displacements he carried out, not so much within Hegelian philosophy but upon it, and upon philosophy as Hegel conceived it. Hence also a whole inversion of themes. Instead of conceiving philosophy as the totality at last capable of thinking itself and grasping itself in the movement of the concept, Jean Hyppolite made it into a task without end set against an infinite horizon: always up early, his philosophy was never ready to finish itself. A task without end, and consequently a task forever recommenced, given over to the form and the paradox of repetition: philosophy as the inaccessible thought of the totality was for Jean Hyppolite the most repeatable thing in the extreme irregularity of experience; it was what is given and taken away as a question endlessly taken up again in life, in death, in memory. In this way he transformed the Hegelian theme of the closure on to the consciousness of self into a theme of repetitive interrogation. But philosophy, being repetition, was not ulterior to the concept; it did not have to pursue the edifice of abstraction, it had always to hold itself back, break with its acquired generalities and put itself back in contact with non-philosophy. It had to approach most closely not the thing that completes it but the thing that precedes it, that is not yet awakened to its disquiet. It had to take up the singularity of history, the regional rationalities of science, the depth of memory within consciousness – not in order to reduce them but in order to think them. Thus there appears the theme of a philosophy that is present, disquieted, mobile all along its line of contact with non-philosophy, yet existing only by means of non-philosophy and revealing the meaning it has for us. If philosophy is in this repeated contact with non-philosophy, what is the beginning of philosophy? Is philosophy already there, secretly present in what is not itself, starting to formulate itself half-aloud in the murmur of things? But then perhaps philosophical discourse no longer has a *raison d'être*; or must it begin from a foundation that is at once arbitrary and absolute? In this way the Hegelian theme of the movement proper to the immediate is replaced by that of the foundation of philosophical discourse and its formal structure.

And finally the last displacement that Jean Hyppolite carried out on Hegelian philosophy: if philosophy must begin as an absolute discourse, what about history? And what is this beginning which begins with a single individual, in a society, in a social class, and in the midst of struggles?

These five displacements, leading to the extreme edge of Hegelian philosophy, and no doubt pushing it over on to the other side of its own limits, summon up one by one the great figures of modern philosophy, whom Hyppolite never ceased confronting with Hegel: Marx with the questions of history, Fichte with the problem of the absolute beginning of philosophy, Bergson with the theme of contact with the non-philosophical, Kierkegaard with the problem of repetition and truth, Husserl with the theme of philosophy as an infinite task linked to the history of our rationality. And beyond these philosophical figures we perceive all the domains of knowledge that Jean Hyppolite invoked around his own questions: psychoanalysis with the strange logic of desire; mathematics and the formalization of discourse; information-theory and its application in the analysis of living beings; in short, all those domains about which one can ask the question of a logic and an existence which never stop tying and untying their bonds.

I believe that Hyppolite's work, articulated in several major books, but invested even more in his researches, in his teaching, in his perpetual attention, in his constant alertness and generosity, in

his responsibilities which were apparently administrative and pedagogic but in reality doubly political, came upon and formulated the
most fundamental problems of our epoch. There are many of us
who owe him an infinite debt.

It is because I have no doubt borrowed from him the meaning
and possibility of what I am doing, and because he very often gave
me illumination when I was working in the dark, that I wanted to
place my work under his sign, and that I wanted to conclude this
presentation of my plans by evoking him. It is in his direction,
towards this lack – in which I feel both his absence and my own
inadequacy – that my questionings are now converging.

Since I owe him so much, I can well see that in choosing to invite
me to teach here, you are in large part paying homage to him. I am
grateful to you, profoundly grateful for the honour that you have
done me, but I am no less grateful for the part he plays in this
choice. Though I do not feel equal to the task of succeeding him, I
know that, on the other hand, if such a happiness could have been
granted us tonight, he would have encouraged me by his indulg-
ence.

And now I understand better why I found it so difficult to begin
just now. I know now whose voice it was that I would have liked to
precede me, to carry me, to invite me to speak, to lodge itself in my
own discourse. I know what was so terrifying about beginning to
speak, since I was doing so in this place where I once listened to
him, and where he is no longer here to hear me.

Translated by Ian McLeod.

NOTES

(All notes are by Robert Young, editor of *Untying the Text*.)

1 Samuel Beckett, 'The Unnamable', in *Trilogy* (London: Calder and
   Boyars, 1959), p. 418.
2 The subject of the debate between Foucault and Derrida. Derrida's
   review of *Madness and Civilization* is reprinted in *Writing and Difference*, trans. Alan Bass (London: Routledge & Kegan Paul, 1978),
   pp. 31–63. Foucault's reply, an appendix to the second edition of *Madness and Civilization* (1972) is translated as 'My Body, This Paper, This
   Fire' in *The Oxford Literary Review* 4:1 (1979), pp. 9–28. Foucault's
   remarks here continue the debate. In *Madness and Civilization* Foucault
   had argued that an 'epistemological break' had occurred between the
   medieval and Classical eras; the pivot of this shift was Descartes, the
   effect of it was to change the 'free exchange' of reason and madness in

the medieval period into the privileging of reason and the exclusion of madness in the Classical period. Derrida argues that this implies a metaphysics of presence or origins, and attempts to show that the division is constitutive of language itself. Here Foucault claims that it is possible to see the division occurring during the history of Greek thought, so disputing Derrida's claim that the *Logos* was always already split, even for the Greeks. The effect of Foucault's remarks is to imply a structure of repetition, which avoids any notion of an original presence, or origins in general. For furthur discussion by Derrida, see 'L'Archéologie du frivole', first published as a preface to Condillac's *Essai sur l'origine des connaissances humaines* (Paris: Galilée, 1973), republished as a separate volume by Denöel/Gonthier, 1976. For further discussions of the debate, see Edward Said, 'The Problem of Textuality: Two Exemplary Positions', *Critical Inquiry* 4:4 (Summer, 1978), pp. 673–714; and Shoshana Felman, 'Madness and Philosophy or Literature's Reason', *Yale French Studies* 52 (1975), pp. 206–28.

3 'The necessity of its form': that is, discourse in its form as constituted by Plato, viz., the laws of logic.

4 Pierre Janet (1859–1947), clinical psychologist, best known for *L'état mental des hystériques* (1892). Janet was Charcot's pupil and successor at the Salpêtrière, the famous Paris Hospital where Freud studied in 1885–6.

5 Foucault here alludes to Alexandre Dumas, *Kean, ou Désordre génie'ie* (1836). The play was adapted by Jean-Paul Sartre in 1954: *Kean* (Paris: Gallimard).

8

The Politics of Discourse*

WILLIAM E. CONNOLLY

POLITICS AND COUNTER-EXAMPLES

The desire to expunge contestability from the terms of political inquiry expresses a wish to escape politics. It emerges either as a desire to rationalize public life, placing a set of ambiguities and contestable orientations under the control of a settled system of understandings and priorities, or as a quest to moralize public life thoroughly, bringing all citizens under the control of a consensus which makes politics marginal and unimportant. Since neither of these orientations is easy to support explicitly today, they typically emerge as methodological themes disconnected from an account of their political implications. By depreciating politics at the level of theory, a politics of depoliticization is covertly endorsed in public life.

This book was designed to dissolve the appearance of neutrality in conceptual analysis, to help render political discourse more self-reflective by bringing out contestable moral and political perspectives lodged in the language of politics. It is a text on the language of politics and the politics of language. There are adjustments I would now make in the readings of 'power', 'interests', and 'freedom' presented in this text, but they are revisions which continue to reflect its basic thesis. Rather than concentrating on those marginal changes, I will here defend, clarify and revise modestly the larger perspective which informs the text itself.

Consider 'power'. My account of the concept power moves within an expressivist philosophy of language. That is, rather than treating concepts merely as vehicles to designate objects or represent the world as it is in itself, I have tried to delineate the point of view from which power is formed in our way of life, the standards and judgements, presumptions and prohibitions, expressed in the

*William E. Connolly, 'The Politics of Discourse', reprinted from William E. Connolly, *The Terms of Political Discourse* (Princeton, N.J.: Princeton University Press, 1983), pp. 213–47, by permission © William E. Connolly.

language of power. If we examine the concepts of persuasion, coercion, force, offer, bribe, deterrence, terror, etc., we see that this family of concepts is rooted in a more basic set of ideas about ourselves as agents capable of autonomous action, self-restraint and coherence, and worthy, because of these capacities, to be treated as responsible agents. In a society where such a conception of self and responsibility has achieved hegemony, the language of social relations will express these deeper conceptions; it will specify their meanings in particular contexts; it will differentiate relationships and actions which honor these standards from those which do not. Its criteria of differentiation will be shaped, in part, by standards of agency and responsibility. Relations, for instance, which inhibit the capacity for autonomous judgement will be differentiated from those which foster it, and those which limit the opportunity to act upon one's own judgement will be distinguished from those which encourage such action. Thus, we distinguish between persuasion and manipulation and between an offer and a threat. Unless our discourse included discriminations of this sort (of course, it houses discriminations along many other dimensions as well), we could not articulate the conception of self and responsibility inscribed in our social practices. More pertinently, if those differentiations were thoroughly absent from the terms of our discourse the conception of self and responsibility they express would be absent from our lives as well.

The language of power in modern life doubtless has more than one use, but it is intimately linked to the conception of self and responsibility operative in that life. Contests over the grammar of power involve debates over the best way to specify these root conceptions or, more fundamentally, the defensibility of the root conceptions themselves. In bringing out linkages between the concept 'power over' and responsibility, I am trying to bring out a rationale implicit in the distinctions we make between relations of power and other social relations. I am also trying to explain why, constituted as we are, we concentrate on a particular set of distinctions in this domain and ignore a much larger set which might be appropriate to us if we were constituted differently. I have suggested, therefore, that the exercise of power over another involves the limiting or impairing of the recipient's capacity for choice or action in some respect and that before such effects are seen as the 'manifestation of some person's or collectivity's power over the recipient, there must be some reasons to hold the bidder responsible for the limitation' (*The Terms of Political Discourse*, p. 97). I have challenged those who claim that there is no linkage between our conception of power and our assessments of responsibility to offer an account of the forms of power (manipulation, coercion, deterrence, etc.) which accounts for their shape and moral import without appealing to our underlying conceptions of agency and responsibility.

Andrew Reeve, in a thought-provoking essay, has challenged this interpretation.[1] He agrees that conceptions of power built around the *intentions* of the bidder are too restrictive to capture the actual and proper grammar of the concept; he believes as well that proposals merely to drop the intentionality criterion generate a concept of power so broad that it loses its ability to do serious work. He does not indicate, however, *why* intention is too restrictive or the alternative too broad. He then goes on to argue that the criterion of responsibility neither captures the range of relations covered by concept of 'power over' nor allows us to discern the rationale implicit within the criteria of inclusion and exclusion constituting the concept 'power over'.

Reeve proceeds by counter-example, delineating cases which seem intuitively to fall inside or outside the orbit of 'power over' in ways which contradict the judgement sustained by the criterion of responsibility. An examination of his counter-examples will help to bring out presuppositions, strengths and limits residing in this mode of argumentation.

First, Reeve believes that I restrict power (I will usually avoid the term 'power over', even though it is the concept to be examined) to those cases where A in some way limits B's ability to form or act upon B's desires, wishes or obligations. 'This has the rather odd consequence, however, that to introduce or fail to remove a constraint will act as evidence of the existence of power, but actually to remove a constraint which B faces, will not.'[2] But the conception I have offered does not have that implication at all. It is clear (I hope) that the term 'power to' covers the ability to achieve some outcome even against difficult odds and even in situations where power over others is essential to the achievement. But can one, on my reading, exercise power over another by removing a constraint? Certainly. A might limit B's capacity for action in one respect and in doing so remove burdens or limits facing B in another. A might, for instance, obstruct B's desires and thereby enhance B's ability to realize particular interests. Moreover, in some of these instances we may conclude that A's exercise of power over B is legitimate. Hence the discussion of legitimate power in the texts.[3]

The connections among agency, power and responsibility do not mean that the exercise of power over agents is never justified, merely that our commitment to treat persons as agents introduces a presumption, expressed in the grammar of 'power', against the imposition of limits or constraints on others. The initial presumption might be overriden, most importantly, perhaps, when a set of limitations helps to foster the capacity for agency itself. The 'oddness' Reeve discerns in my characterization of power dissolves when this dimension is included, but another question remains unanswered: what rationale or set of standards did Reeve invoke when he assessed a reading of power as odd, inappropriate or confused? Is ordinary language assumed to provide rational and sufficient criteria as it now stands or is to be supplemented by some other court of appeal?

Reeve's second counter-example speaks to the connection between assessments of responsibility and assessments of harm to the recipient. Some undesired effects are normally not judged to be harmful and some harmful effects are not normally judged to be the responsibility of agents knowingly entangled in the processes which generate them. For example:[4]

> If A is taking an examination in which the top 10 percent pass, and does as well as he can, knowing that this will impose a disbenefit on weaker candidates, he is Connolly-responsible for a restriction on them, and has power over them.

This judgement, Reeve adds, goes against our normal intuitions.

Consider a counter to the counter-example. Suppose that A is a member of a privileged minority, that he is taking an examination especially geared to his background and training, that the examination is designed to select a small number of employees from a larger candidate pool, that the examination questions are not linked closely to the skills actually appropriate to the job assignment, and that the favored examinees are, or easily could be, aware of these conditions. I would say that the examinees (along with the authors of the examination) share responsibility for a limitation imposed upon those excluded and that they exercise power over the excluded members (as long as the other specified conditions of responsibility are operative). In the example developed by Reeve, I would say that the successful examinee is neither responsible for B's limitation nor exercising power over B.

The two examples are distinguished by particular differences in the contexts in which the agents act. The point in establishing connections among the conceptions of agency, responsibility and power, is to bring out how implicit considerations which help to shape one of these concepts enters in to the constitution of the others as well. Their relations cannot be exhaustively captured in a couple of definitions. That is why I refuse to offer a *definition* of power or responsibility and insist on articulating a *paradigm* of each (*TPD*, p. 103) which allows us to fit the elements of the paradigm to a variety of specific circumstances.

We do not, for instance, say that a change in someone's conduct is the result of coercion if an acquaintance threatened to ignore him in the future should he continue to act on his most fundamental principles. We do not because the threat is trivial by comparison to the importance of the action. In my paradigm of power I say that the agent of power must have access to resources which can limit the range of options 'normally available' to the recipient (*TPD*, p. 102 and footnote, 132). What counts as normally available depends on the norms accepted within a way of life. If, for instance, the ends of growth, productivity and efficiency, which have played a prominent role in our civilization, were to undergo fundamental devaluation, we would assess Reeve's example differently. We might, as some now do, construe the examination as a selection procedure to be a mechanism of power. Such an invocation of implicit norms is inevitably involved in assessments of power and this is so because the concept is closely linked to context-dependent norms of responsibility. If those implicit norms themselves were subjected to a thorough critique, the range of contests over the composition of 'power' would be extended radically. A paradigm of power helps us to discern the complex relations between its grammar and those norms, but it cannot exhaustively detail them. It also helps us to identify points of attack for those who would disconnect 'power' from these associations.

As we shall see later, theories in which the norms of agency and responsibility are treated as arbitrary mechanisms of disciplinary control must also transform the concept of power lodged in our discourse. These alternative theories signify the internal connection in our discourse between power and responsibility.

A further objection to the conceptual link between responsibility and power has been posed by John Gray.[5] Gray contends that sometimes those whose actions severely limit the life chances of others are themselves locked into patterns of 'socialization' or, perhaps more credibly stated, structural determinations which restrict their range of choice and action. Thus, their actions are linked to constraints imposed on others, but they are not responsible for them.[6]

Since those who exercise power, no less than those upon whom power is exercised, have their preferences determined by the culture in which they are immersed and the institutions by which they are surrounded, how can it be justified to impute responsibility to the former but not to the latter?

If this is an objection to themes presented in this book, something has gone amiss. It is actually a restatement of a thesis argued here. I argue (*TPD*, pp. 122–5) that when agents in superordinate positions are themselves locked into a set of structural contraditions, where action in either of two directions available will necessarily impose burdens on others, the language of power itself begins to lose its grip. It is not just that we cannot allocate responsibility: we cannot specify the agents who could be said to exercise power. We might, in these circumstances, stretch the language to say that power is exercised without being able to identify agents who exercise it, but in this book I have concluded that, in an instance of this sort, structural determination should be seen to have superseded the exercise of power. I have done so to endorse the view that power is intrinsically connected to individual or collective agents who exercise it. One could proceed in a different direction, as Michel Foucault has done, by articulating a conception of power which is invested in institutions and divested from agents, but I see no sign that Gray is prepared to follow this path. Foucault's concept of power without agents is bound up with his theory of the agent as an artificial production without moral or epistemic privilege. The counter-example designed to break the connection between power and responsibility has the undesired effect of severing power from agency.[7]

Since I now endorse a theory of the subject (or agent) as an essentially ambiguous *achievement* of modernity, it is incumbent upon me to endorse at least some of the connections among agency, responsibility and power operative in modernity which express such a theory of the subject. I thereby reserve the concept 'power' for those contexts in which power can be said to be *exercised*; I adopt the vocabulary of structural constraints to characterize the parameters within which the exercise of power can occur and the vocabulary of structural determination to characterize those (if there are any) in which the constraints are so tight that there is no space for the exercise of power.

But what can one say in those intermediate conditions where one collectivity, with options available to it, is regularly implicated in transactions which limit the interests, desires or obligations of other collectivities? How do we move from consideration of individual relations of power, agency, and responsibility to those involving collectivities such as organizations, classes, ethnic groups, and regions. It may be that the reach of the traditional language of power, coming from an era in which the web of social institutions was less tightly drawn, is now insufficient to characterize the conditions in which we live. In affirming connections among agency, responsibility and power I intend not merely to *unfold* those already intact in our discourse; it is also necessary to *revise* the language of power to fit more closely the circumstances in which we now live. That is the topic of chapter 5 of this text (see *TPD*, pp. 198–205). 'If part of the point in saying that A has power over B is to charge A with closing B's options unnecessarily it may turn out that the criteria appropriate to establishing such a charge in the society of the local shopkeeper are rather different from those appropriate to the society of the corporate manager (*TPD*, p. 200.).'

This lag between inherited terms of discourse and changing constellations of social life contributes both to the contestability of core concepts and the inherently creative dimension of political conceptualization. We may not be able to *discover* within the inherited web of meanings unambiguous answers to the questions we pose to it. Creativity is required in these instances, but it is a mode of political creativity which must advance on several fronts together if it is to advance securely at all. We might see recent constructions such as 'institutional racism', 'affirmative action', 'bureaucratic responsibility', 'non-decision', and 'citizen entitlement', as elements in a broad, precarious movement to root the concepts of agency/responsibility/power more firmly in the organizational matrix of contemporary life. These political advances in turn help to generate the conceptual space – to generate, if you will, a new fund of examples and counter-examples – in which a conception of power linked to agency and responsibility can be adapted to the conditions of modernity.

These innovations, though creatively linked to conceptions of responsibility within our discourse (*TPD*, pp. 191–205), are not immune to counter-examples; if they succeed it will be because we become convinced first, that the ideals of agency and responsibility are worth retention, and second, that to prize these ideals today is to seek ways to weave them more fully into the fabric of organizational society.

The counter-example, given royal status as a testing procedure in philosophies which pretend that established concepts are in order as they are or claim that a reconstructed system of concepts can impose a rational order on the loose texture of natural language, must play a more modest role when the established terms of political discourse are understood to house heterogeneous standards of conduct. In these circumstances, counter-examples selected by one party in a debate might provide considerations which modify the initial reading or identify anomalies in need of assimilation; but it is always necessary to *decide* whether the counter-example will be allowed to override the thesis or the thesis to override the counter-example. Ordinary language, as a repository of conflicting examples, cannot suffice to govern such judgements, for the question revolves around ascertaining which of the multiple tendencies within it should be given primacy in the instance at issue.

The fetish of the counter-example in contemporary analytic philosophy is a ghostly legacy of defunct philosophies which promised to save philosophy from political engagement by endowing it with a neutral method to adjudicate between competing perspectives. Many who have overtly acknowledged the failure of this latter quest continue to evade the political dimensions of their own enterprise and to treat the counter-example as if it could be a definitive testing devise. The fetish of the counter-example allows analysts to occlude the intimate connection between the discourse of politics and the politics of discourse.

The counter-example plays its most constructive role when it is deployed not only to counter a thesis but to sustain an alternative thesis. For in a debate between articulated alternatives, in which each side offers putative counter-examples with some foundation in established discourse, the contestants will be driven to a deeper question, What considerations can be invoked to ascertain which example should be given primacy?

Felix Oppenheim has not only criticized the conception of power defended in this text, he has formulated an alternative conception to replace it. By exploring the contest between these two conceptions, we will be able to discern more clearly why 'power' is a locus of persistent turbulence in contemporary political thought and why each rival party strives to impose its particular order on it. For these debates are indispensable elements within larger debates over the ideals and standards to be given hegemony in modern life.

Oppenheim opposes the view that certain concepts of politics describe from a normative point of view and the claim that some of these latter concepts are essentially contestable. He promises to explicate a set of neutral, descriptive concepts which all rational social scientists must accept, regardless of their moral or ideological convictions. The quest is important to Oppenheim. For, unless it

can succeed, we cannot hope to have a science of politics and unless
we have a science of politics we cannot, he thinks, hope to bring
reason to political and moral debates. Oppenheim treats ordinary
language as only one test of a good conceptualization. We must be
willing to repudiate its guidance whenever it contains ambiguities
or surrounds descriptive concepts with moral connotations. The
goal is to reconstruct the language of political inquiry to make it a
suitable medium for a science of politics.

To relieve power of the normative 'connotations' which persistently cling to it, Oppenheim defines authority and persuasion as
forms of power. This move, if it succeeds, clearly divorces 'power'
from a moral point of view. For it lumps modes of determining
conduct which are presumptively legitimate in our discourse with
those which are presumptively illegitimate. Why are persuasion and
authority to be treated as instances of power?

> From the point of view of an *effective* language of political
> inquiry, the decisive question is, What is more *important*,
> the differences between rational persuasion and deception/
> deterrence/coercion or the similarities between all these rela-
> tionships of interaction? Different political scientists may give
> different answers, depending mainly on their research topic.
> But all will *agree* that we *need* a single concept tying together
> all methods by which one actor determines another actor's
> conduct. . . .[8]

Why do we need a single concept tying together all methods by
which one actor determines another's conduct? Oppenheim is
vague at this point. He says such a general concept will be more
'fruitful' for inquiry, that this demand corresponds with similar
judgements he has made for other concepts in political inquiry, that
the overarching concept of power recommended will be free of
normative entanglements, and that, because of its purely descriptive
character and generality, it will establish essential preconditions for
the formation of a science of politics. The last contention assumes, I
think, overriding importance for Oppenheim; but it also contradicts his promise to develop one definition of each political concept
suitable for use by theorists supporting alternative theoretical
orientations. This characterization of power is, on Oppenheim's
own reading, incompatible with an interpretive approach to political inquiry because the latter approach only makes sense when
couched within an expressivist philosophy of language, and on
expressivist philosophy contends that the web of concepts a

populace shares expresses in its network of differentiations their most fundamental ideals, standards, and conflicts. The science Oppenheim's definitions serve is not neutral between competing conceptions of political inquiry and I will contend further that the understanding of social life implicit in Oppenheim's concept of power (and associated concepts) supports a specifiable and contestable set of political prescriptions.

The purposes governing differentiations among alternative ways to get people to do what they would otherwise not do might vary in significant ways. We might seek to know the extent to which alternative modes respect and treat the self as a responsible agent. If that were the purpose, conceptions of persuasion, authority, coercion, bribery, etc., residing in our practices could provide a valuable launching pad from which to articulate the desired differentiations. Alternatively, the objective might be to assess techniques for controlling behavior according to their relative effectiveness, range of applicability, efficiency, cost, and completeness. When these latter priorities are given hegemony, the set of differentiations listed above loses much of its pertinence. Another set is needed which gives primacy to the reliability, scope, and efficiency of various modes of control. If we interpret Oppenheim's account to be governed by this latter purpose, we can see why he thinks it 'important', 'fruitful', and 'effective' to draw authority and persuasion into the concept of power and why he construes power to be a master concept into which 'all methods of determining behaviour' should be absorbed. The differentiations built around standards of agency and responsibility must be reshuffled and subjected to a new calculus of differentiation when these ends are given priority.

Oppenheim's 'reconstruction' of 'power' and associated concepts does not represent a neutral language of political inquiry, it expresses a technocratic ideal of politics. One could, of course, elaborate this set of distinctions and identities to show how it subverts a conception of self and societal ends worthy of endorsement. But Oppenheim never provides such a reading of the conception of power he presents. Intentionally or unintentionally, the differentiations he affirms subjugate the norms of agency and responsibility to a technocratic conception of social life. This ideal is so compelling to Oppenheim that he believes it to describe the world as it is fundamentally beneath the rhetoric and normative connotations of everyday discourse. He convinces himself that his concepts describe fundamental realities when they in fact describe an ideal to which he is wedded.

Oppenheim's reconstruction of political concepts constantly runs into two dilemmas. The rationale guiding his constructions can be discerned once the technocratic conception they express is articulated, but that very specification undermines his claim to construct a neutral system of political concepts. He must remain close to ordinary language if his reconstructed language is to influence the audience he strives to reach, but he must deviate from it significantly if he is to disconnect the terms of political discourse from normative ideals and standards they express in everyday life. If he moves far away, he loses contact with the community to which he speaks, and if he stays close the appearance of normative neutrality dissolves. Thus, the necessity for conceptual revision supported by vague justifications. When we discern the links between Oppenheim's 'explication' of power and a technocratic ideal of politics, we can see more clearly why the language of power in our discourse does not mesh perfectly with the criteria of responsibility. We can also see why it is unlikely that a concept of power could be articulated today which incorporates smoothly all the elements now competing for space within this frame. The concept 'power' is composed of heterogeneous elements standing in unstable relations to one another. It is one of the sites of a struggle between rival ideals of the good life competing – though not on equal terms – for hegemony in our civilization. If modernity is marked by rivalries in which efficiency and community, democratic citizenship and the imperative of economic growth, utility and autonomy, rights and interests, domination and appreciation of nature all compete for primacy, it is not surprising – at least to those who accept an expressivist philosophy of language – to see microcosms of this rivalry inside the concepts which help to constitute that way of life. As long as modernity continues to house debates over the character of the good life, the terms of political discourse will provide sites upon which the debates are pursued.

The central terms of political discourse, then, are *contestable* and they are more likely to be *contested* overtly when modes of conceptual analysis which pretend to transcend or neutralize these contests are demystified. The neutralists do not transcend the politics of discourse. They practice an academic politics of depoliticization through reification of the terms of political discourse.

ESSENTIALLY CONTESTABLE CONCEPTS

To say that a particular network of concepts is contestable is to say that standards and criteria of judgement it expresses are open to contestation. To say that such a network is *essentially* contestable is to contend that the universal criteria of reason, as we can now understand them, do not *suffice* to settle these contests definitively. The proponent of essentially contestable concepts charges those who construe the standards operative in their own way of life to be fully expressive of God's will or reason or nature with transcendental provincialism; they treat the standards with which they are intimately familiar as universal criteria against which all other theories, practices, and ideals are to be assessed. They use universalist rhetoric to protect provincial practices.

The thesis of essentially contested concepts (i.e., concepts which are contested or open to contest) has been challenged from several directions. The charge most commonly launched within the Anglo-American tradition of analysis is that the doctrine is too radical: it overlooks resources of reason or logic or tradition or neutral representation which can legitimately dissolve the definitional disputes persistently operative in moral and political philosophy. The Continental tradition of genealogy and deconstruction would criticize the thesis, as it has been developed by Hampshire, Gallie, Lukes, Montefiore, MacIntyre and myself, from the opposite direction. On this view, the proponents of the contestability thesis continue to erect barricades – such as the conception of the self as an agent – which arbitrarily confine the space in which the contests can legitimately move. I will consider the Anglo-American strategy of containment first, saving consideration of the Continental charge that a residue of transcendental provincialism still clings to the contestability thesis until the last section of this chapter.

The first charge is that the doctrine is internally contradictory.[9] It is contradictory to say first that a concept is essentially contestable and second that the particular reading one endorses is superior. Yet the thesis as I endorse it does not include the latter claim; it does not pretend to show that the reading it prefers is demonstrably superior to every other reading it opposes. The thesis claims (1) that a conceptual contest involves rival parties who accept some elements of the concept in common;[10] (2) that the common resources of reason and evidence available can illuminate these debates but are insufficient to reduce the number of interpretations rationally defensible to one; (3) that a strong case can sometimes be made within this remaining area of contestability in support of a particular reading. One argues for one's reading within this space but does not claim to demonstrate its validity. One of the points in emphasizing the contestability of concepts which enter into a way of life is to establish rational space for debate over the terms of discourse. The

thesis expresses an appreciation for politics by encouraging opposing parties to discern a possible element of rationality in the reading
they contest.

Why should the parties not merely suspend judgement in the
circumstances we have characterized? Sometimes that might be
appropriate, and surely advocates of this thesis often do hold their
position on particular issues in a different and more open way once
they have acknowledged an element of rationality in opposing
orientations. The concepts of politics, however, also help to constitute the standards and priorities of political life. Politics is the
sphere of the unsettled, the locus of those issues not fully governed
now by the unconscious play of tradition or the conscious control
of administrative rationality; it is also the sphere in which collec-
tively binding decisions sometimes must be made even though the
available resources of reason and tradition are insufficient to determine the outcome. Politics is, at its best, simultaneously a medium
in which unsettled dimensions of the common life find expression
and a mode by which a temporary or permanent settlement is sometimes achieved. In these circumstances, to endorse a particular
set of standards is to support criteria for decision where decision is
imperative, and to acknowledge that the decision endorsed is contestable is to endorse the case for keeping dissident perspectives
alive even after a political settlement has been achieved. There is no
contradiction in first affirming the essential contestability of a concept and then making the strongest case available for one of the
positions within that range. That's politics.

A second objection rests on the charge that the doctrine of
essential contestability is by its own premises essentially contestable. The doctrine is therefore alleged to be self-refuting. For if its
premises allow *it* to be essentially contested then it is quite per-
missible for people to contest it. Let us look at the logic of arguments of this sort more closely.

The argument is located on the same plane as the following
questions. To what does the correspondence of truth correspond?
Are the criteria of rationality rational? Is the empiricist theory of
knowledge empirically established? Hegel used a version of this
argument to refute the primacy of epistemology presupposed in
empiricist and rationalist philosophies. He argued that the importa-
tion of an external criterion of knowledge (e.g., clear and distinct
ideas, falsifiability, or verification through observation), to test the
truth of an operative mode of consciousness not committed to that
criterion, must run up against one of two unwanted implications.
Either the defense of the criterion imposed invokes the criterion

again (e.g., the doctrine of clear and distinct ideas is known to be true by the character of its clarity and distinctness) or it appeals to another criterion itself in need of grounding. The first argument is viciously circular and the second draws itself into an infinite regress. I think this is a powerful argument and it is probably at the base of those contemporary Continental philosophies which deny the primacy of epistemology continuing to govern Anglo-American analytic philosophy. An argument of this sort can be powerful against doctrines which purport to reveal some demonstrative truth, then, and the argument concerning the dilemma of epistemology helps to launch the contestability thesis.

The most promising way to avoid this dilemma is to present and defend some form of transcendental argument. Such an argument begins by identifying a sphere of experience taken to be undeniable, and it then indicates what capacities the subject of that experience must have for it to be possible. The argument in effect establishes a privileged level of presuppositions at one level to explain undeniable experience at another, and it uses these presuppositions (about the self or reason) to support a larger set of conclusions. The doctrine of essentially contested concepts is incompatible with transcendental arguments of the strongest type, though I have supported a weaker version in this text (*TPD*, pp. 192–8). If one were established to secure a particular moral doctrine specific enough to guide practical judgement in concrete contexts, the thesis of contestability would be refuted.

The affirmation of essential contestability is not self-refuting because it is not presented as a necessary or demonstratable truth. It does not even claim that its counter-thesis cannot be pursued. First, it claims that no previous or current philosophy has been able to secure a set of basic concepts both specific enough to guide practical judgement and immune to reasoned contestability. Second, it anticipates that future attempts to do so will falter unless they establish closure artificially through the exercise of power. Third, it promises to offer internal critiques of current and future doctrines which purport to eliminate rational contestability. We do not *know* that achievements unavailable to us now will necessarily be unavailable in the future. It is therefore not irrational for someone to deny *essential* contestability. But the denial does not have much bite until it is linked to articulation of one theory capable of withstanding the charge of contestability.

I concur with John Gray's reminder that what is open to contestation now may be susceptible to rational resolution later.

My claim that rival positions in political philosophy can be shown to hinge on differing answers to substantive questions of philosophy leaves open, however, the possibility that these questions are susceptible of a conclusive rational resolution. . . . Obviously there is no assurance that there will be sufficient progress in other areas of philosophy to permit the central problems of political philosophy to be resolved conclusively. . . .[11]

The history of political discourse and our best current understanding of language supports the belief that space for contestability will persist in the future, even though that space may be closed politically and/or difficult to recognize by those drawn into a particular practice of discourse. This expectation about the future, however, cannot be demonstrated to be true, for a future populace may generate discursive forms not now conceivable to us.[12]

Ambiguities lodged within the predicate 'essential' are probably responsible for several misreadings of the thesis advanced here. Not only does the predicate signal that these disputes are central rather than trivial or peripheral, some have interpreted it to mean that they are *demonstrably* interminable rather than reasonably expected to be so and that there are no rational grounds whatsoever to guide and inform these debates. I wish to affirm the disputes to be centrally important, to deny that it is demonstrable that they are in principle irresolvable, and to deny that there are no criteria at all to illuminate these contests. Let us consider this last issue.

To say that a contest is essential is not necessarily to affirm the radical relativism several critics have read into the thesis. It may be to contend, as I have done explicitly, that the universal criteria of rationality available to us limit and inform such debates but are insufficient to resolve them determinately. 'It is partly because we share the pertinent norms of responsibility *imperfectly* that contests arise with respect to such political concepts, and it is because we *share* these norms imperfectly that we are provided with some common leverage for limiting the range within which these contests can rationally proceed' (*TPD*, pp. 197–8). The limits recognized in the text flow from an endorsement of Strawson's view that, though the conception of agency and responsibility inscribed in our practices is not identical to those affirmed in other times and places, these are nonetheless 'categories and concepts which in their most fundamental character change not at all' (Strawson, quoted in *TPD*, p. 197). I will contend later in this chapter that the Strawson thesis is too strong, but neither the initial formulation nor the revised account endorses radical relativisim. If that were the thesis we might be able to speak of conceptual differences, but not of contests.

The phrase 'essentially contestable concepts', properly interpreted, calls attention to the internal connection between conceptual debates and debates over the form of the good life, to the reasonable grounds we now have to believe that rational space for such contestation will persist into the future, to the value of keeping such contests alive even in settings where a determinate orientation to action is required, and to the incumbent task for those who accept the first three themes to expose conceptual closure where it has been imposed artificially. The thesis refers to essentially contestable *concepts* to focus attention on the locus of space for contestation, not in some abstract space in which language is deployed as a neutral medium of communication, but in the fine meshes of social and political vocabularies themselves. I would happily accept a retitlement of this thesis as long as it properly accentuated the internal connection between the concepts imperfectly shared in a way of life and the contestable standards, judgements and priorities which help to constitute that life.

CONTESTABILITY AND DECONSTRUCTION

The thesis of essentially contestable concepts, developed within the Anglo-American world, is both a precursor of Continental philosophies of genealogy and deconstruction and a potential target of their assault. Deconstructionists show how every social construction of the self, truth, reason, or morality, endowed by philosophy with a coherent unity and invested with a privileged epistemic status, is actually composed of an arbitrary constellation of elements held together by powers and metaphors which are not inherently rational. To deconstruct these established unities is to reveal their constructed character and to divest them of epistemic privilege. Genealogy is a mode designed to expose the motives, institutional pressures, and human anxieties which coalesce to give these unities the appearance of rationality or necessity. Some forms of deconstruction/genealogy seem to be in the service of nihilism, while others, by bringing out the constructed character of our most basic categories, aim at opening up new possibilities of reflection, evaluation and action.

Michel Foucault, after defining his early project as an archae-

ology exposing the underlying elements holding together the institutional forms and epistemological constructions of past eras, now
characterizes himself as a genealogist of the present. The shift is
merely one of emphasis, since his studies of the history of epistemes,
medicalization, madness, punishment, and sexuality have consistently aimed at distancing contemporaries from the unities which
govern our way of life by bringing out the artificial and constructed
character of these forms. Genealogy is a radicalization of the earlier
project, concentrating on the 'strategies' of power which establish
and maintain the most basic unities of modernity while suspending
any appeal to rationality or truth to understand these constructions.

Foucault's genealogies represent a reversal of the project of interpretation. While interpretation seeks to bring out the rationale
implicit in the practices, say, of tribal society, partly to allow us to
come to grips more reflectively with the underlying priorities and
standards in our own way of life, genealogy strives to distance us
from the rationale implicit in past and present practices. Our modes
of rationality, morality, agency, sexuality, and responsibility,
through a genealogy of the elements from which they are constructed and the forces which bind the constructions together,
become experienced as arbitrary impositions to be opposed, evaded
and resisted. The genealogies appeal to the aspect of our experience
which is contained, subjugated or excluded by these constructions.
Genealogy thus totalizes the project of politicization modestly pursued in the thesis of essentially contested concepts. It is uncertain
(to me) just how far Foucault himself would push this process of
politicization. There are many occasions where he seems to endorse
a politicization complete enough to break up modernity itself, thereby enabling perhaps a new set of artificial constructions to emerge
in its place. At other times it seems possible that Foucault, believing
that the forces of order are always well represented and armed in
the bureaucracies and academies, has decided to focus exclusively
on the genealogical project to provide a counterpoint to the forces
of order and unity. Foucault may see himself as 'the other' (or fool)
of modernity, exposing artificialities it congeals or conceals in the
hope of enhancing space for politics. To redress the current imbalance in favor of ordered constructs he puts all his weight on the
other side of the scale. We cannot explore these alternative possibilities here; we will examine those aspects of Foucauldian genealogy
which make critical contact with the thesis of essentially contestable concepts.[13]

Three Foucauldian themes are particularly pertinent: (1) the thesis that the modern agent or subject is an artificial production of modernity rather than a rational achievement which establishes standards through which to assess modernity; (2) the contention that a social practice construed by interpretationists to be constituted partly by concepts which express its norms and standards is better seen as a 'discursive practice' in which heterogeneous elements such as architectural design, available instruments, concepts, and rules of evidence congeal into a particular structure of mutual determinations; (3) the view of 'power', not as a possession of agents who exercise it to define the options of others, but as a set of pressures lodged in institutional mechanisms which *produce* and *maintain* such privileged norms as the subject or the primacy of epistemology. The key to the last two themes resides in the credibility of the Foucauldian view of the subject. If the subject, for instance, is construed to be an artefact of power rather than an agent who, among other things, exercises power, then clearly the modern tendency to link power closely to agents would have to be revised. And if the concept of the self as subject endorsed in this text were undermined completely, the limits within which contestation can proceed rationally would be broken too. The thesis of essential contestation would give way to the practice of total deconstruction. We will concentrate, therefore, on the Foucauldian account of the subject.

This book endorses the idea of the self as agent and the agent as a center of responsibility. We are seen here as 'agents, capable of forming intentions, of deliberately shaping . . . conduct to rules, of appreciating the significance of actions for other . . ., of exercising self-restraint;' and we are therefore said to be 'worthy of being held responsible for conduct that fails to live up to expected standards' (*TPD*, p. 193). The most basic norms of agency and responsibility, because they are unavoidably presupposed in our daily transactions, are treated here as criteria to guide and limit conceptual contestation: 'those who disagree about the grammar of key political concepts also share, if tacitly, a range of commitments about persons and responsibility . . . some aspects of these shared commitments reflect conventions relative to our social life, while the central core reflects conventions relative to social life as such' (*TPD*, p. 197).

Foucault challenges any such attempt to privilege the norms of agency and responsibility. He does not say that the inhabitants of modernity are not subjects or that the modern subject is a mere fiction; he presents the subject as a real artefact of modernity, as an artificially engendered unity which becomes a vehicle for the extension of disciplinary control over the self. The subject, on this reading, is neither a universal phenomenon, nor a historical achievement which, once attained, allows us to come closer to rationality, truth, and autonomy.

Foucault does not seek to refute the idea of the subject directly, for that would implicate him in standards of truth and rationality bound up with the notion of a subject who recognizes them. His approach is indirect. He constructs genealogies of modern formations which engender the subject, seeking to disconnect us thereby from the standards of reason and truth which presuppose subjectivity. He thus studies the formation of modern forms of reason, sanity, responsibility, and sexuality by linking these contructions to the forms of unreason, sanity, irrationality, and perversity they simultaneously engender and subjugate.

Foucault deconstructs the modern subject by connecting the norms and institutions which form it to the elements of unreason, madness, delinquency, and perversity it thinks it transcends in itself and treats humanely in others. The genealogies typically begin with an era in which these dualities are not yet perfected and proceeds to modernity where they emerge together. The subject is a modern artefact and these institutionally engendered dualities provide its conditions of existence. Thus, if the late Middle Ages confronted ambiguities in madness by treating the mad as the fallen bearers of truths too deep for human articulation and yet susceptible through madness to some dark manifestation, modernity subdues the ambiguity in madness. It contains, confines and treats unreason to protect itself from that which does not fit into its affirmative constructs. That which escapes the control of subjectivity, rationality and responsibility must either be brought back into the fold through modern confessionals (therapy, rehabilitation, and the dialectic of self-consciousness) or confined and controlled by disciplinary mechanisms. The disciplinary mechanisms and the confessionals together produce us as subjects and function to maintain the production from disruption. The mad are today treated as victims of an illness to be cured, never as *signs* that the norms of subjectivity, reason, and responsibility are too demanding of the self to which they are applied. The criminal is either immoral (to be punished) or delinquent (and in need of treatment); he is seldom seen as evidence of the arbitrary character of the norms which produce him. The epistemic privilege invested in the subject is sustained by constituting that which is differentiated from it as a deviation in need of treatment or containment.

These genealogies of the self and its other are buttressed by a genealogy of three epistemes which have taken turns in providing the site upon which theories of the self, language, reason, and knowledge can be articulated and contested. The epistemes of the late Middle Ages and of the Classical Age did not create space for the modern subject; the conceptions of language, knowledge, and truth they allowed did not articulate with the self as a subject. The modern episteme does support this conception of the self, but since no episteme contains the resources to establish or justify itself, to prove the truth of its governing rules and norms, these artefacts of modernity are not proven to embody truth merely because they fill the space available to them. No transcendental argument can be constructed without deploying resources within the modern episteme and no argument deploying those resources can deduce the truth of the episteme itself. What we can do through genealogy is to glimpse limits set by the modern episteme, and this is particularly possible today because the elements it has held together are beginning to break up.

The genealogies at these two levels are together supposed to generate a reversal of the modern orientation to subjectivity and responsibility. Instead of viewing them as universal norms or modern achievements, we glimpse how they are artificially engendered and how the maintenance of the affirmative side constantly requires the production of the other which denies and resists it. The dualities of reason/unreason, rationality/irrationality, responsibility/irresponsibility, normality/abnormality, sanity/insanity constantly engender and sustain each other. Our treatment of deviations and deviants are not unfortunate necessities required to maintain norms transcendentally established, but the institutional means (imprisonment, rehabilitation, confessional, therapy, confinement) by which we protect the dualities themselves from the deconstruction to which they would otherwise succumb.

The power of Foucault's genealogies resides partly in the detail of the account and partly in the metaphors he deploys to unsettle our confidence in metaphors we ordinarily apply in similar contexts. The disruptive use of unsettling metaphors is particularly important in these genealogies, I think, because it draws our attention to ways in which the position we endorse is sustained not by argument or logic, but by the power of a dominant metaphor insinuated into our discourse.

Out of this deconstruction of the subject emerges an alternative picture of (as I shall call it) the bifurcated self of disciplinary society. One part of this self is the free, rational, and responsible agent capable of consenting freely to rules, of being guided by

long-term interests and principles, and of being punished for deviation from those norms to which it has voluntarily consented. This
side of the self is susceptible to social control by appeal to its virtue
or responsibility or by threats of coercion or by the introduction of
incentive systems which make it in its interests to behave in certain
ways. This first side of the self is the site of self-discipline, and part
of the pressure to accept self-discipline flows from its desire to
avoid official definition as 'the other' which can no longer be
treated as a subject. The second dimension of the self is the other
(the double or the shadow) which does not fit neatly into the first
construction. It is the site of impulses, desires, feelings and pressures which are not subjected to rationality and self-control. When
this side achieves hegemony the self is officially defined to be insane
or delinquent or mentally unstable. And these official judgements
license therapy to draw the loose elements more fully into the
control of the subject or they license disciplinary controls to intimi-
date the self into conformity. This second site of the self is the
object of institutional mechanisms of confinement, treatment, rehabilitation, confessional therapy and drug therapy.

If the self remains unsusceptible to control through one of these
sites the mechanisms of disciplinary society turn to the other. The
choice is not governed by knowledge or truth but by strategic
considerations of relative effectiveness in control. 'Individualiza-
tion' itself is a process by which the self is rendered susceptible to
dual strategies of bureaucratic control.

> In a system of discipline, the child is more individualized than
> the adult, the patient more than the healthy man, the madman
> and the delinquent more than the normal and non-delinquent.
> In each case, it is towards the first of these pairs that all the
> individualizing mechanisms are turned in our civilization; and
> when we wish to individualize the healthy, moral and law-
> abiding adult, it is always by asking how much of the child he
> has in him, what fundamental crime he has dreamt of com-
> mitting. . . . All of the sciences, analyses or practices em-
> ploying the root 'psycho' have their origin in this historical
> reversal of the procedures of individualization.[14]

So both sides of the bifurcated self are sites of control, and those
humanists who oppose bureaucrats, technocracy, harsh punishment, and incentive systems to the norms of responsibility, self-
consciousness, civic virtue, therapy or rehabilitation, function as
the disciplinary twins of those they oppose. The two philosophies

of politics complement one another. Those who celebrate the agent as a center of self-discipline, rationality, freedom and self-consciousness are thereby unwitting vehicles of disciplinary society. To seek to dismantle the modern subject, along with its shadow which grows longer the more it is perfected, is to oppose the hegemony of disciplinary society. Anything else plays into its hands.

How does one assess such a genealogy with its charge that modern humanism is a vehicle of disciplinary control? One can try to argue that Foucauldian politics is self-refuting.[15] One can try to show that the genealogies draw inevitably upon norms of rationality they seek to deconstruct and are thus self-reflecting.[16] One can criticize the detail of Foucault's histories. I doubt, however, that any of these strategies would suffice by itself. We need to confront the Foucauldian reversal of the theory of the subject directly to ascertain which elements from this account are compelling and which are not. This tactic, at least, is essential to a doctrine which has asserted that there is an essential sphere of contestability in the political discourse of modernity *and* that conceptions of agency, reason, and responsibility presupposed in those discourses help to set limits within which these contests legitimately proceed.

It appears that a strong case can be made in support of the view that the subject is a modern formation. Hegel, for instance, concurs with Foucault on this point, though he tries to construe the mutually constitutive forms of civil society, the state and the subject to be *achievements* of modernity. And A. H. Adkins has developed persuasive support of the view that the Homeric Greeks construed themselves in ways which deviate sharply from the modern conception of the subject (and from the associated categories of morality and responsibility).

Adkin's interpretation is drawn from a reading of 'ordinary language' in the Homeric myths; it thus coincides nicely with the expressivist view of language I have adopted while challenging a central presupposition within my original account of conceptual disputes. The concepts of the Homeric age, he contends, reveal a self interpreted by participants to house a plurality of 'little selves', each little self functioning as a quasi-independent center of emotion, consciousness, and action. This plurality is only occasionally and 'lightly' organized into a coherent unity.

We are accustomed to emphasize the 'I' which 'takes decisions' and ideas such as 'will' or 'intention'. In Homer there is much less emphasis on the 'I' or decisions. Men frequently act as *kradie* or *thumos* bid them.[17]

Thumos, kradie, ker and *etor* each function within the self as centers of feeling and action; the self is thus experienced as a constellation of 'separate springs capable of impulse, emotion and thought; the existence of, so to speak, separate "little people" within the individual seems natural in the light of Homeric psychology and . . . physiology.'[18]

This conception of self as a multiplicity governed sporadically and loosely by unifying pressures is articulated within a world of multiple gods which intervene competitively in the life of the self; it also emerges within a small, vulnerable social form which is continually susceptible to fate and to the threat of enemy invasion. These forms in turn are associated with norms of responsibility and merit which depreciate intention, motivation, or effort as criteria of assessment and appreciate failure or success in protecting the community.

The terms of discourse in this setting express conceptions of self, responsibility, merit, and worth which are alien to modernity, or better, emerge as minor chords within our lives barely audible within the modes of expression available to us. If Adkins's account is correct, then Strawson has overplayed the hand of rationality in contending, after a careful account of the conception of self and responsibility inscribed in *our* language and *our* reactive attitudes, that these are 'concepts which their most fundamental character, change not at all'. Any argument seeking to defend modern postulates of agency and responsibility must retreat from the claim that these are universal orientations presupposed in all human societies and merely lifted to a peak of realization in modernity.

The work of disparate thinkers such as Hegel, Adkins, and Foucault requires a loosening of the standards of self and responsibility taken in this text to provide the indispensable background to discourse and the criteria for assessing it. Do these studies, though, after the disappearance of Hegelian *Geist*, deconstruct arguments for agency and responsibility altogether? I believe this latter implication is not required and I will close by sketching a set of considerations which might, when properly developed and integrated, sustain a defense of the subject as a precarious and ambiguous achievement of modernity.

Amidst the differences detected by Adkins and others between the modern and a variety of pre-modern conceptions of self, there are also notable continuities. These aliens are recognizably human even if they are unlike us in significant ways. The multiplicity which the pre-Platonic Greeks experienced heavily is also experienced by us occasionally, though we contain and organize it in different vocabularies (e.g., the concept of the unconscious and romantic images of the self which continue to haunt the official understandings of modernity). And this similarity is reversible. The Greeks, after all, experienced the unity of the self lightly.

Moreover we and they are essentially *embodied* selves, and the nature of that embodiment itself helps to shape the form of perception available to us, our spatial and temporal experience, and the experience of the self as implicated in a cycle of birth, maturation through dependence on adults, and death. These experiences, variable to be sure, but containing a universal dimension, help to give a sense of unity to a single life. They allow the self to experience itself to have continuity through time, to have a past and a future. We are also essentially language users, and we bestow a name upon each individual which individuates one and draws one into the discourse of the community as an active, identifiable participant with a past and a future. These are materials from which a loosely bounded transcendental argument concerning the structure of the self can be launched.

There are additional considerations, more particular to our own age, but capable of defense from a variety of directions. The gods, for instance, have retreated from the world, and we could not seriously endorse a conception of self and responsibility which presupposed their competitive intervention in our world and lives. Similarly, the sciences of modernity make it extremely improbable that we could once again endorse a cosmology in which the universe is filled with purpose and meanings to be acknowledged by us. We might develop, partly through a deeper recognition of ourselves as *embodied* selves necessarily implicated in nature, a deeper appreciation of the integrity and complexity of nature than we now manifest, but it is unlikely that we could again invest nature with agency and purpose. We, finally, have access to historical and anthropological accounts capable of making us more aware of the distance between us and other worlds and thus more self-conscious of presuppositions built into our practices and conduct. This developed capacity for self-consciousness is itself one of the elements which enhances our capacity for coherence and agency; it allows us, though incompletely and imperfectly, first, to convert pre-conscious and unconscious elements of conduct into conscious premisses and then to assess these premisses for their internal coherence.

Universal characteristics humans share as essentially embodied selves, and premisses deeply rooted in modernity, together provide materials from which a conception of the subject as an achievement can be defended. The elements particular to modernity may in principle be contestable, but these are contests we are not now in a position to open.

This combination, then, might support a conception of the subject as an inherently ambiguous achievement. We take it to be an achievement because we know that those who have experienced the affirmative side of modern freedom, self-consciousness and citizenship (the subject at the level of political life), invariably seek to retain and extend this experience. Even Foucault's genealogies become exercises in self-consciousness particularly available to the modern self as subject. The subject is arguably an achievement in a second sense as well. Every way of life imposes some sort of order on the chaos and multiplicity which would otherwise prevail, and every way of life must therefore develop some means of setting and enforcing limits. The development of a subject-centered morality may turn out, when compared to other conceivable alternatives, to be the most salutary way to foster order through the consent and endorsement of participants. Democracy is an achievement of citizenship. It requires the subject, capable of adjusting conduct to norms, willing to assume responsibility for commitments, and willing to take the common good into account in its public life when assured that others will too.[19]

After confronting the challenge of Foucauldian genealogy I would, however, also contend that the subject is an *ambiguous* achievement of modernity; the most basic agenda is to ascertain how to reconstitute the achievement to enable us to acknowledge the ambiguities within it, to find ways to temper some of them, and to develop compensatory mechanisms for dealing with others. The subject is an ambiguous achievement because the history of its formation has been marked by a corollary history of the perfection of instruments, enclosures, therapies, and medications to control and contain the other which does not fit into officially designated norms of agency. The formation of the modern self correlates with the modern imperative to co-ordinate more and more aspects of public and private life. To confront the ambiguities in the modern subject is to explore those pressures in modernity to bring more of the self into the orbit of social control through incentive systems, civic virtue, morality, observation, confessional therapies, medical treatment and criminal punishment.

We can recognize and relieve ambiguities in the modern achievement of subjectivity by finding ways to loosen these imperatives which simultaneously require modernity to draw more and more of the self into the orbit of social control and encourage many participants to find ways to elude, resist, and subvert those controls. To loosen the imperatives of social co-ordination would be to relax pressures on both sides of the bifurcated self; it would allow a wider range of conduct to be untouched by normative assessment; and it would allow a larger portion of that conduct which must be normatively appraised to be housed within categories such as the eccentric, the odd, the weird, and the wayward rather than concepts of the irrational, delinquent, sick, obsolete, illegal, or abnormal. For the latter judgements license bureaucratic modes of correction through confessional therapies or disciplinary controls. The way to loosen the reins of social co-ordination is to relax those expansionary imperatives of the civilization of productivity which, to be met, must treat the subject and its shadow as dual sites of strategic control.

I do not claim of course to have presented an adequate theory of the subject here, let alone to have shown how the ambiguities within this achievement could be more fully acknowledged and relieved in our civilization.[20] I merely wish to suggest, first, that the frame in which essentially contested concepts was initially enclosed was too narrowly defined and, second, that even after confronting attempts to deconstruct the modern subject, considerations remain available from which an appreciation of the subject as an ambiguous achievement of modernity can be articulated. To show the subject to be a construction is not to render its deconstruction imperative.

NOTES

1 Andrew Reeve, 'Power Without Responsibility'. See also Alan Ware, 'The Concept of Manipulation and Its Relation to Democracy and Power', *British Journal of Political Science* (Spring, 1981), pp. 163–81.
2 Ibid., p. 83.
3 In general, Reeve ignores the discussion of legitimate power in chapter 3, Power and Responsibility. This allows him to suggest that I think power is immoral or wrong. 'Connolly . . . thinks of power itself as something unpleasant' (p. 85). As the presentation of legitimate power makes clear, I think, in fact, that power one exercises *over* another is

always in need of legitimation, not that power in a good society would be unnecessary or that it must be illegitimate in existing societies. I believe, in fact, that no order could sustain itself without power, though that will not be the *principle* basis of order in a well-ordered polity. It is crucial to recall that, on my reading, while a presumption against exercising power *over* another is operative, it does not apply in exercising power to achieve an end, unless *that* involves power over another.

4 Reeve, *Power Without Responsibility*, p. 84.

5 John Gray, 'Political Power, Social Theory and Essential Contestability', in *The Nature of Political Theory*, ed. D. Miller and L. Siedentop (London: Oxford University Press, 1983). Gray has illuminating things to say about the scope and limits of the thesis of essentially contested concepts, and I will consider that topic shortly. But his discussion of my concept of power contains misreadings of themes advanced in the text. He treats the 'Connolly/Lukes' concepts of power as if the two were one. There are in fact notable differences in our accounts amidst the significant similarities. Gray inteprets me to say (with Lukes) that to exercise power over another is to limit the other's *interests*. I do not, however, restrict power so tightly; I speak of constraints on the interests, desires, or obligations of another and even then leave that which is restricted open-ended. This would be an innocent enough misreading if Gray did not then conclude that the exercise of power for me always limits the capacity for agency. It is, though, on my reading, quite possible for A to restrict B's *desires* in ways which support the realization of B's interests or autonomy. Hence, one of the reasons for the discussion of legitimate power in the text – a topic ignored by Gray. My argument, it will be recalled, is that because the exercise of power over another limits the other in some respect, and because we generally endow persons with the presumptive right to act according to their own judgement, there is a presumption against 'power over' which needs to be overcome if it is to be made legitimate. It is this presumption which helps to account for contests between those who try to extend the conventional criteria of power and those who try to contract it. The first is trying to extend the sphere of presumption and the second to contract it. Finally, partly because of these preliminary misinterpretations, Gray concludes that I look forward to a possible polity in which power is inoperative. That apparently would be a fully legitimate polity for me. But I do not. It is not just that I think full consensus is unrealizable, I think the attempt to realize it is always a form of tyranny. The thesis of essentially contested concepts *is* a thesis about the unrealizability of rational consensus and it supports efforts to help keep the terms of discourse open. In a society of this sort there will be power and, especially, politics.

6 Gray, ibid.

7 Gray may intend to argue that, since I think subordinate constituencies in our civilization are systematically indoctrinated, I should argue that

putative agents of power are similarly constrained. Hence no responsibility and no power. I do not adopt, however, the first premiss. One can have a concept of real interests without concluding that everyone is in fact unconscious of his or her real interests.

8 Felix Oppenheim, *Political Concepts: A Reconstruction* (Chicago: University of Chicago Press, 1981), p. 39.

9 Since the effort in this text to resurrect the thesis of essentially contested concepts developed initially by Gallie and Hampshire, a series of texts on the topic has emerged. They include: Steven Lukes, *Power: A Radical View* (London: Macmillan, 1974); Alan Montefiore, 'The Concept of Politics', in *Neutrality and Impartiality* (Cambridge: Cambridge University Press, 1975); John Gray, 'On the Contestability of Social and Political Concepts', *Political Theory* (August, 1977), pp. 331–48; John Gray, 'On Negative and Positive Liberty', *Political Studies* (December, 1980), pp. 507–26; John Gray, 'On Liberty, Liberalism and Essential Contestability', *British Journal of Political Science* (October, 1978); pp. 385–402; John Gray, 'Political Power, Social Theory and Essential Contestability' op. cit.; Michael Shapiro, *Language and Political Understanding* (New Haven: Yale University Press, 1981), chapter 7; K. I. Macdonald, 'Is "Power" Essentially Contested?' *British Journal of Political Science* (July, 1976), pp. 380–2; Steven Lukes, 'Reply to K. I. Macdonald,' *British Journal of Political Science* (July, 1977), pp. 418–19; Barry Clarke, 'Eccentrically Contested Concepts', *British Journal of Political Science* (January, 1979), pp. 122–6; Fred Frohock, 'The Structures of "Politics"', *American Political Science Review* (September, 1978), pp. 859–70; Amy Gutmann, 'Moral Philosophy and Political Problems', *Political Theory* (February, 1982); pp. 33–48. While Lukes, Montefiore, Gutmann, and Shapiro have generally sought to develop this thesis and explore its implications for political discourse, Gray, Barry, Macdonald, Frohock and Clarke have contested it (the latter eccentrically) in one way or another. Shapiro, it should be noted, probes similarities between this thesis and theories of genealogy and deconstruction advanced by French philosophers such as Derrida and Foucault, a topic we turn to in the last section of this chapter.

10 In *The Terms of Political Discourse*, pp. 30–1, I say that the disputants may share (imperfectly) the point of view from which the concept is formed but contest the central criteria appropriate to it; they may accept many of the same criteria but dispute the point of view from which it is to be formed; they may concur on the criteria and point of view but dispute the extent to which the concept is applicable to the way of life examined. Some analysts would refuse to call this last debate a conceptual dispute, and it is unimportant to the overall thesis if they do so or not, as long as they recognize that disputes of this sort are common and important.

11 Gray, 'Political Power, Social Theory and Essential Contestability', pp. 346–7.

12 One who accepts an intersubjective conception of social life and an expressivist philosophy of language would expect, in fact, that some background dimensions of a way of life potentially contestable will not be available to the self-consciousness of participants. Stuart Hampshire, one of the two originators of the phrase 'essentially contested (or disputed) concepts', explores this phenomenon in *Thought and Action* (New York: Viking Press, 1959) and it is a central theme in Charles Taylor's exploration of the history of debates between designative and expressivist philosophies of language, 'Language and Human Nature', Alan B. Plaunt Memorial Lecture, Carleton University Publication, 1978.

13 I have considered other dimensions of Foucault's work in 'The Dilemma of Legitimacy', in John Nelson ed. *Political Theory Now* (Albany: State University of New York Press, 1983), pp. 307–42; and 'The Politics of Disciplinary Control', paper delivered at the 1982 Convention of the American Political Science Association, Denver, Colorado, September 1–5.

14 Michel Foucault, *Discipline and Punish* (New York: Random House, 1977), p. 193.

15 I have developed a version of this argument in 'The Dilemma of Legitimacy'.

16 Hilary Putnam states such an argument against Foucault in *Reason, Truth, and History* (Cambridge: Cambridge University Press, 1982), but I do not think he has considered carefully Foucault's strategy of bracketing the question of truth as a privileged site and probing the mechanisms which give certain rules in a society that privileged status.

17 Arthur W. H. Adkins, *From the Many to the One* (Ithaca: Cornell University Press, 1970), p. 15.

18 Ibid., pp. 20–1.

19 I have defended this thesis in *Appearance and Reality in Politics* (Cambridge: Cambridge University Press, 1981), especially chapters 4 and 5.

20 I have explored, though in a highly preliminary way, the question of how to relax the growth imperative and thus to foster more 'slack' in the order in 'The Dilemma of Legitimacy', 'The Politics of Reindustrialization', *democracy* (July, 1981), pp. 9–20; 'Civic Disaffection and the Democratic Party', *democracy* (July, 1982), p. 18–27.

9

The Linguistic Model*

FREDRIC JAMESON

Meaning or language? Logic or linguistics? Such are the fateful alternatives which account for the immense disparity between British and Continental philosophy today, between the analytical or common language school and what has become, almost before our very eyes, Structuralism. Origins are as emblematic as the results themselves, and it is therefore fitting, for a moment at the outset, to juxtapose the *Cours de linguistique générale* of Ferdinand de Saussure, published in 1916, three years after his death, from a set of collated lecture notes, with such a characteristic product of the Anglo-American tradition as C. K. Ogden and I. A. Richards's *The Meaning of Meaning*, which first appeared in 1922.

These two works, each immensely influential, have something revealing and symptomatic to tell us about the cultural areas to which their respective influence has been limited. It would be tempting, but not quite accurate, to see in them two mutually exclusive modes of thought, to hold them up as the antithesis between the analytical and the dialectical understanding. It may be more adequate to account for the divergence through some initial ambiguity in their object of study, through the unique structure of language itself, with its twin faces, of which Saussure has said, in a famous image, that it is 'comparable to a sheet of paper: thought being the recto and sound the verso; one cannot cut one side without at the same time cutting the other; and in the same way, in language, one can neither isolate sound from thought nor thought from sound.'[1]

Yet each side is the starting point, not even for a different philosophy, but for a wholly different discipline itself. If we have in his book to deal with the return of linguistics as a model and an informing metaphor to that literary and philosophical realm from which, as a science, it once declared its independence, then it is just as certain that it returns with all the prestige of science itself; while,

*Fredric Jameson, 'The Linguistic Model', reprinted from Fredric Jameson, *The Prison-House of Language* (Princeton, N.J.: Princeton University Press, 1972), pp. 3–39, by permission © Princeton University Press.

with symbolic logic, its philosophical alternative also conquers its methodological autonomy upon the ruins of systematic philosophizing after the death of Hegel.

The Anglo-American approach has of course its philosophical and ideological roots in the long tradition of British empiricism, which in some ways it prolongs. In the same way, it is difficult to assess the originality of Saussure without forming some preliminary idea of the state of linguistics when he came to it, in order to be in a position to appreciate what it was he came to change.

As in the other disciplines, so also in linguistics the Romantic movement, the primacy of the middle classes, was the signal for a thoroughgoing re-evaluation of all outstanding problems, as well as solutions, in new and historical terms. In linguistics, the preference of Classical thought for eternal, changeless, normative laws had resulted in that close identification of language with logic whose codification we know as grammar. The Romantic age replaced grammar with philology; and it was characterized by a sudden proliferation of great historical discoveries (Grimm's law, Bopp's reconstruction of Indo-European, the elaboration of the great schools of Romance and Germanic philology, particularly by German scholars) and the ultimate codification of these discoveries as laws of language by the Neo-Grammarians, and particularly by Hermann Paul, whose ideas may stand as the dominant intellectual current in linguistics during the period when Saussure undertook his first studies.

I

We may assume that the elaboration of dogma coincides with the exhaustion of the vein. In any case, Saussure's innovations may be understood first and foremost as a reaction against the doctrines of the Neo-Grammarians. For the interest in change and evolution, in the reconstruction of proto-languages and the determination of language families and their inner affiliations, had led in the long run to Paul's conviction that 'what is not historical in linguistics is not scientific'.[2] Against this, Saussure's separation of the synchronic from the diachronic, a historical from structural research, is equally absolute, and contains a methodological presupposition which is just as peremptory a value judgement: 'to the degree that something is meaningful, it will be found to be synchronic'.[3]

But Saussure's starting point is more than a mere reaction; it is at the same time a liberation of intellectual energies. For with this distinction between diachrony and synchrony (he seems to have invented the terms in this form, although they were known before him in other acceptations in geology), he is able to demonstrate the existence of two mutually exclusive forms of understanding as well. Historical philology, in this light, proves to have taken as its object only individual changes, isolated facts; even its laws are somehow local and contingent: they are, we may say, scientific but meaningless. Saussure's originality was to have insisted on the fact that language as a total system is complete at every moment, no matter what happens to have been altered in it a moment before. This is to say that the temporal model proposed by Saussure is that of a series of complete systems succeeding each other in time; that language is for him a perpetual present, with all the possibilities of meaning implicit in its every moment.

Saussure's is in a sense an existential perception: no one denies the *fact* of the diachronic, that sounds have their own history and that meanings change. Only for the speaker, at any moment in the history of the language, one meaning alone exists, the current one: words have no memory. This view of language is confirmed rather than refuted by the appeal to etymology, as Jean Paulhan has shown in an ingenious little book. For etymology, as it is used in daily life, is to be considered not so much a scientific fact as a rhetorical form, the illicit use of historical causality to support the drawing of logical consequences ('the word itself tells us so: *etymology, etumos logos*, authentic meaning. Thus etymology advertises itself, and sends us back to itself as its own first principle').[4]

We may express all this in yet another way by showing that the ontological foundations of the synchronic and the diachronic are quite different from each other. The former lies in the immediate lived experience of the native speaker; the latter rests on a kind of intellectual construction, the result of comparisons between one moment of lived time and another by someone who stands outside, who has thus substituted a purely intellectual continuity for a lived one. In short, we may ask what it means to say that, for instance, 'etymology' and *etumos logos* are the same. The same for whom? On what principle is this identity, which crosses generations of individual lives and the extinction of untold numbers of concrete pronunciations, founded? If the question seems unduly ingenious, that is because we are still caught up in all kinds of positivistic presuppositions, because the position of the observer is still being taken for granted and has not yet come to strike us as problematical.

The first principle of Saussure's work is therefore an antihistorical one, and we will understand its meaning better if we see just what role its discovery played in his life. Saussure seems to have been a reluctant revolutionary: his innovations are not the work of someone instinctively out of step with his own time, of someone from the very beginning restless and dissatisfied with the modes of thought he found dominant as a young man, but rather of someone who was his whole life long involved in the teaching and propagation of precisely those diachronic, Neo-Grammarian doctrines against which his posthumous work stood as an attack. His major publication in his own lifetime, the *Mémoire sur le système primitif des voyelles dans les langues indoeuropéennes*, the work by which his contemporaries knew him and which he had published in 1879 at the age of twenty-two, was one of the crowning achievements of the Neo-Grammarian school, a deduction on diachronic principles the effect of which was to demonstrate the hidden regularity of certain sound patterns which had hitherto been taken as 'exceptions' to the 'laws' already codified. It is therefore permitted to conjecture that he arrived at the key notion of the separation between synchrony and diachrony – or, to put it in more positive terms, he developed the concept of a *system* – out of increasing dissatisfaction with his experience of history itself, and with the kinds of thinking and explanation he found possible there, a dissatisfaction based not so much on the absence of general laws as on their very abundance, on their secret hollowness for the mind. In short, one can well understand how in the face of all the tables of sound changes Saussure found himself little by little evolving a distinction between causes that are external to a phenomenon and causes which are somehow instrinsic to it, and this distinction may stand as the definition of the idea of system itself. What is at stake is the whole notion of law itself, as a meaningful explanation satisfying to the mind. To be sure, the patterns of diachronic changes are regular and can be formulated in predictable recurrent patterns; Saussure did so himself in the striking example mentioned above. But this merely empirical fact of regularity has no meaning in the linguistic system because it derives from causes – geographical barriers, migration and population shifts – outside the language itself. The law thus represents, we may say, a leap from the terms of one series (language patterns) to the terms of another (geographical law or population movements).

We may illustrate this disparity perhaps more clearly in an illustration drawn from history itself. I am thinking, for instance, of Pieter Geyl's revision of the classic interpretation of the religious and cultural split between the Protestant Netherlands and Catholic

Belgium.[5] What is in question is no doubt the inevitability of the
boundary line; yet in historical matters, as is well known, we may
take the word 'inevitable' as the sign, not of any deterministic
presuppositions, but simply of the sheer comprehensibility of a
given event in the terms of the historical understanding itself. For
the earlier historians, this split was somehow an 'inevitable' one,
for it reflected a basic cultural difference between the populations
on either side. To the north, the Protestant population resisted the
Spaniards for religious reasons; to the south, the Catholic rebels
against the crown were less intransigent and easier to subdue. Later
on, with Pirenne and his school, we come to another version of this
same thesis, the terms of whose translation, however, reflect pro-
French sympathies rather than the Protestant ones clearly in evidence in the earlier formulation. Pirenne's doctrine of a genuine
autonomous cultural tradition in Flanders that extended back into
the Middle Ages results in the same general conclusion, namely that
the ultimate national boundary was little more than a ratification of
a profound and already existing division between the two areas.

Geyl has little difficulty showing the immediate political and
polemic ends served by these various theses at those conjunctures in
Dutch or Belgian history when they were proposed; his own solution is, as one might suspect, a reductive, debunking one. He is able
to dismiss the earlier theories by pointing out what everyone had
known all along, that there was no greater concentration of Protes-
tantism in the north than in the south, and by showing that the
present-day religious and national frontier falls together with a
geographical one, namely with the beginning of the area of the
great rivers in the north in which the Protestant armies entrenched
themselves, and into which Parma's army was not strong enough to
penetrate. Given this ceasefire line conditioned by natural obstacles,
cultural pacification proceeded briskly on either side and the relative religious homogeneity of present-day Belgium or Holland is not
really a matter for much astonishment.

I have introduced this illustration, not to make any comment on
the historical thesis presented in it, but rather to underline the
various effects on the mind of different types of historical explanations. Geyl's theory is, I would like to say, diachronically satisfying
as the history of history: insofar as it is itself the resolution of a
historical riddle, prepared by the presentation and successive rejection of the earlier historical positions, it has great elegance for the
mind. But in itself, synchronically, there is something more disturbing about it: its thrust is to place the ultimate source of the comprehensibility of history outside human action itself, in the contingent

accidents of the non-human environment; to locate the ultimate term of the chain of cause-and-effect outside history, in geology, in the brute physical fact of the disposition of the geographical terrain. This final term has of course its own history (the origin of the great rivers at an earlier moment in the earth's development, the formation of the deltas, the chemical composition of the soil deposited there), but *that* history is a series which has nothing in common with the series of purely human events, a different series entirely, on a vaster and indeed incommensurate scale. I am even tempted to say that the very notion of the type of series itself, the distinction between internal and external causes, which may strike the reader as an unanalyzed presupposition smuggled into the discussion, is in reality implicit in Geyl's theory itself: for the force of his trick ending depends precisely on a shift from human to inhuman forms of causation.

I am, of course, not suggesting a return to the kind of idealistic history which Geyl's theory is concerned here to refute, and which foresees a holding together, within a common conceptual framework, of such incommensurate realities as human action and geological upheaval. It is, however, worth pointing out that the fact of the great rivers can never have been felt as contingent by the neighboring populations, and must already have been integrated, as a form of meaning, into their respective cultures long before its return upon them, with renewed contingency, in the form of the external influence under discussion here. The very notion of contingency or 'hasard' reminds us that the Saussurean revolution is contemporaneous with theories of 'pure poetry' and with the struggle, within the aesthetic realm as well, to eliminate the last traces of the extrinsic or the contingent from poetic language itself. We may best dramatize the value of Saussure's linguistic solution by pointing out that even for historiography there is yet another solution conceivable, alongside that of Geyl or of the meta-history which he attacks: this would be a type of structural history in which the relationship between Holland and Flanders would be studied within the context of a certain number of oppositions (Catholic-Protestant, Flemish-Walloon), which may then be combined or co-ordinated in a series of permutations or determinate relationships. From such a point of view the earlier combinations would be as little relevant as the previous casts of dice in a given succession.

In any case, it was some analogous feeling for the radical incompatibility of the various explanation systems which must have been at work in Saussure's mind during the elaboration of his own theories. This is still, of course, a negative way of putting it; and in

this sense Saussure's thought is but one among many contemporary
reactions against positivism. It is precisely his notion of a system
which distinguishes him from the idealistic and humanistic, anti-
scientific revolt which we find in the late nineteenth-century
religious revival and in Bergson and Croce and the linguistic movements which developed out of them. Saussure's position has many
affinities with that of Husserl, for like Husserl he was not content
simply to point out the existence of another equally valuable mode
of humanistic and qualitative thought alongside the scientific and
quantitative, but tried to codify the structure of such thought in a
methodological way, thus making all kinds of new and concrete
investigations possible.

   Saussure's dissatisfaction with the older linguistics was in its very
essence a methodological, a terminological one. When one reflects
on the relative obscurity of Saussure during his own lifetime, when
one examines the slight volume of his published work and learns
something of the posthumous history of his manuscripts, it is
difficult to escape the feeling that there is something archetypal
about Saussure's silence. It is that same legendary and august
renunciation of speech of which the gesture of Rimbaud is
emblematic, but which recurs again and again in the early modern
period in different guises and different forms, in the reticence of
Wittgenstein, in Valéry's long abandonment of poetry for
mathematics, in the testament of Kafka and in Hofmannsthal's
'Letter from Lord Chandos'. All of them testify to a kind of geological shift in language itself, to the gradual deterioration in this
transition period to new thought patterns, of the inherited terminology and even the inherited grammar and syntax. 'Wovon man
nicht sprechen kann, darüber muss man schweigen.' Yet the famous
sentence, in that it can be spoken at all, carries its own paradox
within itself. So it is that we learn what we know of those silences,
not through the official art forms which have been emptied of their
meaning, but through secondary and impermanent media, through
reminiscences and snatches of conversation, through letters and
fragments. It is, in fact, in a letter to Antoine Meillet that Saussure's
peculiar anxiety is preserved for us:

>   But I'm sick of it all and of the general difficulty of writing any
>   ten lines of a common sense nature in connection with linguis-
>   tic facts. Having so long busied myself with the logical clas-
>   sification of such facts and with the classification of the points
>   of view from which we examine them, I begin to be more and
>   more aware of the immense labor that would be necessary to

show the linguist *what he is really up to* when he reduces each operation to the appropriate category; and at the same time to show the not inconsiderable vanity of everything one ends up being able to do in linguistics.

In the last analysis, only the picturesque side of a language still holds my interest, what makes it different from all the others insofar as it belongs to a particular people with a particular origin, the almost ethnographic side of language: and precisely I can no longer give myself over without reserve to that kind of study, to the appreciation of a particular fact from a particular milieu.

The utter ineptness of current terminology, the need for reform, and to show what kind of an object language is in general – these things over and over again spoil whatever pleasure I can take in historical studies, even though I have no greater wish than not to have to bother myself with these general linguistic considerations.

Much against my own inclination all this will end up with a book in which I will explain without any passion or enthusiasm how there is not a single term used in linguistics today which has any meaning for me whatsoever. And only after that, I'm afraid, will I be able to take up my work again where I left it.[6]

The transition witnessed by Saussure, and dramatized by the other great moments of verbal impairment alluded to above, may be described as a movement from a substantive way of thinking to a relational one, a transition nowhere quite so acute as in linguistics. The discovery of Saussure was that the cause of terminological difficulties in linguistics resulted from the fact that these terms tried to *name* substances or objects (the 'word', the 'sentence') while linguistics was a science characterized by the absence of such substances:

Elsewhere we find things, objects, given in advance, which you are free to consider from various points of view. Here there are first of all points of view, they may be true or false but there are nothing but points of view in the beginning, with whose help you then subsequently *create* your objects. These creations turn out to correspond to realities when your point of view is correct, or not to correspond as the case may be; but in either case nothing, no object, is given at any time as

existing in itself. Not even when you're looking at the most
material kind of fact, one most obviously having the appearance of definition in and by itself, as would be the case with a
series of vocal sounds.[7]

Thus it is on account of the peculiar nature of language as an
object of study that Saussure is led to strike out in a new direction.
Once again, of course, the dilemma of linguistics is only part of a
vaster crisis in the sciences in general: in physics for instance, where
the alternation between the wave and particle theories of light
begins to cast some doubt on the conception of the atom as a substance, and where indeed the idea of a 'field' is not without analogies
to Saussure's notion of a system. In all these areas, scientific investigation has reached the limits of perception; its objects are no
longer things or organisms which are isolated by their own physical
structures from each other, and which can be dissected and classified in various ways. Saussure's concept of the 'system' implies
that in this new trackless unphysical reality content is form; that
you can see only as much as your model permits you to see; that the
methodological starting point does more than simply reveal, it
actually creates, the object of study.

In personal or psychological terms, this methodological perception is reflected in existentialism, whose leitmotiv – the priority of
existence over essence – is indeed simply another way of saying the
same thing, and of showing how lived reality alters in function of
the 'choice' we make of it or the essences through which we
interpret it: in other words, in function of the 'model' through
which we see and live the world. On a larger scale, it is clear that
this kind of thinking has the gravest implications for the human
studies, for disciplines such as history and sociology whose object
of study is almost as fluid and ill-definable as language itself.
Saussure was of course well aware of this: 'When a science has no
immediate recognizable concrete units, then it follows that such
units are not really essential to it. In history, for instance, what is
the basic unit? The individual, the period, the nation? No one is
sure, but what difference does it make? Historical investigations
may be pursued without a final decision on this point.'[8]

Thus, for units, entities, substances, are substituted values and
relationships: 'All of which simply means that *in language there are
only differences*. More than that: a difference normally presupposes
some positive terms between which it is established; but in language
there are only differences *without positive terms*.'[9] Saussure is here
conceiving value in terms of an economic metaphor, where a given

unit of currency has the same function whether it be gold or silver coin, *assignat* or wooden nickel: in other words, where the positive nature of the substance used is not as important as its function in the system.

In one sense, this distinction between value and substance has something of the force of the mind/body opposition, of the antithesis between mind and matter. One of its advantages for Saussurean linguistics is to make possible a methodological separation of pure sounds (as, for example, the articulations made by a speaker of a language utterly unknown to us) from meaningful sounds, or what Saussure calls acoustic images, the kinds of patterns a language begins to fall into even when we do not yet know it terribly well: that which permits us to recognize and perhaps visually to identify or to spell a foreign word even though we do not yet know its meaning. The distinction had already been anticipated by the two Polish linguists, Kruszewski and Baudouin de Courtenay (the latter later to become the teacher of the Petersburg Formalists)[10] when they foresaw the need for two wholly different kinds of science, the one an investigation of sounds in their pure physicality (phonetics), the other based on an exploration of meaning patterns ('phonologie' or phonemics). We will see the results of such a distinction later on; suffice it to say that we here witness the return of the antithesis between diachronic and synchronic on a new level, for phonetics will deal chiefly with diachronic changes, while to phonemics will fall the task of exploring the synchronic system.

Thus, philosophically, we are faced with a rather peculiar identification between change and matter, on the one hand, and meaning and the atemporal, on the other. It should be noted that the most adequate philosophic analogies are not with the older and rather simplistic versions of the mind/body problem, but, once again, with the newer phenomenological ones, where matter becomes Husserl's *hylé*, and whose most illustrious ontological expression is found in the Sartrean antithesis between the *en-soi* and the *pour-soi*, between facticity and transcendence.

Yet the basic problem of the idea of system remains even after we make abstraction of the purely material substratum: if substances no longer exist in the ordinary sense, then how can relationships function, of what and in what does value consist? The point is that for Saussure the ultimate atomic units, the basic components of the system, are somehow self-defining: inasmuch as they are themselves, whatever they may turn out to be, the basic units of meaning, it is logically impossible to go beyond them and to work up some more abstract definition in terms of which they would function as members of a class. This is what Saussure expresses in a striking phrase. 'The characteristics of the unit are at one with the unit itself. In language as in any semio-logical system, what distinguishes a sign is what constitutes it. Difference creates the characteristic (or the feature) in the same way that it creates value and the unit itself.'[11] Ogden and Richards are very clear on this point when they complain, 'The disadvantage of this account is . . . that the process of interpretation is included by definition in the sign!'[12]

What is meant by all this in a practical way is simply that where in a given language *ng* may be a distinctive feature, in another it will have no functional value whatsoever even if it does happen to occur, so that in this sense no generalizations are possible about the individual components of the linguistic process. Context is everything, and it is the feeling of the native speaker which remains in the last resort the test of presence or absence of distinctive features.

In another sense, of course, we continue to discuss these phenomena in abstract and general terms: the proof, if any were needed, lies in the very project of a 'general linguistics' itself. What has happened is that the mode of abstracting has shifted. Where, in earlier, substantialist thought, abstractions were basically names for the substances (i.e., the 'noun'), the new abstractions aim precisely at the meaning process itself, describe the way the mind distinguishes signs, are resumed in the two words 'identity' and 'difference', which clearly reflect a wholly different conceptual level than the old grammatical categories. (It is worth noting that where relatively substantial categories do survive in Saussure, as in a word like 'phoneme', at that point all kinds of polemics and false problems tend to arise.)

All this – the concept of system, the notion of language as a perception of identities and differences – is thus implicit in the initial distinction between synchrony and diachrony. It is therefore no real service to Saussure's thought to attempt to compromise, as many of his followers have done, by trying to show that this initial distinction is not really so marked, not really so absolute, as its terms might at first glance imply. The plain fact of the matter is that one cannot have it both ways. It was precisely the unrelieved starkness and intransigence of the initial antithesis that proved the most suggestive for future development, and on which the subsequent parts of the doctrine are founded. Once you have begun by separating diachronic from synchronic, in other words, you can never really put them back together again. If the opposition in the long run proves to be a false or misleading one, then the only way to suppress it is by throwing the entire discussion onto a higher dialectical plane, choosing a new starting point, utterly recasting the problems involved in new terms.

It would be wrong, however, to conclude that no diachronic development whatsoever is possible in the Saussurean model , and it is instructive in this light to examine the solution which Roman Jakobson has given to this dilemma in his 'Principes de phonologie historique'.[13] He there points out how a diachronic change – i.e., the loss of as certain sound – results in an imbalance in the synchronic system which must then be modified to adapt to the new state of things. Where before, let us say, the available entities *a, b, c, d* combined with each other in various combinations, now all those combinations must be redistributed among the remaining *a, b, d*. This model of successive, modified synchronic systems served as the basis for Jost Trier's lexicological studies, the most famous illustration of which is the thirteenth-century Middle High German displacement of the opposition *Kunst/List* (both of them subsumed under the general category *Wisheit*) by the idea of *Wizzen*, which replaces *List* but is no longer part of *Wisheit*, so that there now remain three terms in presence of each other rather than the earlier binary antithesis, and the dyad becomes a triad.[14]

Yet as rich and fascinating as such models of historical change may be, they are still not altogether satisfying conceptually. 'If a rupture of the system's equilibrium precedes a given mutation,' Jakobson tells us, 'and if there results from this mutation a suppression of the disequilibrium, then we have no difficulty discovering the mutation's function: its task is to *re-establish the equilibrium*. However, when a mutation reestablishes the equilibrium at one point in the system, it may break it at other points and provoke the need for a new mutation. Thus a whole series of stabilizing mutations are produced. . . .[15] The trouble is that the word 'mutation' is being used in two different ways, or, if you prefer, that there are not one, but two mutations in question here. The first is the initial diachronic change itself ('the rupture of the system's equilibrium'); the second is the manner in which the system is altered to absorb the change (it is for this alteration that Jakobson apparently reserves the term 'mutation'). Clearly, therefore, this solution only postpones the problem and shifts it to another level. No doubt the initial phonetic change is itself comprehensible in terms of historical events, migrations, or by reference to physiolinguistic laws of various kinds. But, as in our example from Dutch history, such explanation constitutes a borrowing from a different causal series, and the ultimate ground of the change still falls outside phonemics and into the realm of the diachronic and the purely phonetic, and remains, as such, meaningless in purely synchronic (Jakobson says 'teleological') terms. Thus, although the diachronic model implicit in Saussure, the theory of mutations, is capable of giving a complex and suggestive picture of historical change, it does not in the long run manage to solve the basic problem of reuniting diachrony together with synchrony *within a single system*. Indeed, the very word 'mutation', borrowed as it is from the older evolutionary model, stands as a symptom of the increasing contradictions of the Saussurean model when pushed to its outer limits.

That this contradiction is already present in Saussure himself can be judged from a close examination of one of his most famous images: language as a game of chess. The first extended comparison[16] is a straightforward one used to illustrate the idea of 'system'. In general the game itself, with its rules, is a synchronic system; its origins in Persia, or the replacement of a lost ivory chessman with a checker – none of these various external events has any bearing on synchrony. Only when the rules themselves are modified are we in the presence of a genuine synchronic event within the system. Yet in the second illustration[17] it is the successive positions of the pieces on the board, the successive moves, which are compared with the various synchronic moments of a language in evolution. Clearly, this analogy, satisfying historically because it makes of the successive synchronic states a kind of meaningful continuity, is not at all in the spirit of Saussurean thinking, for in the chess game, the rules remain the same throughout: whereas in the evolution of a language, it is precisely the rules that change. Saussure himself knows this so well that he indeed is ultimately embarrassed by his own analogy: 'In order for the chess game to resemble the game of language at every point, one would have to suppose an unconscious or unintelligent player' – a sentence we may reverse by saying that precisely the analogy as stated tends to imply that diachronic changes in language are somehow meaningful, 'teleological', in themselves, moves made by some meaningful force immanent in phonetic history.

II

The distinction between synchronic and diachronic is only the enabling act which permits Saussure's doctrine to come into being in the first place. No doubt it is ahistorical and undialectical in that it is based on a pure opposition, a set of absolute contraries, which can never be resolved into any kind of synthesis. Yet once we grant it as a starting point, and move inside the synchronic system itself, we find that matters are there quite different. Here the dominant opposition is that between the *langue*, which is to say the ensemble of linguistic possibilities or potentialities at any given moment, and the *parole*, or the individual act of speech, the individual and partial actualization of some of those potentialities. It is instructive to examine the comments of Ogden and Richards on this distinction, for nowhere else is the difference between the two modes of thought so strikingly illustrated:

> De Saussure does not pause at this point to ask himself what he is looking for, or whether there is any reason why there should be such a thing. He proceeds instead in a fashion familiar in the beginnings of all sciences, and concocts a suitable object – '*la langue*', the language, as opposed to speech. . . . Such an elaborate construction as *la langue* might, no doubt, be arrived at by some Method of Intensive Distraction analogous to that with which Dr Whitehead's name is associated, but as a guiding principle for a young science it is fantastic. Moreover, the same device of inventing verbal entities outside the range of possible investigation proved fatal to the theory of signs which followed.[18]

A passage of this kind makes clear that what Ogden and Richards really object to in Saussure is precisely the dialectical quality of his thought. The vice of Anglo-American empiricism lies indeed in its stubborn will to isolate the object in question from everything else, whether it be a material thing, an 'event' in Wittgenstein's sense, a word, a sentence, or a 'meaning'.[19] (This mode of thought, going back as it does to Locke, is, I believe, ultimately political in inspiration; and it would not be difficult, following the lines pursued by Lukács in *History and Class Consciousness* for rationalizing and universalizing thought, to show how such thinking is characterized by a turning away of the eyes, a preference for segments and isolated objects, as a means to avoid observation of those larger wholes and totalities which if they had to be seen would force the mind in the long run into uncomfortable social and political conclusions.)

Saussure's opposition is dialectical in that it involves a tension between a part and a whole either of which is inconceivable without the other: being relational rather than substantialist, it thus strikes directly at the kind of isolation of a single apparently free-standing element (such as a 'statement') foreseen by empirical thinking. But even the defense of Saussure's 'imaginary construct' must be dialectical, for clearly the initial logical problem is grounded, not in Saussure's terminology, but in the thing itself. It is precisely *because* language is the kind of peculiar entity that it is – nowhere all present at once, nowhere taking the form of an object or substance, and yet making its existence felt at every moment of our thought, in every act of speech – that the word which names it will not be able to function with the neatness of nouns that stand for physical objects. (The parallel with the concept of society is one which naturally imposes itself: Adorno has shown[20] how the antinomies in the idea of society result from the contradictions in the thing itself rather than from some inherent failure in conceptualization. In any case, this parallel is itself one of the reasons Saussure's model has in its turn seemed so suggestive to other disciplines.)

The opposition has another meaning as well, one which Ogden and Richards do not seem to have grasped, and which has crucial methodological implications. The new opposition is a different one from the first, although it uses the same terms and amounts to a different dimension of the same basic reality; and although such terminological uncertainty has often been attributed to the hesitations in Saussure's thought, to the various stages at which the collated courses and lectures were given, and the unfinished, imperfectly systematic nature of this posthumous doctrine, I myself tend rather to attribute it to the relational character of his work in general. As we have seen above, the definition of the basic units of language – word, sentence, sign, phoneme, syntagma – is much less important than the grasping of relationship in a given concrete case. This is not to say that Saussure's thought dissolves into the unverifiable like an Empsonian ambiguity, but rather that its precisions hold only for the specific contexts under examination. In this sense, I do not think that the unfinished character of his work was accidental; he never could have finished it in any traditional sense: in this, as in so much else, in his modesty of personal bearing and the immeasurable range of the work he proposed himself, resembling Mallarmé.

The relationship of part to whole reflects an older logical model, that of the organism, which is no longer useful in the solving of the new kinds of problems posed by the peculiar nature of language. Thus the new form of the opposition will have as its function the untangling from one another of various heterogeneous systems within language itself. The *parole*, for instance, the individual act of speech, is irrelevant for Saussure's science not only to the degree that it is always, and of necessity, incomplete, but also insofar as it is the locus of individual difference, of individual personality and style. To see the relationship of *parole* to *langue* as member to class, however, or as part to whole, as physical event to physical law, would be to reintroduce the positivistic models of the Neo-Grammarians which it had precisely been Saussure's intention to replace.

His solution to this dilemma is ingenious: one may call it situational, or even phenomenological, in that it takes into account the concrete structure of speech as a 'circuit of discourse', as a relationship between two speakers. It is this circuit which we ordinarily forget, when common sense suggests that the relationship of *langue* to *parole* is something inside ourselves, in the individual consciousness, a relationship between the immediate sentence I happen to have pronounced, and my power to construct sentences, my interiorized store of linguistic forms in general. Yet it is possible to break the circuit of discourse in a different place and to come up with a more methodologically suggestive model. This is the originality of Saussure, who separates the *parole* of the speaker from the *langue* of the person who understands him, for whom *parole* is the active, *langue* the passive dimension of speech, for whom indeed, as the Soviet linguist Smirnitsky has perceived,[21] *langue* is not so much the power to speak as it is the power to understand speech. Thus, at one stroke, all purely articulatory matters, all questions of local accent, mispronunciation, personal style, are eliminated from the new object under consideration, becoming themselves problems for a different science, that of the *parole*. The study of the *langue* remains concrete, for we can investigate it by testing the limits and characteristic forms of any native speaker's understanding; yet the investigation is now no longer complicated by the presence of some particular object (like an individual sentence) to which it would stand as a physical law to its experimental manifestation.[22]

The theoretical advantages of this new model can be measured if we compare it to what seems to have been its source in the sociology of Durkheim.[23] Not only does the latter's insistence on the representational nature of social facts strongly resemble Saussure's notion of signs (to be examined shortly); but the very thrust of Durkheim's thought, in its attempt to separate out the personal and individual from the objective and social, is quite consistent with the Saussurean distinction between *langue* and *parole* which we have just been examining. Only Durkheim, in order to assure a methodological foundation for his research, is led to posit the existence of a collective consciousness of some kind which underlies the collective representations, just as the individual consciousness does for the individual ones. Clearly this hypothetical entity merits the kind of criticism we have seen Ogden and Richards mete out to Saussure, in its suggestion of an organic group existence of some kind. But note that where Durkheim must have recourse to an imaginary collective substance, the very peculiarity of Saussure's object, which is the circuit of discourse, permits him to escape any such substantialist illusion, even as a methodological hypothesis. The objection of Ogden and Richards is inappropriate in Saussure's case, for the very construction of his model excludes consideration of any 'collective mind'[24] and indeed forces the attention in wholly different and unrelated directions. It is for this reason also, I think, that the Saussurean model has become more useful for social scientists than that of Durkheim, whose false problems it permits them to avoid.

It is instructive to gauge the originality of this model against yet another projection, namely that which we find in literature, where the application of the idea of the circuit of speech in 'Folklore as a particular type of artistic creation' by Jakobson and Bogatyrev yields instructively different results from Sartre's analysis of the role of the public in *What Is Literature?* For Sartre, the other term of the circuit of discourse, the public, is implicit in the writer himself, and follows logically from the choices of material and the stylistic formulations which are the acts of his own solitude. This is not a psychological identification; or, rather, Sartre's analysis takes place on a level which excludes psychology as such, for it merely shows how a certain selection of material, involving a lengthy presentation of certain things and only the most schematic references to others, as though they were already immediately intelligible to his audience, is in itself a selection of the readership, as a group possessing certain social characteristics, certain familiarities, certain types of knowledge. His illustration is black literature, which will clearly vary in style and tone as it is addressed to the in-group itself, or to white people, to whom so many allusions, so much that is unfamiliar, has first to be explained. Thus the model of Sartre is a relatively individualistic and Kantian one, in which the nature of the individual's relationship to groups outside or to society can be determined by internal analysis of the degree to which his own attitudes and ideas constitute a kind of universality.

Jakobson and Bogatyrev, on the other hand, follow the Saussurean model in their investigation of the relationship of individual creation and individual style to those collective and anonymous objects which are folk tales. No doubt everything in the folk tale originates with the individual, just as all sound changes must; but this necessary fact of invention in the first place is somehow the least essential characteristic of folk literature. For the tale does not really become a folk tale, given the oral diffusion of this literature, with its obvious dependence on word of mouth circulation, until the moment when it has been accepted by the listeners who retain it and pass it on. Thus the crucial moment for the folk tale is not that of the *parole*, that of its invention or creation (as in middle-class art), but that of the *langue*; and we may say that no matter how individualistic may be its origin, it is always anonymous or collective in essence: in Jakobsonian terminology, the individuality of the folk-tale is a redundant feature, its anonymity a distinctive one.

Yet in spite of the suggestiveness of this new distinction between *langue* and *parole*, it is clear that the problem of the relationship of part to whole will return in it in one form or another, if only in the relationship between my understanding of an individual sentence and my power to understand in general. In other words, it is now necessary to go more deeply into the concrete ways in which the *langue* is articulated into a system.

III

We may find a first clue to the nature of these articulations by once more contrasting the terminology of Ogden and Richards with Saussure's equivalents. Where the former, as semanticists, are concerned with words as symbols, the latter is insistent on the definition of language as a system of signs. It is perhaps difficult at first glance for a layman to understand the immense fortune which this Saussurean term has known, not only among linguists, but in other projections as well. Once again, however, the quality of the innovation is clear only against the background of that which is being changed by it.

Saussure's definition of the sign runs as follows: 'The linguistic sign unites, not a thing and a name, but a concept and an acoustic image,'[25] the latter terms being then replaced by a new set, the 'signifié' and the 'signifiant', the signified and the signifier. The point is made further that the sign is wholly arbitrary, that its meaning rests entirely on social convention and acceptation and that it has no 'natural' fitness in and of itself.[26]

Thus, the very construction of the concept of a sign allows us as it were to read backwards through it the various earlier theories it was designed to replace. For one thing, it clearly strikes down the most archaic language theory of all, one still occasionally revived by poets, that of the indissoluble link between words and things, which is to say the apprehension of language as names and naming.

There can no longer be any question of such an intrinsic relationship once the utterly arbitrary character of language has been
made clear. Far more fruitful from the poetic point of view, is the
reversal of this older doctrine by Mallarmé, for whom poetry comes
into being, not as an attempt to restore the old Adamic names, but
rather in reaction against this arbitrary quality of language and as
an attempt to 'motivate' that which in its origin was wholly 'un-
motivated':

> Les langues imparfaites en cela que plusieurs, manque la
> suprême: penser étant écrire sans accessoires, ni chuchote-
> ment mais tacite encore l'immortelle parole, la diversité, sur
> terre, des idiomes empêche personne de proférer les mots qui,
> sinon se trouveraient, par une frappe unique, elle-même
> matériellement la vérité. Cette prohibition sévit expresse, dans
> la nature (on s'y bute avec un sourire) que ne vaille de raison
> pour se considérer Dieu; mais, sur l'heure, tourné à de l'esth-
> étique, mon sens regrette que le discours défaille à exprimer
> les objets par des touches y répondant en coloris ou en allure,
> lesquelles existent dans l'instrument de la voix, parmi les
> langages et quelquefois chez un. A côté d'*ombre*, opaque,
> *ténèbres* se fonce peu; quelle déception, devant la perversité
> conférant à *jour* comme à *nuit*, contradictoirement, des tim-
> bres obscur ici, là clair. Le souhait d'un terme de splendeur
> brillant, ou qu'il s'éteigne, inverse; quant à des alternatives
> lumineuses simples – *Seulement*, sachons *n'existerait pas le
> vers*: lui philosophiquement rémunère le défaut des langues,
> complément supérieur.[27]

Thus the doctrine of the arbitrariness of the sign eliminates the
myth of a natural language. At the same time it serves to throw
psychological considerations of language onto a different plane as
well: for now what distinguishes human beings is no longer that
relatively specialized skill or endowment which is the power to
speak, but rather the more general power to create signs; and with
this, the royal road from linguistics to anthropology is thrown
open.

But there is still more: the force of the Anglo-American terminology, of the word 'symbol', was to direct our attention towards the
relationship between words and their objects or referents in the real
world. Indeed, the very word 'symbol' implies that the relationship
between word and thing is not an arbitrary one at all, that there is
some basic fitness in the initial association. It follows that for such a

viewpoint the most basic task of linguistic investigation consists in a one-to-one, sentence-by-sentence search for referents, and in the purification from language of non-referential terms and purely verbal constructs. The bent or twist of this model leads straight to Basic English, common language philosophy, and semantics as an organized discipline. Such an approach underestimates the weight of sheer historical convention and inertia in language at the same time that it overestimates the importance of 'lack of communication' and of the so-called language barrier in human events.

Saussure, on the other hand, is deflected by his very terminology from the whole question of the ultimate referents of the linguistic sign. The lines of flight of his system are lateral, from one sign to another, rather than frontal, from word to thing, a movement already absorbed and interiorized in the sign itself as the movement from the signifier to the signified. Thus, implicitly, the terminology of the sign tends to affirm the internal coherence and comprehensibility, the autonomy, of the system of signs itself, rather than the constant movement outside the symbol-system towards the things symbolized which we find in Ogden and Richards. Just as the latter implies semantics as its ultimate field of study, so the former points ahead to semiology as its ultimate fulfillment.

The philosophical suggestion behind all this is that it is not so much the individual word or sentence that 'stands for' or 'reflects' the individual object or event in the real world, but rather that the entire system of signs, the entire field of the *langue*, lies parallel to reality itself; that it is the totality of systematic language, in other words, which is analogous to whatever organized structures exist in the world of reality, and that our understanding proceeds from one whole or *Gestalt* to the other, rather than on a one-to-one basis. But, of course, it is enough to present the problem in these terms, for the whole notion of reality itself to become suddenly problematical; and indeed, for semiology, the latter is either a formless chaos of which one cannot even speak in the first place, or else it is already, in itself, a series of various interlocking systems – nonverbal as well as verbal – of signs.

IV

We must now determine the manner in which the individual signs are related among each other, for it is this mode of relationship which will make up the linguistic system as a whole. The starting point must clearly be the realm of sounds, the material dimension of language. But if we remember the distinction insisted on both by Saussure and his spiritual contemporaries in the Slavic world – that between 'pure' sounds and acoustic images, between measurable but meaningless sonorities and those which organize themselves into a kind of perceptual pattern for us – then the way in which to pose the problem is given. At what point do sounds become acoustical images? What does it take for phonetic matter to be transformed into a phonemic organization or system?

Thus posed, the question contains its own answer, for the shift involved is indeed a perceptual one, and presupposes an abandonment of an atomistic, empirical perception of an isolated thing-in-itself, a sound-object that has no connection with anything else, for a relational type of perception, something in the order of the *Gestalt* perception of form against field, or the dialectical tension between part and whole. Yet the latter formulations are not the appropriate ones in this case, for it is the relationship to the opposite rather than to the whole which marks this kind of organization.

The acoustic image of signifier is made up of a series of differential or distinctive features. Our perception of a given phoneme is a differential perception, which is to say that we cannot identify a word as a singular masculine noun without at the same time apprehending it as *not* being a plural, or a feminine word, or an adjective. This type of simultaneously identifying and differentiating awareness holds true all the way down to the smallest meaningful units of the word, namely the phonemes and their particular distinctive features.

Thus language perception follows in its operation the Hegelian law that determination is negation; but it is perhaps Sartre's distinction between internal and external negations which makes its specificity clearest. External negation obtains in analytical thought, and in the world of physical objects juxtaposed side by side. Thus, to say that a table is not a giraffe is to say something true, but non-essential, which affects neither the being of the table nor that of the giraffe, which in other words does not really contribute to the definition of either. But human reality is governed by the internal negation; so that the fact that I am not an engineer, or a Chinese, or a sixty-year-old, says something that touches me profoundly in my very being. So with language: each sound stands in a relationship of internal negation to the other elements of its system.

One may characterize the peculiar reality of language by saying that for it the concepts of difference, distinction, and opposition, which in other fields of thought do not always imply each other, here fall together and are all one and the same. The movement of

Saussure's thought may perhaps be articulated as follows: language is not an object, not a substance, but rather a value: thus language is a perception of identity. But in language the perception of identity is the same as the perception of difference; thus every linguistic perception holds in its mind at the same time an awareness of its own opposite.

Although distinctive features can attain combinations of great complexity, the most basic form they can take is that of a series of binary oppositions. The simplest form of such oppositions, and at the same time the most profoundly dialectical, is a tension between presence and absence, between positive and negative (or zero) signs, in which one of the two terms of the binary opposition 'is apprehended as positively having a certain feature while the other is apprehended as deprived of the feature in question'.[28] Here most clearly the difference between phonemic and phonetic perception is demonstrated: for the first, nothing is present at all (in other words, the non-Russian-speaker listening to Russian is not even aware of what might have been present in the way of sounds); for the second, a determinate absence is heard, is felt. What is at stake is the difference between not-being itself and absence as a *Gestalt* organized around some central emptiness.

Perhaps for the layman nothing illustrates the dependence of the mind on such binary oppositions so well as the apparent exception, in which our differential perceptions click on and off in the void. Thus, by thinking the words 'fish' and 'sheep' rapidly over, first in the singular and then in the plural, the mind can be felt instinctively to work up a feeling of opposition where none is physically or materially present.

Saussure's idea of the system has known its most complete practical application in the science of phonemics, particularly in the works of Trubetskoy and Jakobson. At the same time, one must point out that the more specialized a field of investigation becomes, the more a general linguistics risks breaking into separate and unrelated units, and the more endangered becomes Saussure's insistence on the unity of language as a phenomenon. We may say this in another way by pointing out that there is a difference between this type of binary opposition, and what ordinarily passes under the name of opposition in dialectical thought and which would be more properly described as a contradiction. The former is a static antithesis; it does not lead out of itself as does the latter. In this sense one may wonder whether a system can be generated out of what remain discrete pairs, whether it can become anything but, in the Jakobsonian terminology, a 'bundle' of pairs, an additive grouping of oppositions under the sign of eternal negation. Indeed, I believe that the static structure of the binary opposition is merely another form taken, within the system, by the initial antithesis which was Saussure's starting point, and which here returns, reinteriorized, to set a limit on the dynamism for which it was in the beginning responsible.

v

But there is yet another aspect of Saussure's description of the system which we have not yet taken into account. The level now described is no longer that of the individual sounds and sound patterns but rather the larger dimension of what in traditional grammar used to be called syntax, that of the word and the sentence. This older terminology is, of course, no longer adequate, since, as we have seen, it presupposes fixed units of measurement, substantialist concepts of stable entities, which neither correspond to the fluid nature of language nor offer a purely formal structure through which the latter may be revealed. But just as we were able before to characterize the mode of perception (identity and difference) of the units we no longer felt able to define in themselves, so now, in the necessary absence of any adequate definition of the sentence or of the parts of speech, we are still able to characterize their way of being together, the forms their combinations take.

For Saussure, the signs or units of meaning tend to form two different general kinds of relationships: the syntagmatic and the associative (which, for symmetry and following the glossematicians, we may call the paradigmatic). The syntagma is a horizontal grouping, a succession of meaning-units or words in time. The sentence is therefore one form which the syntagma can take, and in it the relationships governing the units are references backwards and forwards in time. Thus the verb 'reflects' refers us back to a subject, at the same time that it anticipates an ultimate object as well; in an uninflected language like English, a noun tends to imply for the mind the imminence of a verb.

At the same time, however, the word 'reflects' carries in itself another, we might call it a vertical, dimension. For it makes us think of the other words with which we associate it, the noun 'reflection' for instance, and any other words formed on the same stem; the verb 'deflect' and any other words rhyming with it or having a similar internal organization; and hosts of other associations as innumerable, indeed, as are the types of sentence or syntagma that might be formed around the verb taken as a horizontal entity.

We recognize here once again, in disguised form, the primary Saussurean distinction between the diachronic (the temporally successive, horizontal dimension) and the synchronic (the simultaneous and systematically organized vertical one). And as in the *Cours de linguistique générale* as a whole, so also in this particular problem of the priority of the two modes of relationship, it is clear that Saussure's bias is for the synchronic, for the associative or paradigmatic, as against the diachronic or the syntagmatic. The logical priority of the former is already implicit in the model; for it seems clear that the only way the mind can feel the verbal, syntagmatic function of a word like 'reflects' is to bear within itself paradigms of the sentence as a whole, to have already learned, by the associative chain, the verbal function and operation in general.

The syntagmatic dimension, in other words, looks like a primary phenomenon only when we examine its individual units separately; then they seem to be organized successively in time according to some mode of temporal perception. In reality, however, we never perceive them separately: the 'verb' is always felt to be part of a larger unity, which is the syntagma itself, and which now, since it is no longer a series of units but rather a unity of its own, is reabsorbed into associative thought and understood through its resemblance to other syntagmata.

What is involved is the basic distinction between contiguity and similarity, the two basic principles of the association of ideas already implicit in the classic discussions of Locke, Hume, and Kant. Such distinctions are classificatory ones, and aim ultimately at the discovery and formulation of absolute mental laws, of the ultimate patterns and categories according to which the mind, and indeed the brain, work.

In any case, it seems to me that if the theory of binary organization reflected the initial starting point of Saussure's thought formally, as the act of creating an opposition, the present distinction between associative and syntagmatic modes reflects the content of that initial opposition, which, at first outside the system and permitting it to come into being, is now reinteriorized and recurs within the synchronic domain itself. Now it becomes problematical to what degree the object of study is the thought pattern of the linguist himself, rather than that of language, and we here more clearly perceive the moment in which the originality of Saussure's point of departure returns to limit his results: for that initial repudiation of history, which at the very outset resulted in an inability to absorb change into the system as anything but a meaningless and contingent datum, is now reproduced, at the very heart of the system itself, as an inability to deal with syntax as such.

Such are the distinctive features of Saussure's doctrine as a whole, and with the completion of this rapid sketch we take leave of official linguistics. Is it necessary to add that our attitude towards this material is of a wholly different type than that of the linguist himself? Where the latter is intent on the referent, on the object named by the various Saussurean theories, our own interest has been the coherence of the system as a whole in its own right, and its suggestiveness as a model or analogy for other modes of thinking. The linguists have gone on to work Saussure's system through to its logical conclusions, and indeed, with Chomsky, to reverse it, proposing a new linguistic model altogether. We, however, will henceforth be concerned with the afterlife of the original theory in other realms of knowledge, and in particular with its liberating influence, as model and analogy, in the areas of literary criticism, anthropology, and ultimately of philosophy itself.

NOTES

1 Ferdinand de Saussure, *Cours de linguistique générale* (Paris, 1965, third edition), p. 157.
2 Quoted by Milka Ivić, *Trends in Linguistics* (The Hague, 1965), p. 61.
3 Quoted in E. Buyssens, 'La Linguistique synchronique de Saussure', *Cahiers Ferdinand de Saussure* XVIII (1961), pp. 17–33.
4 Jean Paulhan, *La Preuve par l'étymologie* (Paris, 1953), p. 12.
5 See Pieter Geyl, 'The National State and the Writers of Netherlands History', in *Debates with Historians* (London, 1955), pp. 179–97.
6 Letter to Antoine Meillet, 4 January 1894, *Cahiers Ferdinand de Saussure* XXI (1964), p. 93.
7 Quoted in Emile Benveniste, *Problèmes de linguistique générale* (Paris, 1966), p. 39.
8 Saussure, *Cours de linguistique générale*, p. 149.
9 Ibid., p. 166.
10 See Ivić, *Trends in Linguistics*, pp. 97–100.
11 Saussure, *Cours de linguistique générale*, p. 168.
12 C. K. Ogden and I. A. Richards, *The Meaning of Meaning* (London, 1960), p. 5, n. 2.
13 Reprinted in N. S. Troubetskoy, *Principes/ de phonologie* (Paris, 1964).
14 See Ivić, *Trends in Linguistics*, pp. 196–7 and Maurice Leroy, *Les grands courants de la linguistique moderne* (Paris, 1966), pp. 166–7. Since the classic introductory essay to this work is unavailable in

translation, I append some extracts. The opening paragraph, on his method: 'No spoken word is as isolated in the consciousness of its speaker and listener as its phonetic isolation might lead one to conclude. Every word we pronounce carries its own conceptual opposite within it. More than that. Of the totality of conceptual relationships which throng forward at the pronunciation of a given word, that of the contrary or conceptual opposite is only one, and not even the most important. Beside it, above it, a host of other words arise which are conceptually more or less closely related to the one which has been spoken. These are its conceptual family. They constitute among themselves and with the word just spoken an articulated whole, a structure which we may call a word-field or a field of linguistic signs. . . .' (p. 1).

And the following, on the problems of diachrony: 'Such a method does not constitute a denial of history and development. It would be wrong to give Being the priority over Becoming simply in reaction against the excessive domination of historicism in modern thought. The requirement of ever more exact and scientific approximation to the eternal stream of Becoming remains in force, only the question arises how we may unite the examination of fields with that of Becoming itself. If the structure of a field is visible only in the pure being of a motionless state of speech (or one conceived as motionless), if only linguistic and conceptual groups and the interdependence of meanings are to be considered, then history can come into being only as the comparison of static moments, as a description that moves discontinuously from one cross-section to another, ever taking as its object the total field, ever comparing it to earlier and later configurations of the same object. It would depend on the density of the juxtaposed cross-sections to what degree one could ultimately approximate the actual stream of Becoming itself. That real time can never actually be conceptualized in itself is a defect which this method shares with every other one, even with the purely historical method that finds its starting point in the individual word, so that it cannot honestly serve as a reproach. . . .' Jost Trier, *Der deutsche Wortschatz im Sinnbezirk des Verstandes* (Heidelberg, 1931), p. 13.

15 In Troubetskoy, *Principes de phonologie*, p. 334. The notion of a mutation may, however, itself be considered contemporaneous with Saussure's concept of synchrony, for it did not gain currency until its rediscovery by de Vries in 1900 (see Gertrude Himmelfarb, *Darwin and the Darwinian Revolution* (New York, 1959), pp. 268ff).

16 Saussure, *Cours de linguistique générale*, p. 43.

17 Ibid., pp. 125–6.

18 Ogden and Richards, *The Meaning of Meaning*, pp. 4–5.

19 See, for instance, Ludwig Wittgenstein, *The Blue and Brown Books* (New York, 1958), p. 42: 'The sentence has sense only as a member of a system of language; as one expression within a calculus. Now we are tempted to imagine this calculus, as it were, as a permanent background to every sentence we say, and to think that, although the

sentence as written on a piece of paper or spoken stands isolated, in the mental act of thinking the calculus is there – all in a lump. The mental act seems to perform in a miraculous way what could not be performed by any act of manipulating symbols. Now when the temptation to think that in some sense the whole calculus must be present at the same time vanishes, there is no more point in *postulating* the existence of a peculiar kind of mental act alongside of our expression.'

20 T. W. Adorno, 'Society', *Salmagundi*, 10–11 (Fall 1969–Winter 1970), pp. 144–53.

21 N. Slusareva, 'Quelques considérations des linguistes soviétiques à propos des idées de F. de Saussure', *Cahiers Ferdinand de Saussure* xx (1963), pp. 23–41.

22 The originality of Chomsky's transformational grammar seems to derive from a reversal of the Saussurean model, a kind of negation of the negation in which the linguistic mechanisms are relocated back in the *parole* or individual act of speech. See Chomsky's comments on Saussure: 'He was thus quite unable to come to grips with the recursive processes underlying sentence formation as a matter of *parole* rather than *langue*.' (Noam Chomsky, *Current Issues in Linguistic Theory* (The Hague, 1964), p. 23.)

23 See W. Doroszewski, 'Quelques remarques sur les rapports de la sociologie et de la linguistique: Durkheim et F. de Saussure', *Journal de psychologie* xxx (1933), pp. 82–91; and also Robert Godel, *Les Sources manuscrites du cours de linguistique générale de F. de Saussure* (Geneva, 1957), Addendum, p. 282.

24 It is only fair to point out that the expression 'esprit collectif' does figure twice in the *Cours de linguistique générale* (pp. 19 and 140), where it has however no real philosophic significance.

25 Saussure, *Cours de linguistique générale*, p. 98.

26 The word 'natural' is not Saussure's but was added by his editors (see Leroy, *Les grands courants de la linguistique moderne*, pp. 106–8). Émile Benveniste's influential critique of Saussure's doctrine of the 'arbitrary' nature of the sign (in 'La Nature du signe linguistique', *Problèmes de linguistique générale*, pp. 49–55) has always seemed to me both true and misleading. The relationship is of course not arbitrary for the speaker but rather for the analyst himself; and the doctrine of the arbitrary character of the signifier seems to me to play an essential enabling and functional role in Structuralism in general (witness Derrida's doctrine of the trace!), one which, as we shall see below, corresponds roughly to the hypothesis of the unconscious in psychoanalysis.

27 Stéphane Mallarmé, *Oeuvres complètes* (Paris, 1945), pp. 363–4.

28 Troubetskoy, *Principes de phonologie*, p. xxvii.

10

The Epistemology of Metaphor*

PAUL DE MAN

Metaphors, tropes, and figural language in general have been a perennial problem and, at times, a recognized source of embarrassment for philosophical discourse and, by extension, for all discursive uses of language including historiography and literary analysis. It appears that philosophy either has to give up its own constitutive claim to rigor in order to come to terms with the figurality of its language or that it has to free itself from figuration altogether. And if the latter is considered impossible, philosophy could at least learn to control figuration by keeping it, so to speak, in its place, by delimiting the boundaries of its influence and thus restricting the epistemological damage that it may cause. This attempt stands behind recurrent efforts to map out the distinctions between philosophical, scientific, theological, and poetic discourse and informs such institutional questions as the departmental structure of schools and universities. It also pertains to the received ideas about differences between various schools of philosophical thought, about philosophical periods and traditions, as well as about the possibility of writing a history of philosophy or of literature. Thus, it is customary to assume that the common sense of empirical British philosophy owes much of its superiority over certain continental metaphysical excesses to its ability to circumscribe, as its own style and decorum demonstrate, the potentially disruptive power of rhetoric. 'The Skywriters,' says a contemporary literary critic (with tongue in cheek) in a recent polemical article, 'march under the banner of Hegel and Continental Philosophy, while the Common Sense school [of literary criticism] is content with no philosophy, unless it be that of Locke and a homespun organicism.'[1]

The mention of Locke in this context certainly does not come unexpected since Locke's attitude toward language, and especially toward the rhetorical dimensions of language, can be considered as

*Paul De Man, 'The Epistemology of Metaphor', reprinted from *Critical Inquiry 5* (Autumn, 1978), pp. 13–30, by permission © University of Chicago Press.

exemplary or, any rate, typical of an enlightened rhetorical self-discipline. At times it seems as if Locke would have liked nothing better than to be allowed to forget about language altogether, difficult as this may be in an essay having to do with understanding. Why would one have to concern oneself with language since the priority of experience over language is so obvious? 'I must confess then,' writes Locke in the *Essay Concerning Human Understanding*, 'that, when I first began this discourse of the understanding, and a good while after, I had not the least thought that any consideration of words was at all necessary to it.'[2] But, scrupulous and superb writer that he is, by the time he reaches book 3 of his treatise, he can no longer ignore the question:

> But when, having passed over the original and composition of our *ideas*, I began to examine the extent and certainty of our knowledge, I found it had so near a connexion with words that, unless their force and manner of signification were first well observed, there could be very little said clearly and pertinently concerning knowledge, which, being conversant about truth, had constantly to do with propositions. And though it terminated in things, yet it was, for the most part, so much by the intervention of words that they seemed scarce separable from our general knowledge. At least they interpose themselves so much between our understanding, and the truth which it would contemplate and apprehend that, like the *medium* through which visible objects pass, their obscurity and disorder does not seldom cast a mist before our eyes and impose upon our understandings. (Book 3, chapter 9, pp. 87–8.)

Neither is there any question about what it is in language that thus renders it nebulous and obfuscating: it is, in a very general sense, the figurative power of language. This power includes the possibility of using language seductively and misleadingly in discourses of persuasion as well as in such intertextual tropes as allusion, in which a complex play of substitutions and repetitions takes place between texts. The following passage is famous but always deserves extensive quotation:

> Since wit and fancy finds easier entertainment in the world than dry truth and real knowledge, *figurative speeches* and allusions in language will hardly be admitted as *an* imperfection or *abuse* of it. I confess, in discourses where we seek

rather pleasure and delight than information and improvement, such ornaments as are borrowed from them can scarce
pass for faults. But yet, if we would speak of things as they
are, we must allow that all the art of rhetoric, besides order
and clearness, all the artificial and figurative application of
words eloquence hath invented, are for nothing else but to
insinuate wrong *ideas*, move the passions, and thereby mis-
lead the judgement, and so indeed are perfect cheat; and
therefore however laudable or allowable oratory may render
them in harangues and popular addresses, they are certainly,
in all discourses that pretend to inform or instruct, wholly to
be avoided and, where truth and knowledge are concerned,
cannot but be thought a great fault either of the language or
person that makes use of them. What and how various they
are will be superfluous here to take notice, the books of
rhetoric which abound in the world will instruct those who
want to be informed; only I cannot but observe how little the
preservation and improvement of truth and knowledge is the
care and concern of mankind, since the arts of fallacy are
endowed and preferred. It is evident how much men love to
deceive and be decieved, since rhetoric, that powerful instrument of error and deceit, has its established professors, is
publicly taught, and has always been had in great reputation;
and I doubt not but it will be thought great boldness, if not
brutality, in me to have said thus much against it. *Eloquence*,
like the fair sex, has too prevailing beauties in it to suffer itself
ever to be spoken against. And it is in vain to find fault
with those arts of deceiving wherin men find pleasure to be
deceived. (Book 3, chapter 10, pp. 105–6.)

Nothing could be more eloquent than this denunciation of
eloquence. It is clear that rhetoric is something one can decorously
indulge in as long as one knows where it belongs. Like a woman,
which it resembles ('like the fair sex'), it is a fine thing as long as it is
kept in its proper place. Out of place, among the serious affairs of
men ('if we would speak of things as they are'), it is a disruptive
scandal – like the appearance of a real woman in a gentlemen's club
where it would only be tolerated as a picture, preferably naked (like
the image of Truth), framed and hung on the wall. There is little
epistemological risk in a flowery, witty passage about wit like this
one, except perhaps that it may be taken too seriously by dull-
witted subsequent readers. But when, on the next page, Locke
speaks of language as a 'conduit' that may 'corrupt the fountains of

knowledge which are in things themselves' and, even worse, 'break or stop the pipes whereby it is distributed to public use', then this language, not of poetic 'pipes and timbrels' but of a plumber's handyman, raises, by its all too graphic concreteness, questions of propriety. Such far-reaching assumptions are then made about the structure of the mind that one may wonder whether the metaphors illustrate a cognition or if the cognition is not perhaps shaped by the metaphors. And indeed, when Locke then develops his own theory of words and language, what he constructs turns out to be in fact a theory of tropes. Of course, he would be the last man in the world to realize and to acknowledge this. One has to read him, to some extent, against or regardless of his own explicit statements; one especially has to disregard the commonplaces about his philosophy that circulate as reliable currency in the intellectual histories of the Enlightenment. One has to pretend to read him ahistorically, the first and necessary condition if there is to be any expectation of ever arriving at a somewhat reliable history. That is to say, he has to be read not in terms of explicit statements (especially explicit statements about statements) but in terms of the rhetorical motions of his own text, which cannot be simply reduced to intentions or to identifiable facts.

Unlike such later instances as Warburton, Vico, or, of course, Herder, Locke's theory of language is remarkably free of what is now referred to as 'cratylic' delusions. The arbitrariness of the sign as signifier is clearly established by him, and his notion of language is frankly semantic rather than semiotic, a theory of signification as a substitution of words for 'ideas' (in a specific and pragmatic sense of the term) and not of the linguistic sign as an autonomous structure. 'Sounds have no natural connexion with our *ideas*, but have all their signification from the arbitrary imposition of men. . . .' Consequently, Locke's reflection on the use and abuse of words will not start from the words themselves, be it as material or as grammatical entities, but from their meaning. His taxonomy of words will therefore not occur, for example, in terms of parts of speech but will espouse his own previously formulated theory of ideas as subdivided in simple ideas, substances, and mixed modes,[3] best paraphrased in this order since the first two, unlike the third, pertain to entities that exist in nature.

On the level of simple ideas, there seem to be no semantic or epistemological problems since the nominal and the real essence of the species designated by the word coincide; since the idea is simple and undivided, there can in principle be no room for play or ambivalence between the word and the entity, or between property and essence. Yet this lack of differential play immediately leads to a far-reaching consequence: 'The *names of simple* ideas *are not capable of any definitions* . . . (book 3, chapter 4, p. 26). Indeed not, since definition involves distinction and is therefore no longer simple. Simple ideas are, therefore, in Locke's system, simple-minded; they are not the objects of understanding. The implication is clear but comes as something of a shock, for what would be more important to understand than single ideas, the cornerstones of our experience?

In fact, we discourse a great deal about simple ideas. Locke's first example is the term 'motion', and he is well aware of the extent to which metaphysical speculation, in the scholastic as well as in the more strictly Cartesian tradition, centers on the problem of the definition of motion. But nothing in this abundant literature could be elevated to the level of a definition that would answer the question: What is motion?

> Nor have the modern philosophers, who have endeavored to throw off the *jargon* of the Schools and speak intelligibly, much better succeeded in defining simple *ideas*, whether by explaining their causes or any otherwise. The *atomists*, who define motion to be a *passage from one place to another*, what do they more than put one synonymous word for another? For what is *passage* other than *motion*? And if they were asked what passage was, how would they better define it than by *motion*? For is it not at least as proper and significant to say *passage is a motion from one place to another* as to say *motion is a passage*, etc. This is to translate and not to define . . . (Book 3, chapter 4, p. 28.)

Locke's own 'passage' is bound to continue this perpetual motion that never moves beyond tautology: motion is a passage and passage is a translation; translation, once again, means motion, piles motion upon motion. It is no mere play of words that 'translate' is translated in German as '*übersetzen*' which itself translates the Greek '*meta phorein*' or metaphor. Metaphor gives itself the totality which it then claims to define, but it is in fact the tautology of its own position. The discourse of simple ideas is figural discourse or translation and, as such, creates the fallacious illusion of definition.

Locke's second example of a word for a simple idea is 'light'. He takes pains to explain that the word 'light' does not refer to the perception of light and that to understand the causal process by which light is produced and perceived is not at all the same as to understand light. In fact, to understand light is to be able to make this very distinction between the actual cause and the idea (or experience) of a perception, between aperception and perception. When we can do this, says Locke, then the *idea* is that which is *properly* light, and we come as close as we can come to the proper meaning of 'light'. To understand light as idea is to understand light properly. But the word 'idea' (*eide*), of course, itself means light, and to say that to understand light is to perceive the idea of light is to say that understanding is to see the light of light and is therefore itself light. The sentence: to understand the idea of light would then have to be translated as to light the light of light (*das Licht des Lichtes lichten*), and if this begins to sound like Heidegger's translations from the Pre-Socratics, it is not by chance. Etymons have a tendency to turn into the repetitive stutter of tautology. Just as the word 'passage' translates but fails to define motion, 'idea' translates but does not define light and, what is worse, 'understand' translates but does not define understanding. The first idea, the simple idea, is that of light in motion or figure, but the figure is not a *simple* idea but a delusion of light, of understanding, or of definition. This complication of the simple will run through the entire argument which is itself the motion of this complication (of motion).

Things indeed get more complex as one moves from simple ideas to substances. They can be considered in two perspectives: either as a collection of properties or as an essence which supports these properties as their ground. The example for the first model of a substance is 'gold', not unrelated, in some of its properties, to the solar light in motion. The structure of substances considered as a collection of properties upsets the convergence of nominal and real essences that made the utterer of simple ideas into something of a stuttering idiot but, at least from an epistemological point of view, a happy one. For one thing, properties are not just the idea of motion, they actually move and travel. One will find gold in the most unexpected places, for instance in the tail of peacock. 'I think all agree to make [gold] stand for a body of a certain yellow shining colour; which being the *idea* to which children have annexed that name, the shining yellow part of a peacock's tail is properly to them gold' (book 3, chapter 9, p. 85). The closer the description comes to that of metaphor, the more dependent Locke becomes on the use of the word 'properly'. Like the blind man who cannot understand the idea of light, the child who cannot tell the figural from the proper keeps recurring throughout eighteenth-century epistemology as barely disguised figures of our universal predicament. For not only are tropes, as their name implies, always on the move – more like quicksilver than like flowers or butterflies which one can at least hope to pin down and insert in a neat taxonomy – but they can disappear altogether, or at least appear to disappear. Gold not only has a color and a texture, but it is also soluble. 'For by what right is it that fusibility comes to be a part of the essence signified by the word *gold*, and solubility but a property of it? . . . That which I mean in this: that these being all but properties, depending on its real constitution, and nothing but powers either active or passive in reference to other bodies, no one has authority to determine the signification of the word *gold* (as referred to such a body existing in nature) . . .' (book 3, chapter 9, pp. 85–6). Properties, it seems, do not properly totalize, or, rather, they totalize in a haphazard and unreliable way. It is indeed not a question of ontology, of things as they are, but of authority, of things as they are decreed to be. And this authority cannot be vested in any authoritative body, for the free usage of ordinary language is carried, like the child, by wild figuration which will make a mockery of the most authoritarian academy. We have no way of defining, of policing, the boundaries that separate the name of one entity from the name of another; tropes are not just travellers, they tend to be smugglers and probably smugglers of stolen goods at that. What makes matters even worse is that there is no way of finding out whether they do so with criminal intent or not.

Perhaps the difficulty stems from a misconceived notion of the paradigm 'substance'. Instead of being considered as a collection, as a summation of properties, the accent should perhaps fall on the link that binds the properties together. Substances can be considered as the support, the ground of the properties (*hypokeimenon*). Here Locke's example will be 'man'; the question to be accounted for then becomes, What essence is the proper of man? The question in fact amounts to whether the proper, which is a linguistic notion, and the essence, which exists independently of linguistic mediation, can coincide. As the creature endowed with conceptual language, 'man' is indeed the entity, the place where this convergence is said to take place. The epistemological stakes are therefore higher in the case of the example 'man' than in the case of 'gold'. But so are the difficulties, for, in answer to the question 'What essence is the proper of man?' the tradition confronts us with two perhaps incompatible answers. Man can be defined in terms of his outward appearance (as in Plato: *animal implume bipes latis unguibus*) but also in terms of his inner soul or being.

For though the sound *man*, in its own nature, be as apt to signify a complex *idea* made up of animality and rationality, united in the same subject, as to signify any other combination: yet, used as a mark to stand for a sort of creatures we count of our own kind, perhaps the outward shape is as necessary to be taken into our complex *idea signified by the word man*, as any other we find in it . . . for it is the shape, as the leading quality, that seems more to determine that species than a faculty of reasoning, which appears not at first and in some never. (Book 3, chapter 11, p. 115.)

The problem is that of a necessary link between the two elements in a binary polarity, between 'inside' and 'outside', that is to say, by all accounts, that of metaphor as the figure of complementarity and correspondence. One now sees that this figure is not only ornamental and aesthetic but powerfully coercive since it generates, for example, the ethical pressure of such questions as 'to kill or not to kill'. 'And if this be not allowed to be so,' says Locke, 'I do not know how they can be excused from murder who kill monstrous births (as we call them) because of an unordinary shape, without knowing whether they have a rational soul or no, which can be no more discerned in a well-formed than ill-shaped infant as soon as born' (book 3, chapter 11, p. 115). The passage is, of course, primarily a mock argument, a hyperbolical example to unsettle the unquestioned assumption of definitional thought. Yet it has its own logic which will have to run its course. For how could anyone 'allow' something to be if it is not necessarily the case that it is? For it is not necessarily the case that the inner and the outer man are the same man, that is to say, are 'man' at all. The predicament (to kill or not to kill the monstrous birth) appears here in the guise of a purely logical argument. But not much further along in the *Essay*, what is 'only' an argument in book 3 becomes an ethically charged issue in book 4, chapter 4, which is entitled 'Of the Reality of Knowledge'.[4] The problem there under discussion is what to do with the 'changeling'; the simple-minded child so called because it would be natural for anyone to assume that this child has been substituted by mistake for his real offspring. The substitutive text of tropes now has extended to reality.

The well-shaped *changeling* is a man, has a rational soul, though it appear not: this is past doubt, say you. Make the ears a little longer and more pointed, and the nose a little flatter than ordinary, and then you begin to boggle; make the

face yet narrower, flatter, and longer, and then you are at a
stand; add still more and more of the likeness of a brute to it,
and let the head be perfectly that of some other animal, then
presently it is a *monster*, and it is demonstration with you that
it hath no rational soul and must be destroyed. Where now (I
ask) shall be the just measure, which the utmost bounds of
that shape that carries with it a rational soul? For since there
have been human *foetuses* produced, half-beast and half-man,
and others three parts one and one part the other, and so it is
possible they may be in all the variety of approaches to the
one or the other shape and may have several degrees of
mixture of the likeness of a man or a brute, I would gladly
know what are those precise lineaments which, according to
this hypothesis, are or are not capable of a rational soul to be
joined to them. What sort of outside is the certain sign that
there is or is not such an inhabitant within? (Book 4, chapter
4, p. 175.)

If we then are invited by Locke, in conclusion, to 'quit the common
notion of species and essences', this would reduce us to the mindless
stammer of simple ideas and make us into a philosophical 'changeling', with the unpleasant consequences that have just been conjec-
tured. As we move from the mere contiguity between words and
things in the case of simple ideas to the metaphorical correspondence of properties and essences in substances, the ethical tension
has considerably increased.

Only this tension could account for the curious choice of examples selected by Locke when he moves on to the uses and possible
abuses of language in mixed modes. His main examples are
manslaughter, incest, parricide, and adultery – when any non-
referential entity such as mermaid or unicorn would have done just
as well.[5] The full list of examples – 'motion', 'light', 'gold', 'man',
'manslaughter', 'parracide', 'adultery', 'incest' – sounds more like a
Greek tragedy than the enlightened moderation one tends to associate with the author of *On Government*. Once the reflection on the
figurality of language is started, there is no telling where it may
lead. Yet there is no way *not* to raise the question if there is to be
any understanding. The use and the abuse of language cannot be
separated from each other.

'Abuse' of language is, of course, itself the name of a trope:
catachresis. This is indeed how Locke describes mixed modes. They
are capable of inventing the most fantastic entities by dint of the
positional power inherent in language. They can dismember the

texture of reality and reassemble it in the most capricious of ways, pairing man with woman or human being with beast in the most unnatural shapes. Something monstrous lurks in the most innocent of catachreses: when one speaks of the legs of the table or the face of the mountain, catachresis is already turning into prosopopeia, and one begins to perceive a world of potential ghosts and monsters. By elaborating his theory of language as a motion from simple ideas to mixed modes, Locke has deployed the entire fan-shape or (to remain within light imagery) the entire spectrum or rainbow of tropological totalization, the anamorphosis of tropes which has to run its full course whenever one engages, however reluctantly or tentatively, the question of language as figure. In Locke, it began in the arbitrary, metonymic contiguity of word-sounds to their meanings, in which the word is a mere token in the service of the natural entity, and it concludes with the catachresis of mixed modes in which the word can be said to produce of and by itself the entity it signifies and that has no equivalence in nature. Locke condemns catachresis severely: 'he that hath *ideas* of substances disagreeing with the real existence of things, so far wants the materials of true knowledge in his understanding, and hath instead thereof *chimeras*. . . . He that thinks the name *centaur* stands for some real being, imposes on himself and mistakes words for things' (book 3, chapter 10, p. 104). But the condemnation, by Locke's own argument, now takes all language for its target, for at no point in the course of the demonstration can the empirical entity be sheltered from tropological defiguration. The ensuing situation is intolerable and makes the soothing conclusion of book 3, entitled 'Of the Remedies of the Foregoing Imperfections and Abuses (of Language)', into one of the least convincing sections of the *Essay*. One turns to the tradition engendered by Locke's work in the hope of finding some assistance out of the predicament.

I

Condillac's *Essai sur l'origine des connaissances humaines* constantly advertises, perhaps even exaggerates, its dependence on Locke's *Essay*. It contains at least two sections that explicitly deal with the question of language; in fact, its systematic commitment to a theory of mind that is in fact a theory of the sign makes it difficult to isolate any part of the treatise that is not modeled on a linguistic structure. Two sections, however, openly and explicitly deal with language: the chapter on the origins of language, 'Du langage et de la méthode', which makes up the second part of the *Essai*, and another section, 'Des abstractions' (part 1, section 5). From Rousseau to Michel Foucault, the former section (which elaborates the notion of '*langage d'action*') has received much attention. But the chapter on abstract terms also deals with language in a more inclusive way than its title would seem to indicate. It can be shown, though this is not my present purpose, that the subsequent chapters on '*langage d'action*' are a special case of the more inclusive model and history set up in this section. Read in conjunction with Locke's 'On Words', it allows for a wider perspective on the tropological structure of discourse.

At first sight, the brief chapter seems to deal with only one rather specialized use of language, that of conceptual abstractions. But 'abstractions' are defined from the start in a way that considerably expands the semantic field covered by the term. They come into being, says Condillac, 'by ceasing to think [*en cessant de penser*] of the properties by which things are distinguished in order to think only of those in which they agree [or correspond: the French word is *conviennent*] with each other'.[6] The structure of the process is once more precisely that of metaphor in its classical definition. Some 130 years later, Nietzsche will make the very same argument to show that a word such as 'leaf' [*Blatt*] is formed by 'making what is different equal [*Gleichsetzen des Nichtgleichen*]' and by 'arbitrarily dropping individual differences [*beliebiges Fallenlassen der individuellen Verschiedenheiten*]'.[7] And a few years after Condillac, Rousseau will make the same argument in his analysis of denomination in the second *Discourse*.[8] It is entirely legitimate to conclude that when Condillac uses the term 'abstraction', it can be 'translated' as metaphor or, if one agrees with the point that was made with reference to Locke about the self-totalizing transformation of all tropes, as trope. As soon as one is willing to be made aware of their epistemological implications, concepts are tropes and tropes concepts.

Condillac spells out these implications in what reads like the plot of a somewhat odd story. He implicitly acknowledges the generalized meaning of the term 'abstraction' by insisting that no discourse would be conceivable that does not make use of abstractions: '[abstractions] are certainly absolutely necessary [*elles sont sans doute absolument nécessaires*]' (section 2, p. 174). On the other hand, he cautions at once against the threat their seductive power constitutes for rational discourse: just as certainly as they are indispensable, they are necessarily defective or even corruptive – 'however corruptive [*vicieux*] this contradiction may be, it is nevertheless necessary' (section 6, p. 176). Worse still, abstractions are capable of infinite proliferation. They are like weeds, or like a cancer; once you have begun using a single one, they will crop up everywhere. They are said to be 'marvelously fecund' (section 7, p. 177), but there is something of Rappaccini's garden about them, something sinister about those vigorous plants that no gardener can do without nor keep in check. Even after their ambivalent nature has been analyzed on an advanced level of critical understanding, there is very little hope they can be mastered: 'I don't know if, after all that I have said, it will at last be possible to forego all these "realized" abstractions: many reasons make me fear the opposite is true' (section 12, p. 179).[9] The story is like the plot of a Gothic novel in which someone compulsively manufactures a monster on which he then becomes totally dependent and does not have the power to kill. Condillac (who after all went down in the anecdotal history of philosophy as the inventor of a mechanical statue able to smell roses) bears a close resemblance to Ann Radcliffe or Mary Shelley.

From the recognition of language as trope, one is led to the telling of a tale, to the narrative sequence I have just described. The temporal deployment of an initial complication, of a structural knot, indicates the close, though not necessarily complementary, relationship between trope and narrative, between knot and plot. If the referent of a narrative is indeed the tropological structure of its discourse, then the narrative will be the attempt to account for this fact. This is what happens in the most difficult, but also the most rewarding, section of Condillac's text.

Paragraph 6 starts out with a description of first or simple ideas in a manner reminiscent of Locke; the main stress is on ideas rather than on *first*, for Condillac stresses the conceptual aspect of all ideas, regardless of order. He contrasts a reality, which is presumably that of things in themselves, with what he calls, somewhat tautologically, 'a true reality [*une vraie réalité*]'. This true reality is not located in things but in the subject, which is also the mind as *our* mind (*notre esprit*). It is the result of an operation the mind performs upon entities, an aperception (*apercevoir en nous*) and not a perception. The language which describes this operation in Condillac's text is consistently, and more so than in Locke's, a language of mastery of the subject over entities: things become 'truly real' only by being appropriated and seized upon with all the etymological strength implied in *Begriff*, the German word for concept. To understand is to seize (*begreifen*) and not to let go of what one has thus taken hold of. Condillac says that impressions will be considered by the mind only if they are 'locked up [*renfer-*

mées]' in it. And as one moves from the personal subject '*nous*' to the grammatical subject of all the sentences '*notre esprit*' it becomes clear that this action of the mind is also the action of the subject.

Why does the subject have to behave in such a potentially violent and authoritarian way? The answer is clear: this is the only way in which it can constitute its own existence, its own ground. Entities, in themselves, are neither distinct nor defined; no one could say where one entity ends and where another begins. They are mere flux, 'modifications'. By considering itself as the place where this flux occurs, the mind stabilizes itself as the ground of the flux, the *lieu de passage* through which all reality has to pass: '. . . these "modifications" change and follow each other incessantly in [our mind's] being, which then appears to itself as a ground [*un certain fond*] that remains forever the same' (section 6, p. 176). The terminology is a mixture of Locke and Descartes (or Malebranche). The subject seen as a compulsive stabilization that cannot be separated from an unsettling action upon reality performed by this very subject is a version of a Cartesian *cogito* – except that the function performed in Descartes's second and third 'Meditation' by hyperbolic doubt becomes here, in the tradition of Locke, a function of empirical perception. Hyperbolic doubt, a mental act in Descartes, now extends to the entire field of empirical experience.

The self-constitutive act of the subject has, in Condillac (as in Descartes), a much more openly reflexive status that in Locke. The verb most frequently associated with the subject 'mind' is 'to reflect [*réfléchir*]': 'since our mind is too limited to *reflect* . . .'; 'the mind cannot *reflect* on nothing. . . .' To reflect is an analytical act that distinguishes differences and articulates reality; these articulations are called abstractions, and they would have to include any conceivable act of denomination or predication. This is also the point at which an act of ontological legerdemain enters the system: the subject (or mind) depends on something which is not itself, here called 'modifications' ('certain sensations of light, color, etc., or certain operations of the soul . . .'), in order to be at all, but these modifications are themselves as devoid of being as the mind – cut off from its differentiating action, they are nothing. As the other of the mind, they are devoid of being, but by recognizing them as similar to itself in this negative attribute, the mind sees them, as in a specular reflection, as being both itself and not itself at the same time. The mind 'is' to the extent that it 'is like' its other in its inability to be. The attribute of being is dependent on the assertion of a similarity which is illusory, since it operates at a stage that precedes the constitution of entities.

How will these experiences, taken abstractly, or separately, from the entity [the mind] to which they belong and to which they correspond only to the extent that they are locked up in it, how will these experiences become the object of the mind? Because the mind persists in considering them as if they were entities in themselves. . . . The mind contradicts itself. On the one hand, it considers these experiences without any relation to its own being, and then they are nothing at all; on the other hand, because nothingness cannot be comprehended, it considers them as if they were something, and persists in giving them the same reality with which it at first perceived them, although this reality can no longer correspond to them.

Being and identity are the result of a resemblance which is not in things but posited by an act of the mind which, as such, can only be verbal. And since to be verbal, in this context, means to allow substitutions based on illusory resemblances (the determining illusion being that of a shared negativity) then mind, or subject, is the central metaphor, the metaphor or metaphors. The power of the tropes, which Locke sensed in a diffuse way, is here condensed in the key metaphor of the subject as mind. What was a general and implicit theory of tropes in Locke becomes in Condillac a more specific theory or metaphor. Locke's third personal narrative about things in the world becomes here the autobiographical discourse of the subject. Different as the two narratives may be, they are still the allegory of the same tropological aporia. It now also becomes more directly threatening since we, as subjects, are explicitly inscribed within the narrative. One feels more than ever compelled to turn elsewhere for assistance and, staying in the same philosophical tradition, Kant would seem to be the obvious place.

II

Kant rarely discusses the question of tropes and rhetoric directly but comes closest in a passage from the *Critique of Judgment* that deals with the distinction between schemata and symbolic language. He starts out from the term 'hypotyposis' which, used, as he does, in a very inclusive way, designates what, after Peirce, one might call the iconic element in a representation. Hypotyposis makes present to the senses something which is not within their reach, not just because it does not happen to be there but because it consists, in whole or in part, of elements too abstract for sensory representation. The figure most closely akin to hypotyposis is that of prosopopeia; in its most restricted sense, prosopopeia makes accessible to the senses, in this case the ear, a voice which is out of earshot because it is no longer alive. In its most inclusive and also its etymological sense, it designates the very process of figuration as giving face to what is devoid of it.

In section 59 of the *Critique of Judgment* ('Of the Beautiful as a Symbol of Public Morality'), Kant is primarily concerned with the distinction between schematic and symbolic hypotyposes. He begins by objecting to the improper use of the term 'symbolic' for what we still call today *symbolic* logic. Mathematical symbols used in algorithms are in fact semiotic indices. They should not be called symbols because 'they contain nothing that belongs to the representation [*Anschauung*] of the object.' There is no relationship whatever between their iconic properties and those of the object, if it has any. Things are different in the case of a genuine hypotyposis. A relationship exists but it can differ in kind. In the case of schemata, which are objects of the mind (*Verstand*), the corresponding aperception is *a priori*, as would be the case, presumably, for a triangle or any other geometrical shape. In the case of symbols, which are objects of reason (*Vernunft*) comparable to Condillac's abstractions, no sensory representation would be appropriate (*angemessen*, i.e., sharing a common ratio), but such a similarity is 'understood' to exist by analogy (*unterlegt*, which could be translated by saying that an 'underlying' similarity is created between the symbol and the thing symbolized). Kant then illustrates at some length the distinction between an actual and an analogical resemblance. In an analogy, the sensory properties of the *analogon* are not the same as those of the original, but they function according to a similar formal principle. For example, an enlightened state will be symbolized by an organic body in which part and whole relate in a free and harmonious way, whereas a tyranny will be properly symbolized by a machine such as a treadmill. Everyone understands that the state *is* not a body or a machine but that it functions like one, and that this function is conveyed more economically by the symbol than by lengthy abstract explanations. We seem at last to have come closer to controlling the tropes. This has become possible because there seem to be, for Kant, tropes that are epistemologically reliable. The denominative noun 'triangle', in geometry, is a trope, a hypotyposis which allows for the representation of an abstraction by a substitutive figure, yet the representation is fully rational and '*angemessen*'. By showing that one can move from the symbolic order, which is indeed imprecise and therefore exists in the restrictive mode of the *only* (the word '*blosz*' recurs four times in the passage), to the rational precision of the schemata, while remaining within the general tropological field defined by the hypotyposis, the epistemological threat that disturbed Locke and Condillac seems to have been laid to rest. The solution is dependent, however, on a decisive either/or distinction between symbolic and schematic language. Representation is either schematic or symbolic (*entweder Schemata oder Symbole*) and the critical mind can decisively distinguish between both.

At this point in the argument, Kant interrupts his exposition for a digression on the all-too-often-overlooked prevalence of figures in philosophical discourse, an important question which 'would deserve a more exhaustive examination'. But this is not the time nor place for such an examination – which he, in fact, never undertook in a systematic way. The terminology of philosophers is full of metaphors. Kant cites several examples, all of them having to do with grounding and standing: 'ground [*Grund*]', 'to depend [*abhängen*]', 'to follow from [*fliessen*]' and, with a reference to Locke, 'substance'. All these hypotyposes are symbolic and not schematic, which means that they are not reliable from an epistemological point of view. They are 'a mere translation [*Übertragung*] from a reflexion upon a represented object into an entirely different concept, to which *perhaps* no representation could ever correspond [*dem* vielleicht *nie eine Anschauung direkt korrespondieren kann*]' [emphasis mine]. The appearance of the word 'perhaps' in this sentence, even though it sounds like a casual side remark, is most surprising. It has been the point of the entire argument that we know for certain whether a representation directly corresponds to a given concept or not. But the 'perhaps' raises the question of how such a decision can be made, whether it is in the nature of things or whether it is merely assumed (*unterlegt*). Is the distinction between schemata and symbol itself *a priori* or is it merely 'understood' in the hope of having it perform the definitional work that cannot be performed directly? From the moment this decision can be said, even in passing, to be 'perhaps' possible, the theory of a schematic hypotyposis loses much of its power of conviction. Things happen, in the text, as if Kant had not at first been aware of the metaphorical status of his own term '*unterlegen*' when he used it in support of a crucial distinction between two modes of support. The considerations about the possible danger of uncontrolled metaphors, focused on the cognate figures of support, ground, and so forth, reawaken the hidden uncertainty about the rigor of a distinction that does not hold if the language in which it is stated reintroduces the elements of indetermination it sets out to eliminate. For it is not obvious that the iconic representation that can be used to illustrate a rational concept is indeed a figure. In the second *Discourse*, Rousseau confronts a similar question[10] but concludes that the particular representation that any general concept necessarily engenders is a psychological epiphenomenon related to memory and to the imagination and not a conceptual trope that belongs to the realm of language and knowledge. What Kant calls a schematic hypotyposis would then not be a cognition at all but a mere mnemotechnic device, the equivalent of the mathematical sign in the area of the psychology of perception rather than of language. In that case, the sentence which emphasizes that the decision as to whether a representation can be adequate to its object is of the order of the 'perhaps', is more rigorous than the either/or distinction, despite or rather because of its vagueness. If the distinction between *a priori* and symbolic judgements can only be stated by means of metaphors that are themselves symbolic, then Locke's and Condillac's difficulties have not been overcome. Not only our knowledge of God, to which the passage under examination returns at the end, but the knowledge of knowledge is then bound to remain symbolic. He who takes it for schematic and gives it the attributes of predictability and transcendental authority that pertain to the objective reality of entities unmediated by language is guilty of reification (the opposite figure of prosopopeia); and he who thinks that the symbolic can be considered a stable property of language, that language, in other words, is purely symbolic and nothing else, is guilty of aestheticism – 'whereby nothing is seen as it is, not in practice either'.

In all three instances, we started out from a relatively self-assured attempt to control tropes by merely acknowledging their existence and circumscribing their impact. Locke thought that all we needed to banish rhetoric from the councils of the philosophers was an ethical determination of high seriousness coupled with an alert eye for interlopers. Condillac limits the discussion to the sphere of abstractions, a part of language that appeals neither to poets nor to empirical philosophers; he seems to claim that all will be well if we abstain from taking these cumbersome terms for realities. Kant seems to think that the entire question lacks urgency and that tidy critical housekeeping can rehabilitate rhetoric and make it epistemologically respectable. But, in each case, it turns out to be impossible to maintain a clear line of distinction between rhetoric, abstraction, symbol, and all other forms of language. In each case, the resulting undecidability is due to the asymmetry of the binary model that opposes the figural to the proper meaning of the figure. The ensuing anxiety surfaces obliquely in the case of Locke and Condillac; it would take a much longer demonstration to indicate that Kant's critical philosophy is disturbed by similar hesitations, but the somewhat surprising theological allusion at the end of our passage may be a symptom. The manifest effacement of such anxiety-traces in the texts is much less important, however, than the contradictory structures of the texts themselves, as it is brought out by a reading willing to take their own rhetoric into consideration.

III

As Kant just taught us, when things run the risk of becoming too difficult, it is better to postpone the far-reaching consequences of an observation for a later occasion. My main point stresses the futility of trying to repress the rhetorical structure of texts in the name of uncritically preconceived text models such as transcendental tele-ologies or, at the other end of the spectrum, mere codes. The existence of literary codes is not in question, only their claim to represent a general and exhaustive textual model. Literary codes are subcodes of a system, rhetoric, that is not itself a code. For rhetoric cannot be isolated from its epistemological function however negative this function may be. It is absurd to ask whether a code is true or false but impossible to bracket this question when tropes are involved – and this always seems to be the case. When-ever the question is repressed, tropological patterns re-enter the system in the guise of such formal categories as polarity, recurrence, normative economy, or in such grammatical tropes as negation and interrogation. They are always again totalizing systems that try to ignore the disfiguring power of figuration. It does not take a good semiotician long to discover that he is in fact a rhetorician in disguise.

The implications of these parallel arguments for literary history and for literary aesthetics are equally controversial. An historian caught in received models of periodization may find it absurd to read texts that belong to the Enlightenment as if one were reading Nietzsche's *Über Wahrheit und Lüge im aussermoralischen Sinn* or Jacques Derrida's *La Mythologie blanche*. But if we assume, just for the sake of argument, that these same historians would concede that Locke, Condillac, and Kant can be read as we have here read them, then they would have to conclude that our own literary modernity has re-established contact with a 'true' Enlightenment that remained hidden from us by a nineteenth-century Romantic and realist epistemology that asserted a reliable rhetoric of the subject or of representation. A continuous line could then be said to extent from Locke to Rousseau to Kant and to Nietzsche, a line from which Fichte and Hegel, among others, would very definitely be excluded. But are we so certain that we know how to read Fichte and Hegel in the properly rhetorical manner? Since we assume that it is possible to co-ordinate Locke and Nietzsche by claiming that their similarly ambivalent attitudes toward rhetoric have been systematically overlooked, there is no reason to assume *a priori* that a similar argument could not be made with regard to Fichte or Hegel. It would have to be a very different argument, of course, especially in the case of Hegel, but it is not inconceivable that it can be made. And if one accepts, again merely for the sake of argument, that syntagmatic narratives are part of the same system as paradigmatic tropes (though not necessarily comlementary), then the possibility arises that temporal articulations, such as narratives or histories, are a correlative of rhetoric and not the reverse. One would then have to conceive of a rhetoric of history prior to attempting a history of rhetoric or of literature or of literary criticism. Rhetoric, however, is not in itself an historical but an epistemological discipline. This may well account for the fact that patterns of historical periodization are at the same time so productive as heuristic devices yet so demonstratively aberrant. They are one way of access, among others, to the tropological structure of literary texts and, as such, they necessarily undermine their own authority.

Finally, our argument suggests that the relationship and the distinction between literature and philosophy cannot be made in terms of a distinction between aesthetic and epistemological categories. All philosophy is condemned, to the extent that it is dependent upon figuration, to be literary and, as the depository of this very problem, all literature is to some extent philosophical. The apparent symmetry of these statements is not as reassuring as it sounds since what seems to bring literature and philosophy together is, as in Condillac's argument about mind and object, a shared lack of identity or specificity.

Contrary to common belief, literature is not the place where the unstable epistemology of metaphor is suspended by aesthetic pleasure, although this attempt is a constitutive moment of its system. It is rather the place where the possible convergence of rigor and pleasure is shown to be a delusion. The consequences of this lead to the difficult question whether the entire semantic, semiological, and performative field of language can be said to be covered by tropological models, a question which can only be raised after the proliferating and disruptive power of figural language has been fully recognized.

NOTES

1 Geoffrey Hartman, 'The Recognition Scene of Criticism', *Critical Inquiry* 4 (Winter, 1977), p. 409.

2 John Locke, *An Essay Concerning Human Understanding*, ed. John W. Yolton, 2 vols. (London and New York, 1961), 2: book 2, chapter 9, p. 87. All further references will appear in the text.

3 An apparent exception to this principle would be book 3, chapter 7, where Locke pleads for the necessity of studying particles of speech as well as nouns. But the assimilation of particles to 'some action or insinuation of the mind' of which they are 'tracks' reintegrates them at once into the theory of ideas (p. 73).

4 Examples used in logical arguments have a distressing way of lingering on with a life of their own. I suppose no reader of J. L. Austin's paper, 'On Excuses', has ever been quite able to forget the 'case' of the inmate in an insane asylum parboiled to death by a careless guard.

5 In the general treatment of mixed modes, Locke lists 'adultery' and 'incest' (p. 34). In the subsequent discussion of the abuses of language, he returns to the problem of mixed modes and gives as examples manslaughter, murder, and parricide, as well as the legal term often associated with manslaughter, 'chance medley'. Mermaids and unicorns are mentioned in another context in book 3, chapter 3, p. 25.

6 E. B. de Condillac, *Essai sur l'origine des connaissances humaines* (1746), ed. Charles Porset (Paris, 1973), book 1, section 2, p. 194. All further references will be from book 1, chapter 5, and will appear in the text; here and elsewhere, my translation.

7 Friedrich Nietzsche, *Über Wahrheit und Lüge im aussermoralischen Sinn*, ed. Karl Schlecta, 3 vols. (München, 1969), 3: p. 313.

8 J.-J. Rousseau, *Deuxième Discours (Sur l'origine et les fondements de l'inégalité)*, in Jean Starobinskied, *Oeuvres complètes*, 5 vols. (Paris, 1964), 3: p. 148.

9 The French word '*réaliser*' is used in a precise technical sense. The abstractions are mistaken for 'real' objects in the same way Locke speaks of the danger of mistaking words for things. The reason for this error becomes clear later in the text.

10 Rousseau, *Deuxième Discours*, p. 150.

11
Literary Production as a Politicizing Practice

MICHAEL J. SHAPIRO

THE PERSISTENCE OF THE KANTIAN QUESTION

And things, what is the correct attitude to adopt toward things?

Samuel Beckett, *The Unnamable*.

Beckett's question evokes a substantial part of the history of philosophy, for in one form or another, the familiar philosophical systems since Plato give this question a privileged place. For present purposes we can begin with Kant, because his reorientation of the question still resounds in the depths of the philosophy of the social sciences. According to Heidegger, who inherited but then recast Kant's question, Kant turned the question, 'what is a thing?' into the question, 'who is man?'[1] Kant's new formulation was liberating inasmuch as it frees us from the tyranny of the object. Rather than looking for meaning in the world of things, Kant turned the gaze inward, positing the structure of human consciousness as the formal, *a priori* condition for our apprehension of things. But Kant's reorientation remained quarantined within the relentless grammatical metaphor of Enlightenment philosophy. Knowing remained for Kant a relationship between subjects and objects.

The Kantian revolution thus attacked one privilege, the privilege of the object and substituted another, the privilege of the subject of consciousness. This privileging of the subject of consciousness is wholly compatible with the practice of science as it is understood within the still dominant grammatical trope of Enlightenment thinking. What Kant neglected, and what science as a practice brackets are the social practices or ways of being in the world that constitute man in any historical period. In focusing on the fact of objectification, the crafting of the things as something shaped by the subject's consciousness, Kant ignored the prior condition of the subject. As Heidegger put it, 'He [Kant] does not inquire into and determine in its own essence that which encounters us prior to objectification into an object of experience.'[2]

Heidegger viewed Kant's approach to the subject as a form of idolatry inasmuch as a fixed, conceptualizing subject fixes objects in a permanence that belies their predication on human practices. As soon as we reject Kant's subject and replace it with an historically, socially and linguistically embedded one, we need an approach to understanding that rejects representation as the mode of relation between the subject and the world of objects. Science, to the extent that it rests on a neo-Kantian subject, rests on an idolatrous metaphysics, objectifying phenomena on the basis of a model of certainty of representation. Opposing this model of science, Heidegger states, 'Science always encounters only what *its* kind of representation has admitted beforehand as an object possible for science.'[3]

What science neglects, according to Heidegger, is what he called the 'ground plan', that which is embedded in the practices of an age and which links and constitutes man, determining being in such a profound way that it gives rise to the questions of research. It is illusion, therefore, that things give themselves to thought.[4] Science as calculation and research has, in the modern age, rested on an epistemology of representation connected to a notion of man as a being with a viewpoint. According to this metaphysics of science, then, man is at the centre of the problem of meaning, regarding his viewpoint as wholly conceptual or voluntary.[5] But this viewpoint, like the world that it beholds, harks back to something prior in the structure of human existence. Heidegger displaces the ego subject, the subject of consciousness from the centre of knowledge and puts in its place an historical, changing subject constituted as a set of skills and/or practices, including (and especially) linguistic practices which 'house' human existence.[6] The philosophy of modern science (and that of the social sciences) remains within the metaphysics of the subject of consciousness whose relationship to objects is one of representation and who thereby construes all experience as mediated by intentional content (this perspective includes the 'perceptions' of empiricism and the 'ideational acts of consciousness' of phenomenology). Heidegger pointed out that a science of any kind, even one that operates within such a cognitivist self-understanding, inevitably expresses the background practices from which it arises and which gives it its predicates. As he put it, '. . . the sciences still speak about the Being of beings in the unavoidable suppositions of their regional categories. They just don't say so.'[7]

Heidegger can be read in a way that provides a new set of

orienting questions in response to Beckett's query about how to adopt a correct attitude toward things. Within Heidegger's perspective, 'things' are associated with historical processes, processes which constitute a subject whose identity emerges within a set of practices. The problem of human understanding in historical, political, or other modes is, within this perspective, provided with a new domain of projection, the processes and conditions of possibility that give rise to the world of human subjects and 'things' which express man's changing conditions of existence. For purposes of inquiry this projection proceeds within the frame of the 'how' rather than the traditional 'why' and 'what' questions of scientific inquiry. The question that becomes relevant involves the various mechanisms for the production of both who man is and what his world is, and this issue of how man comes about and how the world is produced can be construed traditionally – within the genre of historical analysis of traditions of practice – or speculatively – within the poetic or literary genre, a genre which, in its modern realization, foregrounds its own practices to both show how such practices produce the person and the world and to show how alternative subjects and things can be produced.

THE PROBLEM OF GENRE AND POLITICAL UNDERSTANDING

> . . .she applied for his reasons. Now though he had none, as we have seen, that he could offer, yet he had armed himself so well at this point, forewarned by the study that he had made of his catspaw mind, that he was able to pelt her there and then with the best diligent enquiry could provide: Greek and Roman reasons, Sturm und Drang reasons, reasons metaphysical, aesthetic, erotic, anterotic and chemical, Empedocles of Agrigentum and John of the Cross reasons, in short all but the true reasons, which did not exist, at least not for purposes of conversation.
>
> Samuel Beckett, *More Pricks Than Kicks.*

Heidegger's attack on the primacy of the 'viewpoint' and his alternative, which understands the world of persons and things as produced by prior practices embedded in language in general and speech practices in particular, provides an opening for the old 'humanistic' genres that were, until recently, proscribed by those interested in the human sciences. If science, at one end of the continuum, has traditionally operated with a view of language as a transparent tool, an instrument devoid of ideational or otherwise practical content, literature, at the other end has seen language as opaque, and has accordingly seen its charge as one of penetrating the opacity in order to recover the commitments and practices contained in language. An increasing interest in the literary genre by social scientists has led to modes of social and political analysis which both cast the social processes under investigation within aesthetically oriented imagery and foreground the language of inquiry itself. Describing this shift to aesthetic imagery in social theory, Clifford Geertz has recently noted that it involves, 'the casting of social theory in terms more familiar to the gamester and aesthetician than to plummers and engineers', and that it reflects an appreciation that language is necessarily opaque rather than clear, that its figures, its grammatical and rhetorical tropes (whether they are live and explicit or dead and therefore naturalized) constitute persons and objects rather than simply adding extra means of expression.[8]

With this altered view of language and the complicity between the literary genre and social/political thought come the discursive objects that guide literary endeavours. Perhaps the most notable contribution that literary theory has lent to social and political understanding is the idea of the text. Not surprisingly, when the text metaphor is used in social and political theory such that, for example, human action, events and situations become 'readable', there develops an impetus to see that reading within a politicized language. Accordingly, modern thinkers have seen that reading as 'polemical' (Ricoeur),[9] 'rhetorical' (Gadamer),[10] 'violent' (Foucault)[11] or, more directly, 'political' (Jameson, who argues that the political perspective is, 'the absolute horizon for all reading and all interpretation').[12] Moreover, the structure, form or construction of the text itself becomes understood with political imagery, e.g., Foucault's notion of the 'discursive practice' – the combination of discursively engendered objects, concepts, enunciative modes and themes – which creates privileged places for some subjects who are constituted as agents of knowledge while others are relegated to silence, and Jameson's notion of the 'ideology of form', the sedimented, archaic practices sequestered in the style of the text which coexist in both social and artistic practices and harbour structures of domination.

The more radical views of reading – e.g., Foucault's and Jameson's – contrast with more traditional hermeneutic approaches in a way that addresses fundamental issues about how interpretation relates to social and political understanding. At the more traditional end of the continuum is Gadamer, who has recently tried to politicize his notion of hermeneutic understanding by conceiving of the process of understanding as involving embeddedness in a practical, politically oriented conversation. To the extent that he politicizes his approach, it is by problematizing the stance or perspective of the interpreter such that hermeneutics becomes a kind of practical activity that involves both the situatedness and activity of the interpreter.[13] But Gadamer's approach maintains the privilege of genre in that he holds to the Aristotelian notion that there is a being intrinsic to that which is being interpreted. For example, in speaking of legal interpretation, he remarks that there is a nature or being to the legal text that plays a directing role in producing the principles of legal interpretation.[14] Given this respect for genre – the legal in this case – Gadamer's politics of interpretation is ultimately more collaborationist than partisan.

Foucault, by contrast, holds to a radical partisanship model of political interpretation and, accordingly, takes a firm stand against the hermeneutic tradition. Employing his violence imagery for reading the text of human events, Foucault has substituted genealogy for the traditional hermeneutics:[15]

> ... if interpretation is the violent or surreptitious appropriation of a system of rules, which in itself has no essential meaning, in order to impose a direction, to bend it to a new will, to force its participation in a different game, and to subject it to secondary rules, then the development of humanity is a series of interpretations. The role of genealogy is to record its history: the history of the concept of liberty or of the ascetic life; as they stand for the emergence of different interpretations, they must be made to appear as events on the stage of historical process.

A genre for Foucault is an historical production to be described rather than embraced. His lack of respect for the integrity of the genre of the text emerges in his historical investigations in which he consistently replaces the discourses of various professions and disciplines – e.g., the medical, penal, and psychiatric – or even the discourse of state power with a discourse that emphasizes control, subjugation and domination. For example, he discusses 'rights' (a discursive entity produced within the modern nation state) not within a legalistic discourse, which emphasizes the role of rights in establishing legal access to privileges, but in terms of the dimensions of power that have been generated by the development of this kind of human identity – persons with 'rights'. As he puts it, 'Right should be viewed, I believe, not in terms of a legitimacy to be established, but in terms of the methods of subjugation that it instigates.'[16]

This approach to knowledge, which essentially rewrites prevailing discursive formulation, is an increasingly familiar mode of post-structuralist analysis, and is sometimes referred to as 'textualism'. In its more radical formulations, textualism is clearly accompanied by a hyper-politicizing consciousness. Before elaborating the implications of modern textualism for purposes of understanding its politicizing tendencies, however, one needs a view of the political that articulates well with textualist philosophical conceits. This view of the political, immanent in his later studies, is characterized by Foucault as an 'analytics of power'.

THE DOMAIN OF THE POLITICAL

> But what they were most determined for me to swallow
> was my fellow-creatures. In this they were without mercy.
> I remember little or nothing of these lectures. I cannot have
> understood a great deal. But I seem to have retained certain
> descriptions, in spite of myself.
>
>   Samuel Beckett, *The Unnamable*.

There is an intimate connection between Foucault's anti-hermeneutic method and the political understanding toward which his investigations move. Rather than looking for meanings in the texts of various social practices – he argues that there is no meaning in the sense of an intent or cognized human goal beneath the surface of various sets of statements of a discipline or practice – he looks at what the statements *are* and why *they* rather than some other statements, conveying power for other kinds of subjects, are there. The 'are' of the statements thus amounts to the statements' strategic significance, the resources they deliver to kinds of subjects.[17] Moving from his concern with the statement as a resource to the genealogical understanding of the modern age, Foucault focuses his analyses on how practices which are immanent in the discourses they form produce us as kinds of subject/objects – e.g., with such individualized identities as the 'onanistic child', the 'hysterical woman' or collective identities such as the 'population'.[18] For example, speaking of the new discursive object, the 'population', he notes:

> One of the great innovations in the techniques of power in the eighteenth century was the emergence of 'population' as an economic and political problem: population as wealth, population as manpower or labour capacity, population balanced between its own growth and the resources it commanded. Governments perceived that they were not dealing simply with subjects, or even with a 'people', but with a 'population'.

Foucault is not asking what a population is in the sense of looking for the referent of the term. It is not the traditional problem of definition, but rather the issue of how population as an idea grew out of the practices of an age and found its way into discourse as a technique of power. For Foucault, the prevailing discourses, those which harbour subjects and objects linked to the structure of domination, are productions of power rather than mere descriptions. Seeing power as immanent in what we *are* in any age, Foucault orients his analyses toward the processes by which humans are turned into subjects. For example, speaking about the proliferation of penalties in the history of penology, he notes that we must read power not as a mechanism to halt illegal actions but as a force that differentiates illegalities, creates multiple identities, and places a surcharge on them.[19] This politicizing approach of Foucault is not merely an interest in description or even the critique of ideology, for he contends that by capturing the way that power makes us what we are, the way that it creates various discursive identities that are both collective in scope (the 'population') or individualizing (the citizen with 'rights'), we can resist power.[20]

> Maybe the target nowadays is not to discover what we are but to refuse what we are. We have to imagine and to build up what we could be to get rid of this kind of political 'double bind', which is the simultaneous individualization and totalization of modern power structures.

But first, we must be able to 'read' power, and Foucault's pedagogy has been to teach us how to conduct this reading. When we begin to approach the understanding of the political domain within the context of reading (dis-covering power) and writing (the process by which power is inscribed and thus the mode of deconstructing power by the rendering of alternative discursivities) we legitimize, as political pedagogy, the range of thinking produced by modern textualists who have turned the reading/writing imagery into an anti-authority epistemology. The pedagogy that has come out of Foucault's reading and writing is not exhortation, for there is none of the conventional signs of the pedagogic discourse. The genre is more literary. Foucault politicizes through his writing, through the production of rhetorical and grammatical tropes that dislodge privileged subjects, objects, events and modes of conduct. By writing in a figural language antagonistic to conventional discourse, Foucault shows how power resides in the production of discursive entities that become fetishized and parade around as literal descriptions. His violent imagery for creating subjects, using, for example, 'the penetrating of bodies' for the traditional ideas of socialization and training replaces pacifying figures which collaborate with existing power, with a figure that challenges it. Foucault's writing, in short, serves to disinherit the powers that enjoy an abundance bequeathed in prevailing discursive practices.

TEXTUALISM

I would like to think that I occupy the center, but nothing is less certain.

Samuel Beckett, *The Unnamable.*

Contemporary textualism has to be given credit for providing vehicles for moving interests ordinarily exclusively associated with literary studies into a central place in social and political theory. A consideration of the wide variety of orientations that fit within the general idea of textualism would interrupt the plot. For present purposes it suffices to highlight those positions that generate the most access from literary concerns to the domain of the political. The first and perhaps most significant contribution relates to Beckett's remark above about the location of the subject. While phenomenology as an interpretive strategy displaces the authority of the object and replaces it with the intentional consciousness of the subject, textualism denies epistemic privilege to both the object or referent of a statement and to the subject/author of the statement. What replaces the referent and the intentional consciousness of the subject is the text.

This displacement of the speaker/writer as a locus of possible meanings is indebted to Saussurean linguistics. Departing from traditions which locate meaning in a relationship between a name and its referent, Saussure developed the position that meaning emerges from the relational structure of signifiers. With this as background, the textualist sees language not as a set of symbols whose function is exhausted by the process of representation but as a set of signs which are part of a system for generating objects. Textualism, with its emphasis on the sign promotes two views relevant to the argument here. The first is that there is a value system embedded in the process of signification which is responsible for producing the objects, acts, and events we entertain in our conscious awareness. In speaking of the emphasis on signs rather than symbols, Jameson has expressed this contribution of textualists well.[21]

> Its privileged object is ... seen as the unconscious value system or system of representations which orders social life at any of its levels, and against which the individual, social acts and events take place and become comprehensible.

The second contribution of textualism is that it privileges literature as the mode of discourse in which the process of signification that produces the world of subjects and objects can be experienced. Because the style of literary discourse is such as to foreground its own productive mechanisms (at least in the case of certain modernistic forms of writing), objects and subjects are seen as productions rather than as natural phenomena, lying outside of human productive activity. Roland Barthes is among the most prominent of those who have promoted the literary genre as one that avoids the naturalizing of the sign and literary criticism as a denaturalizing analytic practice. This position emerged in his early work in which he construed mythologies as unself-reflective forms of writing which naturalize phenomena and thereby hide political content in signs. In his later writings he emphasized the way language naturalizes to the extent that it is treated as a transparent tool instead of a producer of a content.[22] Against such a naturalization of the sign, Barthes promoted a view of the text as a tissue of codes, separate fragments that invoke different readings, subjects and values but never provide a single, definitive reading for the text as a whole[23] It is the tissue of codes, however, rather than the author that controls the text, for the text is run by 'the order of the signifier', no one discourse or code can claim privilege with respect to founding an appropriate interpretation.[24]

Jacques Derrida has also exalted the pluralistic nature of the text, and has produced vigorous critiques of attempts to locate an originating consciousness behind the production of a text or referent. The development of a text involves for Derrida a process of writing which he characterizes as a free play of signification, understandable more from the inner structure that it exercises than the series of referents that it produces. Given this play of signification in the text, Derrida, in his analyses of the writings of various thinkers, invariably tries to show how their texts harbour something that eludes them, elements of mythology or commitment in the opacity of the text which the writer misses because of treating the discourse as a neutral channel from intention to objective.[25] For example, in his analysis of Benveniste's attempt to show how the language-thought distinction is invalid, Derrida shows that Benveniste makes use of something he is attempting to dismiss. The language that Benveniste uses to deal with the thought-language relationship already contains the acceptance of a rigid distinction between the two (e.g., the concept of 'category', which depends for its meaning on a language-thought distinction).[26] There is no way, according to Derrida, to get outside of language to assess thoughts or consciousness. Accordingly, one cannot juxtapose language to something else which is thought to be less mediated or interpreted. Consciousness is manifested *in* writing; it is not an originating event to be expressed once it is generated.

In accord with this view Derrida develops a model of the Freudian subject *as* memory rather than a person with a consciousness who *has* a memory.[27] Memory is constructed, by Derrida, as a series of writings and erasures. Consciousness is thus a form of writing, and a given subject is constituted by the selections made from the systems and process of differences in the play of signification. Similar to Derrida's notion that the Freudian subject *is* memory, is Lacan's suggestion that it is inappropriate to say that a ego is frustrated. Rather, for Lacan, the ego is constituted *as* frustration.[28] But, and this is central to how his analysis privileges writing, Derrida sees the development of memory as constituted by fiction, by imaginative discourse (contrary to the classic Platonic distinction between reality and imagination) whereas Lacan sees fiction as a clue to truth, a truth that lies outside of the realities produced by fictionalizing.[29]

Because, for Derrida, in thinking one is always writing, creating a text, the approach to interpreting the written text, like the text itself, is shot through with non-present meaning, a meaning that eludes the writer. Self-consciousness, for the writer/interpreter, then, can only consist in a thoroughgoing suspicion of the language produced (and thus the thinking and reality produced) in the process of interpretation. Accordingly, after deconstructing the thought of Levi-Strauss, Derrida produces a brief meditation on his own writing and acknowledges his figurative use of childrearing.[30]

Derrida shows, with this gesture, the pervasiveness of textuality, the inability to get outside the production of the world as a form of writing. This position, the political significance of which Derrida never seems to approach directly, relates importantly to the domain of the political nevertheless. By exposing the density of commitment in writing (or thinking *as* writing) that eludes the consciousness of the author/writer, Derrida shows how the conclusions in social and political thought are engendered in the writing process. The production of a text *and* its interpretation can thus be seen as ideologizing processes.

What Derrida does not provide is a purchase on the world, a way of thinking/writing that foregrounds the political dimension. Foucault's strategy has been to characterize the kind of subject/object that has been scripted by modernity and to denote the collective groupings (disciplines, agencies, etc.) that have disproportionately contributed to that scripting. As Said has put it, Foucault allows the text to, 'assume its affiliation with institutions, offices, agencies, classes, academies, corporations, groups, guilds, ideologically defined parties, and professions'.[31] Foucault's historical and political problematics guide his readings while Derrida remains self-conscious about his own mythologizing but does not render that self as one that sides with those subjects he imagines as participating in a world resistant to subjugation and domination as does Foucault.

THE PROBLEM OF THE FETISH

> The creation of the world did not take place once and for all time, but takes place every day. Habit then is the generic term for the countless treaties concluded between the countless subjects that constitute the individual and their countless correlative objects.
>
> Samuel Beckett, *Proust.*

Textualism as an approach to interpretation feeds off other radical epistemological strategies inasmuch as it is an attack on fetishes, on objects which enchant to the extent that they appear natural, universal or in some way beyond human artifice or invention. A major dimension of the establishment of fixed modes of authority among members of a society is the transformation of processes and possibilities into objects and *faits accomplis*. We are thereby left with totems or idols which, when they are no longer recalled as arrests of the activities they represent, become objects of worship, things which one sees as external or outside of – to use Beckett's metaphor – treaty making. From a political point of view, the fetish performs the ideological function of removing power and authority from the realm of direct contention. This recalls the Foucaultian model of political understanding sketched above inasmuch as the fetish – kinds of scripted human subjects in Foucault's Nietzschean version of it – reflects or represents practices involving domination and subjugation. To point out or to dislodge the fetish is to show how it can be read politically as a product of power rather than a thing.

Various thinkers in different epistemological camps have attacked the fetish within different linguistic frames of reference but in ways that are stategically similar. All of these radical epistemologies – including the Marxian, Freudian, Nietzschean and post-structuralist – see the world of objects available to our immediate consciousness as a product of our discursive habits, a product that stands for (and hides) processes of production. The Marxian approach to the fetish, growing out of Marx's notion of the fetishism of commodities, was best elaborated by Lukacs under the rubric of reification.[32] Lukacs, like Heidegger, attacked the radical distinction between subject and object as the philosophical support for reification. His position, as Goldman has noted, is that, 'objects exist only as correlates to a subject in relation to this subject's praxis'.[33] To attack reification is to show that we have become so habituated to things that emerge *from* our practices, we have lost the subjectivity that things carry as a result of their being produced *in* our practices and that we have thus lost our ability to analyse human relations and practices. The Marxist epistemological orientation is thus an attempt to recover the human relations lost in the reified discursive world of things.

Accordingly, the Marxist hermeneutic is a hermeneutic of suspicion which construes things (fetishes) as masks hiding processes. What is to be recovered in Marxist interpretation are the human relations that are hidden in such things as the commodity. Marx's reading of society was, in effect, an attempt to divulge a hidden text.

The Freudian hermeneutic can be similarly construed, even though it operates within a therapeutic rather than a political problematic. For Freud, the role of analysis is one of making a person's hidden text transparent or available to that person. The world of fetishes – things that appear in fantasy life – are to be reduced to the underlying psychic processes that produce them. This understanding of the Freudian model of consciousness as the recovery of a lost text is encouraged by Freud's use of the mystic writing pad as an analogy for levels of consciousness. In order to show how a psychic text can be created without being available to immediate consciousness, Freud suggested that we conceive of the establishment of a psychic history as a form of writing. The medium of that writing is a mystic writing pad, a tablet with a plastic sheet over a wax surface. On such pads – still popular as children's toys – a pull on the plastic sheet to separate it from the wax surface makes the writing disappear from the sheet. To render this as a dynamic of consciousness, Freud argued that as the self engages in its own construction through a writing process, much that is written is lost to immediate consciousness (the plastic overlay). But the hidden text remains (as an impression in the wax) and remains there to be recovered.[34] The epistemological imagery is thus very similar for Marx and Freud, notwithstanding the vast difference in problematics directing their interpretive activities.

With Nietzsche we find yet another attack on the fetish. Like Marx and Freud, Nietzsche's interpretive approach seeks to show how the world that is experienced in ordinary imagery or the language of everyday affairs is mistakenly taken for an external reality of things that stand apart from human practices and contrivance. But, importantly, Nietzsche's approach is not interpretive in the traditional sense in that he saw no truth behind the mystifications in the world available to consciousness. As he put it, 'What then is truth. A mobile army of metaphors, metonyms, and anthropomorphisms . . . to be truthful means using the customary metaphors – in moral terms: the obligation to lie according to a fixed convention, to lie herd-like in a style obliging to all.'[35] The text to be recovered for Nietzsche is the record of human contrivances wherein the world has been donated ('we put value into things and this value has an effect on us after we have forgotten that we were the donors').[36] The problem of the fetish is in part the problem related to turning values into things. But more important than the 'things' that hide human values, are actions. The primary fetish for Nietzsche was the fetish of the subject, an invention that people add to actions and events.[37]

> The subject is a fiction that many similar states in us are the effect of one substratum; but it is we who first created the 'similarity' of these states: our adjusting them and making them similar is the fact, not their similarity which had rather ought to be denied.

Nietzsche's perspectivism – his view that subjects can never gain a comprehensive view of the world of things because that world is engendered from the practices or modes of being of humans – along with his view of the subject as a fetish – turned his attention to language. His particular interest in poetics, that form of language most self-conscious of its own style, stemmed from his view that it is in the tropics of language that we see the production of reality. Knowing is always caught within productive tropes and is thus an aggressive act to be understood not causally but aesthetically. To see how knowing produces the world is to pay attention to the textuality of human linguistic practices, the rhetorical and grammatical tropes that produce subjects and values. Nietzsche conveyed his notion that the style of language creates subjects, objects and actions with careful attention to the style of his own writing. As Derrida has pointed out, for example, Nietzsche would produce purposeful contradictions in his own text in order to *show* that 'truth' is plural.[38] In general, Nietzsche argued that the troped up world can only be understood as a process, a process that must be recovered philologically. His analyses, therefore, sought to discover the linguistic formations that have given rise to what we 'know'. For Nietzsche, as was the case for Heidegger, understanding the world as a presence requires an understanding of the 'how' of the construction of that world. Knowing within this context for Nietzsche is thus a kind of action or practice, not a unified form of consciousness. Nietzsche, more than any other philosopher, tied the trope intimately to the problem of knowing and understanding.

METAPHORS AND OTHER TROPES

Habit is the ballast that chains the dog to his vomit.
Samuel Beckett, *Proust*.

Beckett, in this brief fragment, challenges habituation not only through an implicit denunciation of it both as limit (the chain image) and as distasteful (the vomit) but also through his own transgression or habit breaking. Because he uses a mixed metaphor the statement has a jarring, dehabitualizng effect. It calls attention to itself because it does not work in the way expected of properly conceived metaphoric expressions. Dogs and chains 'work' all right as a metaphor for limit, but chains and vomit do not, their linking up refuses the mind its accustomed rest.

Habituation to a reified world of subjects and 'things', the failure to realize the structures of value, legitimation and power sequestered in the way the world is discursively engendered, is in part a failure to penetrate the tropes in prevailing discursive practices. The commitments and legitimations involved in the rhetorical and grammatical dimensions of discursive practices are ignored to a large extent because of a venerable metalinguistic position evident in the histories of philosophy and political thought. There is an epistemology of rhetoric whose tenacity has militated against an effective challenge to our habituation to language and the 'things' it puts over on us. That disabling epistemology of rhetoric has been effectively identified recently in the writings of philosophers and literary theorists who, influenced by Nietzsche's notion of metaphors as productive, equal-making enactments, have characterized tropes as aggressive and ideological, while traditional approaches, which see language as reproductive of thought, have conceived of metaphor as additional adornment to that process of reproduction.

For Aristotle, who began the tradition within a reproductive model of language, to make a good metaphor was predicated on the 'seeing' of a similarity. This he proferred within the context that knowledge is a function of 'right talking'.[39] Locke promoted a primarily semantic view of language, regarding good or knowledge-related language as that which could serve as a conduit between thought and things. Within this view, he constructed his notion of figures of speech as elements that corrupt the relationship between an idea about things and the things themselves.[40] But, as de Man has demonstrated, Locke's own discourse violates his view of language in general and figurative language in particular. He points out how Locke's view of the relationship between ideas and language, in which he consigns ideas to the extra-discursive realm of 'simples', is confounded because one cannot separate thought and language. Within a semiological rather than a semantic approach to language it becomes evident that it is the structure of relationships among linguistic entities that produces our things or 'simples'. An 'idea' is not a thing that stands outside of language waiting to be expressed or spoken about. It comes from the Greek *eide* which means light. To understand 'idea', then, is to appreciate the way that it is figuratively constructed. Metaphors cannot corrupt ideas, for 'idea' *is* a metaphor.[41]

Given the pervasiveness of the figural, our traditional distinction between figural and literal language breaks down, and we are left with the recognition that some expressions are obviously or explicitly figural and some are not. In the case of the latter, the figurative is simply taken for the literal. Because aspects of our meanings, our enactments of reality are embedded in our discursive practices, how we create our world is not easily available to conscious deliberation. It is un- or non-consciously that we engender or celebrate our social and political world inasmuch as the given structure of legitimation, power, and domination is immanent in discourse producing both our self-understandings and the 'things' we speak about.

If pruning away figures of speech in order to have a clear vision of the world is a misguided stategy for political understanding, our strategy has to be one of planting and nourishing a crop that will force out the older varieties or at least provide competition and challenge. This gardening metaphor for an epistemological shift translates into the promotion of the literary genre as a means for opposing the ideational commitments entrenched in linguistic practices which, within the old epistemology of 'clarity', go unnoticed. The creation of a new terrain of meaning requires the production of new figures opposing those of the old meaning system. Writers who have made this a practice, according to Derrida, include Renan, Nietzsche, Freud, and Bergson, 'all of whom, in their attentiveness to metaphorical activity in the theoretical or philosophical discourse, proposed or practiced the multiplication of antagonistic metaphor in order to better control or neutralize their effects.'[42]

In a sense, then, theoretical discourses, when they are oriented toward literariness, that is when they are constituted with a self-consciousness of their own figural practices, are politicized. They are politicized in that they oppose the authority and legitimacy sequestered in incumbent figures. To see such literariness as political requires, as recent post-structuralist thought has suggested, an adjustment in our metalinguistic conceits so that we see metaphor, for example, as ideational, value creating and aggressive instead of as a figure which either succeeds or fails at creating clarity. As Derrida has pointed out the old view of metaphor in terms of clarity is owed to the predominant metaphor of metaphor, the 'heliotrope' or trope based on the sun wherein metaphors are evaluated on the basis of the ability to shed light.[43]

When we see metaphor in particular and figural language in general from the point of view of their polemical effects, we become more sensitive to the politicizing implications of discursive selection. As I have suggested elsewhere, for example, there is a conservative bias in the increasing tendency to model political processes on language borrowed from information processing activities (whence we come to view political participation as 'providing input' thereby accepting an outsider status for all such 'input' providers).[44] Or, similarly, as Baudrillard has suggested, there is a disguised political model promoted when we borrow from the domain of the 'enjoyment of consumer goods' to speak about social stratification. Whereas one (like Baudrillard) might want to see inequality politicized, understood as control over economic and political decisions, the consumer discourse conjures away the issue of class antagonisms or conflicts of interest into a statistical dichotomy between two groups of consumers between whom the gap is narrowing. Such a choice of figuration, according to Baudrillard, creates an alibi for modern democracies.[45]

There is a political dimension of figuration, whether it is in the direction of mystification and legitimation, serving prevailing structures of power and authority, or in the direction of resistance, politicizing a domain that has been naturalized or obnubilated by a figuration that is too familiar, or too distantly associated with interest and power to evoke the idea that the issue of control is problematic. In this latter instance, politicization comes through the refiguration of the field. The metaphor involved in bringing together two previously remote linguistic domains creates what Ricoeur has called a 'predicative impertinance', the creation of a productive clash between semantic fields.[46] Thus, for example, Foucault's placing of education, jurisprudence, and psychiatry, among other things, within the frame of 'carceral functions' can be regarded as a literary gesture with political significance. The employment of a discourse borrowed from a punitive domain and lent to 'helping' or ameliorative domains has the effect of problematizing what were, within their more familiar discursive frames, unproblematic institutional, descriptions.

THE EXPLICITLY LITERARY

> He had a strong weakness for oxymoron.
> Samuel Beckett, *More Pricks Than Kicks*.

While all writing, all discursive employments have a literary dimension, a style that contributes to the meanings of the statements, it is the explicitly literary or poetic that sees itself as governed not only by the referents it assembles but also (and often primarily, especially in the case of modernist writing) by a concern with how its language works. As an exercise of imagination, literature foregrounds the vehicle (linguistic effects) for imaginative production while more realistic or denotative discourses bracket imaginative operations, ignoring the way that the discourse produces things, and focus rather on speaking about things. The brief examples in this section from literary works are selected for the presence of linguistic self-consciousness, the extent to which they promote a form of interpretation through their style. In contrast to more denotational discourses that are predicated on a social code with its reified subjects, objects and relationships, the literature I shall consider here is code questioning, code breaking and code producing.[47]

To highlight this consciousness of codes, literary discourse often makes use of metalinguistic emphases, focusing not on the relationship between language and objects but on the structure of the codes that produce objects and actions, i.e. on the practices that are presupposed in utterances that do not reflect explicitly on their metalinguistic presuppositions. Thomas Mann implicitly offers several relevant metalinguistic meditations in his Joseph novels. For example, at the beginning of the third novel, the point at which Joseph is pulled from the pit and finds himself in the custody of wandering merchants, the dialogue begins thus:[48]

Where are you taking me?' Joseph asked Kedeema, one of the old man's sons as they were setting up the sleeping-huts, in the rolling, moonlit lowland at the foot of the mountains called Fruitlands.

Kedeema looked him up and down.

'Thou'rt a good one!' said he, and shook his head in token that he did not mean good at all but various other things such as pert or queer or simple. 'Where are we taking thee? But are we taking thee anywhither? No, not at all. Thou art by chance with us, because our father hath purchased thee from harsh masters, and thou goest with us whither-ever we go. But taking thee that cannot be called.'

'No? then not,' responded Joseph. 'I only meant: whither doth God lead me, in that I go with you?'

'Thou art and remainest a funny fellow,' countered the Ma'onite, 'and thou hast a way of putting thyself in the centre of things till one knoweth not whether to wonder or be put out. Thinkest thou thou "Come-hither", that we are a-journeying in order that thou mayest arrive somewhither where thy God will have thee to come?'

Whereas much literary discourse achieves its effects with the use of lexical tropes such as the metaphor discussed above, this passage, like many in realist prose relies on the use of the grammatical trope. Man here makes use of what Jacobson has referred to as 'the poetic resources concealed in the morphological and syntactic structure of language . . . the poetry of grammar'.[49] Jacobson demonstrates grammatically oriented poetics in an analysis of the Mark Antony funeral oration from Shakespeare's *Julius Caesar*. Before considering the Mann passage here, Jacobson's analysis is worth reviewing because of the structural similarity in the two strategies. First of all, Jacobson notes that throughout the oration, Brutus's claims are rendered in abstract terms as belief states instead of reported facts:

The Noble Brutus hath told you Caesar was ambitious

Shakespeare manipulates the grammar of the oration as Antony 'lampoons Brutus's speech by changing the alleged reasons for Caesar's assassination into plain linguistic fictions.'[50]

I speak not to disprove what Brutus spoke.
But here I am to speak what I do know.

What Shakespeare/Antony manipulates through the play of the grammar of the passage as the oration unfolds is responsibility for action or the legitimation of models of agency. To show this, Jacobson cites the contrast between Brutus's claim, 'He was ambitious', and Antony's query, 'Did this in Caesar seem ambitious?' There is a clear transfer here of agency from the agent to the action. So apart from the obvious irony (which produces a good deal of the oration's effects as well), the grammatical shifts have the effect of changing the locus of the indictment. With this shift Antony is again disclosing that 'these reified attributes [e.g., ambition] are nothing but linguistic fictions'.[51] There are then additional shifts as ambition (as an abstract noun) becomes part of a 'concrete passive construction'.[52]

Ambition should be made of sterner stuff.

and (as a predicate noun) part of an interrogative sentence:[53]

Was this ambition?

Mann's opening to *Joseph in Egypt* has a grammatical play

which has an effect parallel to that which Jacobson extracts from
the funeral oration. What is shown is how linguistic constructions
are not simply statements about facts or deeds but rather are
implicit vehicles for agency and responsibility. The modes of action
and agency that distribute responsibility and thereby create what
are regarded as deeds are inextricably linked with the grammar that
delivers them.[54] Grammatical tropes thus have the effect of
problematizing and thus politicizing modes of agency inasmuch as
what becomes at issue is the locus of legitimacy. For example, the
model of agency that Joseph begins with is one in which the
Ma'onites are responsible for his destiny:

> Where are you taking me?

This is a sentence which nominates the Ma'onites as the actors
and Joseph as an object being controlled. Kedeema responds by
rejecting the grammar and the model of agency immanent in it.
Noting that his father has purchased Joseph, i.e., that Joseph is an
object of the action called a purchase, Kedeema states that as for
Joseph's destiny,

> Thou goest whither-ever we go.

and he goes on to note that this grammatical construction cannot
be translated to make them responsible for taking him somewhere.

> But taking thee that cannot be called.

Joseph's second grammatical attempt to hold on to a destiny
model of his journeying (a model intimately tied to the mythological structure of the Old Testament) fails also.

> Whither doth God lead me, in that I go with you?

This is also not the grammar of agency that Kedeema can accept,
and he again chides Joseph (through an opposing grammatical
construction) for attempting to place himself at the centre of the
Universe. (Here the grammatical structure of the novel seems to be
conveying the idea that we have a story about the new historical
construction of a type of ego that we can derive from the biblical
Joseph's story.)

It is easy for the *reader* moving through Mann's Joseph novels to
place Joseph at the centre of the Universe, for the story line revolves

around him, and his journeys downwards and upwards, the swings of fortune he experiences, provide a major continuity and an emotional purchase for the reader. But at another level, that of the grammatical style of his language, Mann's novels foreground the problem of meaning, the difficulty of penetrating the text of a people's rules for legitimacy, authority and responsibility. The difficulty that Joseph has in speaking to the Ma'onites at the beginning of his major journey downwards mirrors the difficulty Mann experienced as he did his research in preparation for writing the novels. He saw himself explicitly attempting to penetrate the world of the Old Testament which, for him, meant developing a style that would be an amalgam of the author and the subject matter which, he felt, had its own style.[55] Joseph, like Mann, blends styles throughout the novels, for Mann regarded Joseph as a transparent figure in whom various traditions were mingled. This mingling is conveyed in the passage under analysis and throughout the novels as the resolution of grammatical variation, the movement toward a shared grammar and thus a shared model of agency and responsibility.[56]

Mann's political orientation in the Joseph novels clearly works in the direction of reconciliation and integration. He was, as he noted in reflecting on the enterprise of the novels, seeking that which unifies humanity, the typicality of that which is human residing in diverse cultural traditions.[57] But much literary production operates without this unificationist persuasion and works, instead, toward a destruction or sundering of the linguistic props that give us our legitimized subjects, objects, actions and events. Instead of seeking to unify codes and bring people together within the same linguistic universe, much of the modernist writing seeks to question, problematize or destabilize codes. One way that literary discourse produces this kind of effect is through what Russian Formalists have called defamiliarization. Shklovsky attributes this practice to Tolstoy who, he claims, 'makes the familiar seem strange by not naming the familiar object. He describes an object as if he were seeing it for the first time, an event as if it were happening for the first time. In describing something he avoids the accepted names and instead names corresponding parts of other objects.'[58]

Samuel Beckett's technique is also a form of defamiliarization, but unlike Tolstoy's, it is linguistically self-conscious in a radical way. He takes familiar figures of speech and dislocates them, using unfamiliar figures or antagonistic ones to oppose stock forms of thinking and legitimation. Part of Beckett's effects are achieved through jarring the reader's sensibilities with mixed metaphors and

oxymorons that do not allow the kind of comfortable purchase on
reality that comes from treating language as a transparent medium.
For example, in his opening story in *More Pricks Than Kicks* the
issue or problem turns ultimately on an oxymoron that occurs in
the second to last line. The story, 'Dante and the Lobster', features
Bellaqua Shuah, a namesake (with the first name) of a character in
Dante's *Purgatorio* who, if one simply follows the story line, has
the task of bringing home a lobster for dinner. At least that is the
story from Bellaqua's point of view. From other points of view,
including the lobster's, events beyond Bellaqua's control conspire
to achieve the result of getting the lobster to his Aunt's table.
Beckett, like Mann in the example above, uses grammatical structure to convey the different points of view (e.g., the lobster's in such
lines as, 'Always assuming, of course, that the lobster was ready to
be handed over.'). But when we heed the figures of speech, another
kind of theme or story emerges, one which recalls the title of the
story, a juxtaposition which, like the figures *in* the story do not
seem to work well together and therefore have a jarring effect
(Dante and a lobster?)

After Bellaqua gets the lobster home to his Aunt's table he is
horrified to learn that it is alive and is to be plunged into boiling
water in this state.[59]

> She lifted the lobster clear of the table. It had about thirty
> seconds to live. 'Well,' thought Bellaqua, 'it's a quick death,
> God help us all.'
>   It is not.

The familiar way to read the passage, one which is not attuned to
the lexical trope, is as a debate about whether this death is slow or
fast and thus whether the lobster must endure much suffering. But
the expression, 'quick death', is arresting and defies the easy interpretation because it is an oxymoron. From the old English, Old
Teutonic and Nordic languages comes the opposition between the
'quick' and the 'dead' (an opposition still 'quick' in Christian
prayer). Quick still retains the meaning, 'characterized by the presence of life'. Once we become aware of the oxymoronic quality of
'quick death', our reading changes, and we see Dante's and the
Christian view of death as non-death (a view connected to the
notion of salvation) or living death. This is a view that clearly
denies death, and that it comes from a Christian or God-related
ideology becomes explicit. The 'God help us all' coupled with the
'quick death' no longer seems to be just an exclamation but rather a

recognition that the idea of God is connected to the idea that death is not really death. The last line also changes. The 'No it's not' is not simply a captious reaction to the idea that the death of the lobster will involve minimal suffering but rather a response to the contradictory notion that death is not death.

The issue thus leaves the narrow terrain of the question of whether, indeed, lobsters suffer when plunged alive into boiling water and enters the broader field of questions about the legitimate control over the concept of death. Why a lobster to represent such an issue? Beckett seems to think it smacks of Christian symbolism, noting, for example, that when seen from above it is a 'cruciform'.[60] By presenting the issue with rhetorical play, Beckett is showing how the Christian idea of death as non-death is more than a proclamatory position, trumpeted from the pulpit. It has taken up residence more subtly within the rhetorical structure of common speech practices.

How should one describe, then, what it is that Beckett does with his mixed metaphors, oxymorons and neologisms. If we equate literary discourse with the exercise of imagination, we get some help from Bachelard whose notion of the role of imagination resonates well with Beckett's style. 'Imagination is always considered to be the faculty of *forming* images. But it is rather the faculty of *deforming* the images offered by perception.'[61] Beckett, like Foucault, Derrida and de Man seems to view the rhetorical figures used to convey knowledge or thinking as particularly inapposite, because much of his deforming energy has gone into producing imagery antagonistic to the prevailing forms used to convey epistemological commitments. He likens the mind to a cat's-paw that grasps aggressively in the process of understanding, and at times, the imagery becomes even more violent:[62]

> His plan therefore was not to refuse admission to the idea, but to keep it at bay until his mind was ready to receive it. Then let it in and pulverize it. Obliterate the bastard. . . . Flitter the fucker, tear it into pieces like a priest. So far so good. But by what means? Bellaqua ransacked his mind for a suitable engine of destruction.

Beckett's wrenching of prevailing understandings by substituting conflicting imagery – thinking as flittering, pulverizing, etc. – is in accord with his notion that the subject is a victim of the dominant models of reason represented in prevailing speech practices. In his *The Unnamable* he anticipates Foucault's conception of power as a

force that produces us, gives us an identity and enforces a garru-
lousness that satisfies a growing surveillance aimed at rendering us
predictable and fitting us into a set of legitimized identities that
serve reason and order. The character in *The Unnamable* laments
his pacification and resulting predictability, his absorption into
prevailing models of one's destiny.[63]

> I have my faults, but changing my tune is not one of them. I
> have to go on as if there was something to be done, something
> begun, somewhere to go. . . .

Of course part of the effect of this passage is achieved through
the use of the ironic tone.[64] The suggestion really is that the fault
lies elsewhere. Being predictable is a condition not a fault. The fault
lies in construing consciousness as an independent causal force
which, if it were, would render us *un*predictable. Beckett's view,
ironically expressed here, of consciousness as epiphenomenal to
something else – language practices – is further conveyed by the
metaphor of the 'tune' which contributes by suggesting that there is
a conductor. The pedagogy of *The Unnamable* is similar to
Foucault's approach to power. Power achieves its effect; grammatically speaking *it* is the actor, and rhetorically speaking, *it* speaks
through the mouth of the subject who subjugates himself with his
own utterances.[65]

> I don't know why with their billions of quick and their
> trillions of dead that's not enough for them. I too must
> contribute my little convulsion, mewl, howl, gasp, rattle,
> loving my neighbour and blessed with reason.

Beckett's writing, like Foucault's, is part of his resistance to
power. His wildly shifting word play constitutes enactments that
seek both to show how identities are epiphenomenal to speech
practices and to resist them. Thinking and understanding are
among his major targets, for, like Foucault, Derrida, and de Man,
he attacks the illusion that thinking is a relationship between a
conscious subject and a world of objects. In a literary way, Beckett
conveys the position that it is the background of practices, the sites
and locations available to the subject that produce the things that
emerge in thought/language. Beckett's form of literary production,
like Foucault's resemanticizations and refiguration, reveals domination and subjugation in discursive practices and shows how subjects
made by power are fetishized. His use of the figure of speech is a

weapon against the deadening habituation to the world troped up in ordinary speech and then treated as if it were delivered in literal language. We can leave Beckett with a passage that achieves its effects with both the lexical and grammatical figures.[66]

> I myself have been scandalously bungled, they must be begin-ning to realize it, I on whom all dangles, better still, about whom, much better, all turns, dizzily, yes yes, don't protest, all spins, it's a head, I'm in a head, what an illumination, sssst, pissed on out of hand.

With his grammatical figure, the passive voice in the first sent-ence, Beckett conveys the notion that the subject, the 'I' is a product rather than an active, directing consciousness. In his substitutions of figures – 'dangles', 'turns', – he shows how the illusion of the 'I' at the centre of reality is merely a function of grasping at rhetorical devices. That the 'I' is in the head, finally, is also an illusion. It is not in the head in the sense of being a directing, originating conscious-ness. Heaping scorn on this Cartesianism, Beckett places the 'I' in a place where it *receives* the action. It is in a head, but the kind where it gets pissed on.

LITERARY READINGS OF THE NON-LITERARY

> I say what I'm told to say, that's all there is to it, and yet I wonder, I don't know, I don't feel a mouth on me, I don't feel the jostle of words in my mouth.
>   Samuel Beckett, *The Unnamable.*

Literary discourse, particularly in its modernist guise is hyper-politicizing. By producing alternative forms of thought *in* language, it makes a political point. By virtue of its departures from linguistic normality, it points to the way that institutions hold individuals within a linguistic web. But it goes beyond this demonstration. It deforms images to show how accepted models of the real are productions of grammatical and rhetorical constructions, and it forms antagonistic imagery that provides sites for resistance to domination. A failure to exercise a literary self-consciousness, then, amounts to the adoption of a depoliticizing posture, the acceptance of institutional imperatives. Following Beckett's musings, one might say that all those who write in a primarily denotative genre cannot feel the words in their mouths. While the poetic or literary takes language as its object, the non-literary discourses, those that subordinate or bracket their literariness, aspire to making their language neutral (unchewy?).

But all writing, whatever its genre, is susceptible to a literary reading, to a concern with the relationship between its style or linguistic practices and the argumentation about things that it presents. That literary analysis travels well across genres has been demonstrated ably by Hayden White in his literary analyses of historical writing. He argues that in addition to providing information and explanations or interpretations at an explicit level, historical, factually oriented accounts of events convey messages about the attitudes that the reader should adopt with respect to the 'data' and interpretations.[67] Leaving aside the obvious epistemological problem involved in separating the 'facts' and 'interpretations' from the values and attitudes that the style of writing implicitly promotes – and White does this very explicitly – his analyses show how historians build stories and develop tropes that produce the attitudes toward historical events.

What White fails to point out, namely that 'events', so called, become events only when shaped by the problematic and style of the discourse, is demonstrated by Northrup Frye in his recent literary analysis of the Bible. Frye shows how the metaphoric and metonymic structures of biblical language constitute the biblical facts and events as well as the interpretive structure for developing an appreciation of the discursively engendered facts and events. For example, he shows how explanatory accounts in the Bible contain a rhetorical structure that arranges words in the form of a continuous prose such that a notion of causality for biblical events is almost inevitable.[68] All the Bible's tropic effects become coherent, Frye shows, in the context of the basic plot of the Bible. Like White's demonstration that simple historical accounts of 'facts' and 'events' take place within an 'emplotment' (a story designed to produce attitudes) is Frye's demonstration that the Bible is a story with 'a specific social function ... a program of action for a specific society'.[69]

Within this program, the Bible then constitutes the facts and events discursively. For example, what man *is* is partly based on an identity produced, according to Frye, by 'the legal metaphor that runs through the Bible, and sees man as under trial and subject to judgment'.[70] Similarly, events described fit in with a purpose, the legitimation or rationalization of centralized authority – in the case of the Bible this is an authority based on the Covenant with God. As Frye points out, the account in Exodus bears only an oblique relationship to the historical condition of Egypt's control over the Nation of Israel. 'The evidence from history seems to suggest that Israel continued to be nominally subject to Egyptian power through most of the period covered by the Judges.'[71] The Exodus story is thus not just an account of control, legitimate or illegitimate, however it might be construed to aid and abet future anti-imperialist movements. It is a deliverance story implicating God as an actor in such a way as to strengthen the legal bond between Him and the 'children of Israel'. That the story is oft repeated and that it is ritualized in period festivals designed to re-enact the deliverance myth shows, according to Frye, how myths function. They are inseparable from notions of what is to be done. They justify actions that serve the authority the myth is designed to legitimate. The prose of the Bible, while seemingly innocent in places where it is primarily descriptive instead of proclamatory, is a legitimater of modes of conduct and commitments of fidelity by dint of the way its style, the structure of the prose narrative, produces subjects, objects, events, and interpretive orientations. Frye sums up this case:[72]

> Accuracy of description in language is not possible beyond a certain point. The most faithfully descriptive account of anything will always turn away from what it describes into its own self-contained grammatical fictions of subject and predicate and object. The events the Bible describes are what some scholars call 'language events', brought to us only through words; and it is the words themselves that have the authority, not the events they describe.

Such a literary reading of prose styles can be used to politicize (in the sense of questioning the model of authority implicit in the style) even the more stylistically austere analyses that constitute the current corpus of public policy and public administration studies in the discipline of political science. When we examine such non-literary discourses – discourses that do not conceive of themselves as literary in orientation – from a literary standpoint as White and Frye have done with historical and biblical discourse respectively, we are seeking to pay attention to the 'jostle of words' that the speaker/writes hardly notice. And when this attention is paid from a political standpoint we are, as Foucault has done with various disciplinary practices, politicizing both by highlighting the discursive practices in the text and by offering alternatives.[73]

For purposes of a brief exercise of this kind, I shall conclude this analysis with a discussion of James Q. Wilson's *The Investigators*, a study of the FBI and the DEA (Drug Enforcement Administration).[74] I select this particular study, not because it is very distinguished for its unconscious ideologizing. Indeed, from most perspectives – at least all those that do not trespass into the issues of style and the way that writing engenders its object, events and meanings – it is an excellent study in the problem of 'implementing' public policy. Like all Wilson's studies, it is well conducted ('well written' in the sense that its claims are reasonable and even ingenious within the scope of the enterprise Wilson sets for himself). The interpretive frames that the study evokes involve the code of science and its criteria for truth and the code of responsibility that goes with a no-nonsense, business mentality. To the extent that one stays within the boundaries of these codes, the study delivers useful truths.

When we put *The Investigators* into a literary genre by dint of a stylistic interpretation, we are raising questions about what it is that Wilson does and how he does it. We can begin with his self-understanding of what he was up to.[75]

> My motive for offering this analysis is not necessarily to make the work of the FBI or the DEA better or more rational, or to expose to public scrutiny additional problems in organizations that have, of late, been beset by controversy. Rather, it is my hope to explain how carrying out tasks within a governmental setting exposes managers and executives to constraints that render the devising of efficient and effective means to attain organizational objectives especially difficult or unlikely. In short, this is an account of the consequences of practicing public administration.

This sounds innocuous enough, but we should not allow this brief statement of motives to throw us off the trail of Wilson's polemical programme. Recall how Mark Antony pleaded a similar innocence with his modest claim about coming to bury Caesar instead of praising him. Then his discourse took over, and, as Jacobson showed us, the grammatical tropes did the job so that by the time he got through, the audience was indignant. No, motives are not the place to look, at least not if motives as viewed as initiating, causal conditions. Wilson's approach to motives suggests that the value impetus that a discourse contains relates to the exogenous purposes of its immediate author (he who writes it down), what that author thought he/she was up to in getting started.

More than 40 years ago, C. Wright Mills pointed out that motives should not be seen as 'the expression of prior elements within the individual'.[76] Without rehearsing much of what has led up to this part of the analysis, I want to note, in agreement with Mills, that discourses contain a valuational impetus not so much by dint of what prompts them but by virtue of what they contain and how they act, how they create or perpetuate subjects (persons with identities), things, relationships, and contexts of agency. What is thought is *in* a discourse. It is not an initiating circumstance but part of what is said and how it is said. This is in fact the insight that Lacan offers on motives in his resurrection of speech as the privileged domain for the psychoanalytic practice.[77]

What I suggest, therefore, with respect to *The Investigators*, is that we de-authorize it, carry it over into a genre that is not the one in which its 'author' thought himself to be toiling. Within the genre of the reading I shall offer, *The Investigators* is an authority perpetuating mythology which can be explicated as myth from two perspectives. The first is that suggested by Frye. Myth, from his perspective is not a concept meaning 'not really true'. In its fundamental (Greek) sense it simply means, 'charged with a special seriousness and importance'. The stories relating to aspects of a society that are told and retold as myths are those which legitimate the existing order and provide justifications for conduct conducive to order maintenance. Any discursive strategy that incorporates the prevailing language helps to legitimate the authority in existing institutions and thus has a mythical element. It is collaborating in telling a story, at least at an implicit level, that is designed to remind the society's members what has to be done. When stories are deliberately told with this mythic function in the foreground, the descriptively oriented language that one finds in historical accounts or social and political inquiries is subordinated to the exhortative language and the imperative mood which explicitly promotes a myth (e.g., 'Go and do thou likewise').

But when the mythic function is in the background, there is an absence of exhortation, and the justifications for conduct are implicit in the grammatical and rhetorical tropes of a discourse whose surface appearance is primarily reportage and inference making. It is clear, from the mythic elements in Wilson's study, even though those elements are not foregrounded, that the work of the FBI and DEA ought to be done in the way it is being done, once some minor irrationalities that obtain because of flaws at the level of organizational incentives are taken care of. Myth, as Frye points out, is inseparable from what ought to be done, and Wilson is telling us, indirectly, what ought to be done.[78]

Before dealing with any of the specific mythic elements in *The Investigators*, we should consider the second perspective from which the study can be read as mythological. This is Roland Barthes's perspective in which myth is viewed as a type of speech, speech that is 'not defined by the object of its message but by the way in which it utters this message'.[79] Without going into the details of how Barthes constructs his notion of the 'way' of an utterance, it should suffice to note that a myth for Barthes is a second order semiological system. The relationship between the original signifier and signified is a sign that contains another signifier-signified relationship. For example, when Barthes saw, on the front cover of the magazine, *Paris Match*, a Negro soldier saluting the Tricolour, he read the picture as a mythology. In this case, the mythic element is in the second order relationship which says, 'that France is a great Empire, that all her sons, without any colour discrimination, faithfully serve under the flag, and that there is no better answer to the detractors of an alleged colonialism than the zeal shown by this Negro in serving his so-called oppressors.'[80] In keeping with what I have said above motives, Barthes notes that the motive behind a myth is not the intentions of a person/author but rather a force intrinsic to the myth. It is the concept that motivates the form in which the myth develops. In the case of the saluting Negro soldier, the motivating concept is an apology for imperialism.

Wilson's mythological function is also one of apology, a genre of apology that is very much a part of modern mass culture. Barthes has described this genre succinctly:[81]

> To instill in the Established Order the complacent portrayal of its drawbacks has nowadays become a paradoxical but incontrovertible means of exalting it. Here is the pattern of this new-style demonstration: take the established value you want to restore or develop, and first lavishly display its pettiness, the injustices which it produces, the vexations to which it gives rise, and plunge it into its natural imperfection; then, at the last moment, save it *in spite of* or rather *by* the heavy curse of its blemishes.

Barthes's examples of how this genre works are from films and books dealing with organizational pettiness, intrigue, and venality in institutions like the Army and the Church, films and books which rescue and legitimize these institutions by contrasting the small blemishes and inefficiencies that occur when order is being maintained with the advantage of having that order (e.g., the film, *From Here to Eternity*). The myth compresses, Barthes suggests, to the message, '. . . what is this trifling dross of order, compared to its advantages . . . What does it matter, after all, if Order is a little brutal or a little blind when it allows us to live cheaply.'[82]

This genre of apology that Barthes demonstrates is a very close fit with that of *The Investigators*. Throughout the study, the FBI and DEA are shown to engage in actions that are not consonant with the alleged missions of their agencies. These shortcomings are then attributed to flaws in the agencies' incentive systems applied to the behaviour of individual functionaries. The conduct encouraged in these functionaries results in a failure to 'realize organizational goals' (primarily a failure to adopt the appropriate criteria for selecting 'priority offenders'. Ultimately, the investigators in both agencies end up responding to political criteria for targeting various classes of 'offenders'. But in Wilson's telling, the worst shortcoming, the politicizing of the conduct of the investigators (and of the agencies at all levels), turns out to be a strength. Here is the dénouement of the mythic story of the investigators, worth quoting at length:[83]

> Excessive zeal in conforming to political demands has led the FBI to undertake some inquiries that had only partisan justification, and a preoccupation with maintaining public support has led it and the DEA to exaggerate their statistical accomplishments and to stimulate public concern over crime, subversion, and drug trafficking. But the same sensitivity to the political environment has also meant that, broadly speaking, these agencies have done what the public wanted done. When crime was on the increase, the FBI went after criminals; when public concern over threats to domestic security was at its peak, the FBI investigated subversives. . . .

Wilson has told us, from his own reckoning, that excessive concern with its image has led the FBI and DEA into various minor administrative shortcomings, primarily in the form of overly rigid demands for conformity within the organizations which has produced conduct at the investigative level that leaves something to be desired. But, to repeat Barthes's insight into this kind of apology for power, 'what is this trifling dross of order compared to its advantages?' Here we have from James Q. Wilson a mythology that is, at the first level an analysis of the implementation of public policy and at the second, the mythic level, a legitimation of part of the established order. It is hard to avoid this kind of conclusion once we are using the mythological framework, for it does not take a minute reading of the above quotation to see an 'excessive zeal' for maintaining the story line of the myth. First we are told that the FBI and DEA are so politicized that they exaggerate their accomplishments by the way they report statistics and that they 'stimulate public concern over crime, subversion, and drug trafficking'. But then these same agencies that are characterized as producing the way the public deploys its concerns with respect to categories of wrong doing are described (in the very next sentence) as being responsive to public wants ('But the same sensitivity to the political environment has also meant that . . . these agencies have done what the public wanted done'). Surely this is a contradiction. If you produce the wants and then respond to them, it is not convincing to make the case that those wants are responsible for initiating your activities. Only a dedicated mythologist, one committed to a story that gets the job done – which in this case is the job of selling our investigative agencies – could be willing to subordinate such contradictory details to the plot as a whole.

The literary reading reveals, then, a mythic story; it transforms an austerely written policy analysis into a legitimating pamphlet, a celebration of part of the existing order (moreover the part that is perhaps most difficult to celebrate from the point of view of values such as justice and fairness, etc.). This celebration is evident, not only when one takes the plot and the genre of the story as a whole. It is evident also when one does a closer, more detailed literary reading, paying attention to the lending discourses that govern the writing and produce kinds of subjects, objects and modes of conduct. These details help the perpetuating myth from the point of view of Frye's notion of myth. They help get the job done.

The most important thing to notice is that, at the level of its language, *The Investigators* is largely ghost written. It incorporates the discursive patterns (and thus the 'motives' – yes, J.Q.'s motives are 'their' motives) of the prevailing institutions and their legitimations. The FBI is described and analysed within that agency's discourse, and likewise for the DEA. We are invited into a world of subject/objects called 'investigators', 'informants', 'criminals', and 'extremists' and their various actions or performances, all described within the code of business or administrative job performance. The investigators have 'tasks' and function in the context of such things as 'performance measures', while their adversaries (the criminals *et al.*)

remain equally in character and engage in 'violations', 'subversion', 'drug trafficking', etc. Wilson worships all the fetishes or idols that the practice of federal level law enforcement has erected, even though he is aware of processes immanent in them. For example, on the 'criminal,' he states that what gets criminalized is a function of political pressures felt by the agencies, but he then goes on to treat the 'criminal' as a thing, a kind of object for the investigator. The temporal dimension of understanding, the processes wherein things become criminalized are bracketed, and we are shown a frozen world of 'things' that are the fixtures in the environment of the actors whose activities Wilson is promoting, the investigators.

Even within the popular political discourse, that concerned at an explicit level with issues of justice and fairness, one might wonder about a practice like 'instigation' in which an investigator and his informant encourage someone to commit a criminal act in order to get sufficient evidence for a successful prosecution. Such activities are spoken of as 'proactive' as opposed to 'reactive' methods of investigation. What some might call entrapment, bullying, infringement of rights, etc., gets sequestered within a neutralizing Latinism.

What Wilson's language does becomes even more apparent in the context of what it fails to do, self-consciously politicizing the field he works. What is 'drug trafficking', for example, if we call off all legitimation bets for the moment and enter the issue with an historical as well as a politicized consciousness. In such a situation, we might wonder about the difference between 'drug trafficking' and 'drug marketing'. Why are 'the investigators' not hanging around the executives in the marketing divisions of large pharmecautical companies? What is the process wherein some harmful substances have been encouraged and some discouraged by official agencies? In the case of the 'dangerous drugs' produced by the pharmaceutical companies, controls consist of esoteric warnings (mostly in Greek and Latin) to the physicians whose medical training has promoted the substances in the first place. Those products that do not survive the loose screening of our FDA get marketed in places such as Latin America whose citizens are not protected by our regulatory agencies.

What historical sequence of events and what power-related process gives rise to the differential identification of the marketing versus the trafficking person? In response to such a question what one would find is what Foucault has shown in his analysis of what he has called the proliferation of illegalities. The historical processes involved in this proliferation can be politically characterized;

they relate to a growing structure of domination. The penalties on behalf of which the investigators operate are 'facts' or 'things' that harbour historical processes. Let us listen for a moment to someone not co-opted by the motives of power:[84]

> Penalty would thus appear to be a way of handling illegalities of laying down the limits of tolerance, of giving free reign to some, of putting pressure on others, of excluding a particular section, of making another useful, of neutralizing certain individuals and of profiting from others. In short, penalty does not simply 'check' illegalities; it differentiates them, it provides them with a general 'economy' and, if one can speak of justice, it is not only because the law itself in the way of applying it serves the interests of a class, it is also because the differential administration of illegalities through the mediation of penalty forms part of those mechanisms of domination.

In contrast to this kind of politicizing statement, what we get from Wilson is a rhetoric of legitimation in the form of the traditional cliches of power and a grammar of absolution. To the extent that Wilson has a political programme, it is not that of Foucault, that of showing how domination and subjugation, the allocation of punishment versus support is embedded within the discourse of the administration of penalities. Rather it is one of supporting the existing enforcement system of those penal codes. One of his major grammatical tropes, which appears throughout the study is what Wilson calls the 'task', a concept which he nominates as an actor. In his preferred model for running investigative agencies, the tasks determine the investigators' behaviour. Where is power in such a grammar? It has fled from the scene after it set up the 'task' which Wilson promotes as the privileged actor. This control by the task is preferred by Wilson to what he calls the bogey of rational and effective law enforcement, the top-down perspective in administration where the organization's executives control conduct through incentives and performance monitoring.[85]

Finally, the major metaphor of *The Investigators*, the 'task' (again) when viewed as metaphor instead of as literal description undermines even the limited political motive that Wilson tacitly acknowledges, that of enhancing the already politically determined pursuits of the investigators. A 'task' is not just a job or piece of work outside of the context of organizational exigencies. As a metaphor for some kind of activity it borrows from the domain of

fiscal management in hierarchical (top-down) structures. It is derived from *taxa, taxare*, a Latin verb meaning, 'a fixed payment to a
king, lord or feudal superior'.[86] Even without benefit of the
metaphoricity of 'task', it should be evident that a task calls forth
activity only in the sense that the person who is charged with the
task has to defer to a superior, be that superior an individual person
or an institutionalized collectivity whose power relations are implicit in each instance of an authorized task: Wilson's political programme turns out to be vacuous. In addition to saying, *qua* his
mythology, that we must celebrate the FBI and DEA, he is saying
that instead of running these agencies from the top-down, we
should run them from the top-down.

How should we talk about the activities of the investigators?
Above, quite inadvertently, I referred to their activities as 'pursuits'.
For the sake both of continuity and political conscientiousness I
will stick with this characterization. To pursue is, 'To follow with
hostility or enmity; to seek to injure (a person) to persecute, to
harass, worry, torment.'[87]

NOTES

1 Martin Heidegger, *What is a Thing?* trans. W. B. Burton/Vera Deutsch
  (South Bend, Indiana: Regnery/Gateway, 1967), p. 244.
2 Ibid., p. 141.
3 Martin Heidegger, 'The Thing', in *Poetry, Language, Thought* trans.
  Albert Hofstadter (New York: Harper & Row, 1971), p. 170.
4 Martin Heidegger, 'The Age of the World Picture', in *The Question
  Concerning Technology* trans. William Lovett (New York: Harper &
  Row, 1977).
5 Ibid.
6 On these aspects of Heidegger's thinking, see Hubert L. Dreyfus,
  'Holism and Hermeneutics', *Review of Metaphysics* 34 (September,
  1980), and, 'The Dasein as a Whole', review of Martin Heidegger's
  The Basic Problems of Phenomenology, *Times Literary Supplement*,
  17 September 1982, p. 1011.
7 Martin Heidegger, 'The End of Philosophy and the Task of Thinking',
  in *On Time and Being* trans. Joan Stambaugh (New York: Harper &
  Row, 1972), p. 59.
8 Clifford Geertz, 'Blurred Genres: The Refiguration of Social Thought',
  The American Scholar 49 (Spring, 1980), pp. 165–79.
9 Paul Ricoeur, 'The Model of the Text: Meaningful Action Considered
  as a Text', in Paul Rabinow and William M. Sullivan eds. *Interpretive
  Social Science: A Reader* (Berkeley and Los Angeles: University of
  California Press, 1979), pp. 73–102.
10 Hans-Georg Gadamer, 'On the Scope and Function of Hermeneutical

Reflection', in *Philosophical Hermeneutics* trans. David E. Linge (Berkeley and Los Angeles: University of California Press, 1976), pp. 18–43.

11 Michel Foucault, 'The Order of Discourse', trans. Ian McCleod in Robert Young ed. *Untying the Text* (Boston: Routledge & Kegan Paul, 1981), pp. 48–78.

12 Fredric Jameson, The *Political Unconscious* (Ithaca, N.Y.: Cornell University Press, 1981).

13 Hans-Georg Gadamer, *Reason in the Age of Science* trans. Frederick G. Lawrence (Cambridge, Mass.: M.I.T. Press, 1982), p. 90.

14 Ibid., p. 136.

15 Michel Foucault, 'Nietzsche, Genealogy, History', in Donald F. Bouchard ed. *Language, Counter-Memory, Practice* (Ithaca, N.Y.: Cornell University Press, 1977), pp. 151–2.

16 Michel Foucault, 'Two Lectures', in *Power/Knowledge* trans. Colin Gordon (New York: Pantheon, 1980), p. 96.

17 Michel Foucault, *The Archeology of Knowledge* trans. Alan Sheridan (New York: Pantheon, 1972) p. 120.

18 Michel Foucault, *The History of Sexuality* trans. Robert Hurley (New York: Pantheon, 1978), p. 25.

19 Michel Foucault, *Discipline and Punish: The Birth of the Prison* trans. Alan Sheridan (New York: Pantheon, 1977), p. 275.

20 Michel Foucault, 'Afterward, The Subject and Power', in Hubert L. Dreyfus and Paul Rabinow, *Michel Foucault: Beyond Structuralism and Hermeneutics* (Chicago: University of Chicago Press, 1982), p. 216.

21 Fredric Jameson, *The Prison House of Language* (Princeton, N.J.: Princeton University Press, 1972), p. 10.

22 For the former, see Roland Barthes, *Mythologies* trans. Anette Lavers (New York: Hill and Wang, 1972), and for the latter, Roland Barthes, 'Literature Today', in *Critical Essays* trans. Richard Howard (Evanston, Ill.: Northwestern University Press, 1972), pp. 151–62.

23 For an example of Barthes's later approach to texts as tissues of codes, see his 'Textual Analysis of Poe's "Valdemar"', in Robert Young ed. *Untying the Text,* pp. 133–61.

24 Roland Barthes, 'From Work to Text', in Josue Harari ed. *Textual Strategies* (Ithaca, N.Y.: Cornell University Press, 1979), pp. 73–81.

25 See Jacques Derrida's analysis of Rousseau in *Of Grammatology* trans. Gayatri Chakravorty Spivak (Baltimore: Johns Hopkins University Press, 1974), and his analysis of Plato, in 'Plato's Pharmacy', in *Dissemination* trans. Barbara Johnson (Chicago: University of Chicago Press, 1981), pp. 61–172.

26 Jacques Derrida, 'The Supplement of Copula: Philosophy before Linguistics', in Josue Harari ed. *Textual Strategies,* pp. 82–120.

27 Jacques Derrida, 'Freud and the Scene of Writing', in *Writing and Difference* trans. Alan Bass (Chicago: University of Chicago Press, 1978), pp. 196–231.

28 Jacques Lacan, 'The Function and Field of Speech and Language in Psychoanalysis', in *Ecrits* trans. Alan Sheridan (New York: W. W. Norton, 1977), pp. 30–114.
29 See Spivak's 'Translators Preface', in Derrida, *Of Grammatology*, p. lxiv, for a comparative analysis of Lacan and Derrida.
30 Jacques Derrida, 'Structure, Sign and Play in the Discourse of the Human Sciences', in *Writing and Difference*, p. 278–94.
31 See Edward Said, 'The Problem of Textuality: Two Exemplary Positions', *Critical Inquiry* 4:4 (Summer, 1978), pp. 673–714, and also Jonathan Culler, 'Jacques Derrida', in John Sturrock ed. *Structuralism and Since* (New York: Oxford University Press, 1979), pp. 154–80.
32 Georg Lukacs, 'What is Orthodox Marxism?' in *History and Class Consciousness* trans. Rodney Livingstone (Cambridge, Mass.: M.I.T. Press, 1971), pp. 1–26. Jameson has restated Lukacs's position on reification as, 'The transformation of human relations into an appearance of relationships between things'. See his 'Reflections in Conclusion', in Ernst Bloch ed. *Aesthetics and Politics* (New York: Schocken, 1979), p. 212.
33 Lucien Goldman, *Lukacs and Heidegger* trans. William Q. Boelhower (Boston: Routledge & Kegan Paul, 1977), p. 70.
34 Sigmund Freud, 'Note on the Mystic Writing Pad', quoted in Jacques Derrida, 'Freud and the Scene of Writing', in *Writing and Difference*, pp. 222–3.
35 Friedrich Nietzsche, 'On Truth and Lie in the Extra-Moral Sense', quoted in Eric Blondel, 'Nietzsche: Life as Metaphor', in David Allison ed. *The New Nietzsche* (New York: Delta, 1977), p. 167.
36 Quoted in Tracy Strong, 'Texts and Pretexts: Reflections on Perspectivism in Nietzsche', paper delivered at the North American Nietzsche Association meeting, The American Philosophical Association, 1980.
37 Friedrich Nietzsche, *The Genealogy of Morals* trans. Francis, Golffing (New York: Doubleday, 1956).
38 Jacques Derrida, 'The Question of Style', in Allison, *The New Nietzsche*, p. 187.
39 Aristotle's conception of science as 'right talking' is developed in John H. Randall, *Aristotle* (New York: Columbia University Press, 1960).
40 Paul de Man, 'The Epistemology of Metaphor', in Sheldon Sachs ed. *On Metaphor* (Chicago: University of Chicago Press, 1978), pp. 11–28.
41 Ibid.
42 Jacques Derrida, 'White Mythology: Metaphor in the Text of Philosophy', in *Margins of Philosophy* trans. Alan Bass (Chicago: University of Chicago Press, 1982), pp. 207–72.
43 Ibid.
44 See my 'Structuralist, Post Structuralism and Political Understanding', paper delivered at the International Political Science Association meeting, Rio, Brazil, August, 1982.
45 Jean Baudrillard, 'Sign Function and Class Logic', in *For a Critique of*

252 *Michael J. Shapiro*

the Political Economy of the Sign trans. Charles Levin (St. Louis: Telos Press, 1981), pp. 29–62.

46 Paul Ricoeur, 'The Function of Fiction in Shaping Reality', *Man World* 12 (1979), pp. 132–3.

47 Julia Kristeva speaks of the literature-code relationship in this way in 'From one Identity to Another', in *Desire in Language* trans. Thomas Gora, Alice Jardine and Leon Roudiez (New York: Columbia University Press, 1980), pp. 124–47.

48 Thomas Mann, *Joseph in Egypt* trans. H. T. Lowe-Porter (New York: Alfred A. Knopf, 1938), p. 3.

49 Roman Jacobson, 'Linguistics and Poetics', in Thomas A. Sebeok ed. *Style in Language* (Cambridge, Mass.: M.I.T. Press, 1960), p. 375.

50 Ibid.

51 Ibid., p. 376.

52 Ibid.

53 Ibid.

54 This is analysed at length by Kenneth Burke in his *Grammar of Motives* (Berkeley and Los Angeles: University of California Press, 1969).

55 Thomas Mann, *The Theme of the Joseph Novels* (Washington D.C.: Library of Congress, 1942), p. 9.

56 Mann explicitly states that he saw Joseph as a 'transparent figure'. Ibid., p. 15.

57 For example, a poem sung to Joseph's father, Jacob, represents this by blending Hebrew cadences with the versification of German Romantic poetry, according to Mann. Ibid.

58 Victor Shklovsky, 'Art as Technique', in *Russian Formalist Criticism* trans. Lee T. Lemon Marion J. Reis (Lincoln: University of Nebraska Press, 1965), p. 13.

59 Samuel Beckett, *More Pricks than Kicks* (London: Chatto and Windus, 1934), p. 22.

60 Ibid., p. 21.

61 Gaston Bachelard, *On Poetic Imagination and Reverie* trans. Colette Gaudin (Indianapolis, Indiana: Bobbs-Merrill, 1971), p. 19.

62 Beckett, *More Pricks than Kicks*, p. 53.

63 Samuel Beckett, *The Unnamable* trans. Samuel Beckett (New York: Grove Press, 1958), p. 66.

64 See Kenneth Burke's discussion of the ironic trope in *The Grammar of Motives*, p. 503.

65 Beckett, *The Unnamable*, pp. 66–7.

66 Ibid., p. 119.

67 Hayden White, 'Historicism, History and the Figurative Imagination', in *Tropics of Discourse* (Baltimore: Johns Hopkins University Press, 1978), p. 105.

68 Northrup Frye, *The Great Code: The Bible and Literature* (New York: Harcourt Brace Jovanovich, 1981), p.81.

69 Ibid., p. 49.

70 Ibid.

71 Ibid.
72 Ibid., p. 60.
73 William Connolly has done this with a discourse in the philosophy of the social sciences. See his literary deconstruction of Richard Rorty in *Raritan*, forthcoming.
74 James Q. Wilson, *The Investigators* (New York: Basic Books, 1978).
75 Ibid., p. ix.
76 C. Wright Mills, 'Situated Actions and Vocabularies of Motive', *American Sociological Review* 5 (December, 1940), p. 904.
77 Lacan, 'The Function and Field of Speech and Language in Psychoanalysis'.
78 Frye, *The Great Code*, p. 33.
79 Barthes, *Mythologies*, p. 109.
80 Ibid., p. 116.
81 Barthes, 'Operation Margarine', in *Mythologies*, p. 41.
82 Ibid., p. 42.
83 Wilson, *The Investigators*, pp. 213–14.
84 Foucault, *Discipline and Punish*, p. 272.
85 See *The Investigators*, chapter I, for this argument.
86 *The Shorter Oxford English Dictionary on Historical Principles* (Oxford: The Clarendon Press, 1933).
87 Ibid.

Index